GROWING UP FAST

AN ORDINARY MAN'S EXTRAORDINARY
LIFE IN OCCUPIED JERSEY

Bob Le Sueur

Seeker
Publishing & Distribution
in the Channel Islands

Published in 2020 by
SEEKER PUBLISHING
Units 1 & 2 Elms Farm
La Route de la Hougue Mauger
St Mary
Jersey   JE3 3BA

www.seekerpublishing.com

Origination by
SEAFLOWER BOOKS
www.ex-librisbooks.co.uk

Printed by
CPI Antony Rowe
Chippenham, Wiltshire

ISBN 978-1-9162118-2-7

CONTENTS

FOREWORD

A few years ago I was involved in the making of a TV documentary on the Occupation of the Channel Islands. Naturally, I wanted to talk to anyone who had been in Jersey during that time and who might be considered an authority on the subject. Whenever and whoever we asked about this, one name always came up: Bob Le Sueur, who was, we were told, without doubt one of the most important voices of the Occupation still living. Off we went along the east coast and found the white house just above the beach where Bob lived. We knocked on the door and Bob let us in. Yes, he would be happy to talk to us, anytime we liked. We were grateful and delighted, but we did not then imagine how important an interview this was to be for us. Just how special, however, we were soon to learn, as Bob sat us down and told us of the time he had spent in Jersey during those now distant years of World War II.

Robert Winter Le Sueur was working as a young (and handsome) insurance clerk when the German soldiers of 216th Infantry Division came marching into St Helier on that hot July day in 1940, the first day of the Occupation. And he was still working at his job in May 1945 when the islands were liberated. He was lucky to be alive, for during those five years of occupation, Robert, or Bob as he was and is popularly known, had taken it upon himself, in the name of common decency, to provide help and find refuge for many wretched victims of German oppression and cruelty. There was one man in particular that Bob helped: he was called Feodor Polycarpovitch Burriy, known as 'Bill' because, Bob told us, the good people of St Ouen, in which parish he was first hidden, had great difficulty in pronouncing any one of his three Russian names. Had Bob been caught helping a Russian slave-worker, he might have been imprisoned, transported to a concentration camp or even shot but, despite this, he persisted in helping Bill and as many fugitives from vicious German captivity as was within his power. Riding about the island on his rickety bicycle with lengths of hosepipe replacing proper tyres, Bob marshalled his helpers, organised safe houses and kept a kindly and caring eye on all involved in the perilous enterprise.

Bob spoke of many of his experiences during the Occupation. As he spoke it became abundantly clear that here was a man who knew and felt more about the Occupation and its effect on his fellow islanders than could ever be adequately captured in any documentary. He had befriended kind-hearted Louisa Gould, who was to meet a tragic end in the Nazi labour camp of Ravensbrück. He had worked with the would-be revolutionary, Norman Le Brocq, and encountered the stern local bureaucrat, Clifford Orange—Bob knew all the major players in the Occupation drama. This gentle and softly-spoken Jerseyman had seen it all.

'What,' I asked him, 'is the most important thing to say about those years of occupation?'

'People,' Bob replied after a pause. 'People you've known well, or thought you knew well, when faced with difficult circumstances, the naturally kind, good-hearted people can become saintly, while those with a mean streak in them become—I must be careful of the word I am using here—well, just what they are.'

It can be said without fear of contradiction that Bob himself belongs to that first category of good-hearted people. Now it is true that Bob has not been canonised, but he was, after an unconscionable time, awarded the MBE. Who has deserved it more? And who could have given a better personal account of the experience of occupation in that most terrible of wars, than appears in *Growing Up Fast*? It is, of course, hugely well informed in all the domestic and political aspects of the Occupation. The traumas, the terrors, all the humour, the unexpected laughter, all the sadness and the tears of those years are here in the pages of what is a beautiful book about an extraordinary time: the reminiscences and observations of a remarkable man, Robert Winter Le Sueur, MBE.

It is truly a privilege and a pleasure to have met him.

John Nettles
May 2020

INTRODUCTION

Bob Le Sueur is a man for whom the phrase 'a stiff upper lip' may have been written. At the age of ninety-nine he still insists on standing in the presence of any member of the opposite sex despite what he terms his 'advancing decrepitude', and would not even contemplate being seen in public without carefully combed hair and a scrupulous shave.

He is a man of precision, with an astonishing recall of facts, dates and people not only from his own experience but from history, literature and the many places of the world that he has visited.

A former teacher of English, Bob has a love of words and a rich vocabulary which he expresses in a voice still strong and powerful.

In recounting a story he will fix you with an unblinking glare if there is a strong point to be made, and hold you in a dramatic pause until relenting and continuing with his tale. Woe betide you if you should ask a foolish question or advance an opinion which is not based on sound reasoning as a lifetime of debate has left him with a keen ear for inexactitudes.

Bob's mother instilled in him from the very earliest age that it was one's social duty never ever to betray any emotion in public. Great delight or deepest despair should be greeted with an upper lip stiffer than a well-starched shirt collar; but crucially one should always have empathy for the discomfort of others. Her influence has given him great modesty, impeccable manners and a strong sense of injustice, together with a determination to offer help to anyone who might need it regardless of their background.

But don't let the stiff upper lip fool you. When he speaks of the day his friends and hundreds of others were deported by the Germans there are tears in his eyes and his voice trembles with pride at the bravery of those who kept calm and carried on despite the terrible injustice being done to them.

Those who have met him will be very aware of Bob's great intellect; he surely would have graced any university lucky enough to have received him. Sadly circumstances prevented him from such advancement, and Berger's bookshop and local debating groups became his higher education. This helped to rationalise clearly his motives for helping the escaped Russian slave known as Bill and many others, beyond a simple desire to resist. He was not attempting to oppose the Germans. He was trying to help the Russians, his fellow men. For him, it is a very important distinction.

All of this didn't necessarily make it easy to write his story. Bob's sangfroid and heartfelt unwillingness to be portrayed as any kind of hero means that he resolutely plays down what he did during those dark days of Occupation, and it was often hard to draw from him how he felt about some of the challenging moments that he faced. He is a sometimes unwilling icon of those years who has become sought after by the media not only in the island but also across the world for his memories and opinions. 'I was an ordinary man who lived through extraordinary times,' he tells them. He certainly has an extraordinary generosity of spirit. This is a man who after four and a half years of privations kept a precious bar of chocolate, earned by giving his blood at the hospital, for six months while existing on undercooked vegetables in order that he might share it with his friends at Christmas.

I believe that Bob, and people like him, became essential to the self-esteem of an island which had been overrun by the Germans without a shot being fired in its defence. When it was all over people wanted, per-haps needed, to believe that there had been some kind of brave opposition to their occupiers, that Jersey did not simply roll over and collaborate as some might have us think. Of course there were those who took action of various kinds, from sabotaging German cars to daubing 'V' signs on walls. Some spread the BBC news which they had heard on their illicit radios, or like Bob helped to feed, clothe and shelter the desperate men who had escaped from the Nazis' slave labour camps. Some spoke about it afterwards, but few with Bob's modest eloquence. Seventy-five years since Liberation, Bob has become the voice of a generation and I am privileged to have been able to help him tell his story.

This book is not the history of the Occupation. More than forty thousand Jersey people lived in the island during the war and the experience of every single one of them was different. The experiences of the thousands of Germans were different again. Rather, this is the history of Bob's Occupation, seen through his eyes and his experiences. Where his recollections have differed to reported fact I have attempted, with the inestimable help of Ian Ronayne, to reconcile the two. I am very grateful to Ian for his meticulous work.

Whatever his protestations to the contrary, we should be in no doubt that what Bob undertook in helping Bill and his fellow countrymen was very dangerous indeed. Twenty-two Jersey people died after being imprisoned by the Germans for crimes ranging from listening to the radio to theft. Louisa Gould, the woman who took Bill into her home, died in the hell of Ravensbrück without betraying Bob to the Germans. Had Bob been caught he would surely have faced the full weight of the Nazi justice system as a prime mover in helping a series of wanted men evade capture and punishment.

But perhaps the most telling fact is that after five years of repression, of seeing his friends deported and his family starved, Bob's biggest regret is that he never shook the hand of a young German solder he encountered on Liberation Day. His extraordinary humanity meant that on that day of all days, when he could quite understandably have cheered and jeered a defeated enemy, he wanted to begin the process of reconciliation. Like that other great Occupation historian Michael Ginns he saw that the key to the future was not through bitterness or recrimination but understanding and friendship.

In his later life Bob was able to spread that message, through his teaching and his work with Amnesty International and various African educational projects. He has been an inspiration to many people in many countries, and surely well deserved to receive the MBE from Prince Charles.

Jersey should be fiercely proud that people such as Bob and his friends did what they did, giving the lie to those who say there was no opposition to the Nazis and their terrible practices in this island. How many of them risked everything and then just drifted back into their everyday lives we will never really know, because many of them were simply far too modest to talk about it.

Once their generation is gone, who will we look up to?

Chris Stone

PREFACE

A warm summer's day in Jersey, 2019. The sun is shining down on the glistening sea around the harbour walls. A small crowd is seated in front of a memorial commemorating the German bombing of St Helier which heralded the beginning of the island's Occupation seventy-nine years before. The parish Procureur invites an old man seated in the front row to speak. The old man stands, not without considerable difficulty, but waves aside offers of help and shuffles with slow steps to the microphone. He is offered a chair. He refuses. He lifts his head and his piercing eyes fix the crowd as he begins to speak. His voice is at once deep, commanding and confident. They are transfixed.

'My name is Bob Le Sueur. I was swimming in the sea when the bombs began to fall....'

Chapter One

SHOULD WE STAY OR SHOULD WE GO?

Ours was a beautiful wireless. It sat in pride of place on the dining-room table, its sturdy wooden frame decorated with fretwork depicting a sunset over the sea, with a cloth screen visible behind the waves which covered the speaker. It reflected the view from the window, which looked out over the expanse of St Aubin's Bay just across the main road. Our house 'Horizon View', on the south coast, was well named and we enjoyed a panoramic vista from St Helier in the east to Noirmont Point in the west. The sun of a glorious late summer day streamed in, glittering off the water.

The wireless was controlled by my father, who was known by his traditional Jersey Christian name of Winter. My mother Lizzie, who came from French parents, controlled almost everything else in her own subtle way. The BBC educated, informed and entertained us, and helped to develop my interest in world events.

It was 3 September 1939. Three days before, Germany had shocked the world by invading Poland, and it was therefore no surprise that I had delayed my morning swim to gather around the wireless with my mother and father to hear the latest news from the continent. We knew that the Prime Minister, Mr Chamberlain, was to address the nation at eleven o'clock. I had followed developments in Germany with an educated ear; my school, Victoria College, had somehow induced myself and my fellow students to believe we were to be the most highly educated males in the island and as such we would bear great responsibility for making decisions in our community later in life. We had all been encouraged to know what the words Marxism, Fascism, and Socialism actually meant. Unlike other teachers who we sometimes teased badly, I almost worshipped the man who taught us modern history, who warned us that we should know as much as possible about the threats facing the world.

Consequently when Mr Chamberlain announced wearily that 'this country is at war with Germany', I heard his words with no great amazement. My father though was dismayed. He had fought in the First Word War, with all the terrible experiences that had entailed and I distinctly remember him repeating sadly, 'I never thought this would happen again. They told us we were in the war to end all wars ...'.

My thoughts were equally morose. I was convinced I would be dead within days, my nineteen-year-old life snuffed out by untimely conflict. I fortified myself with the thought of Sir Francis Drake playing bowls on Plymouth Hoe when news came of the Spanish Armada's impending arrival. He had calmly carried on his game, so I resolved to continue in the same spirit. Picking up my towel, I strode out of the house and across the road to have my swim. After all, I never knew when I might have the chance of another. As I floated on my back in the sun-kissed sea I thought how crazy it was that we were surrounded by the beauty of nature, only now preparing to muck it all up with the violence of war.

After lunch I pedalled off to the house of one of my nearby friends to suggest we make a trip to swim on the north coast, fully expecting that area to be made off limits very soon due to invasion precautions. But when I arrived I found him very busy helping his father to rig up material across all the windows for The Blackout. Undeterred, I headed to the nearby pool at Havre des Pas where I found a throng of people splashing about and enjoying the sun. There was a very artificial mood of defiance, the shouts of the men a little too loud and the shrieks of the women a little too shrill. They were determined to show the world they would not be put off from their freedoms by the threat of war.... As the sun set, our first night of blackout darkness began.

The Air Raid Precaution, or ARP, man, who had already been appointed, came to our house early on since we were on the coast. One of our lights could be seen through the thin curtains, and we were ordered to remove the bulb until thicker drapes could be found. So ended 3 September 1939, the first day of conflict. I lay down with my gas mask that night unsure of what the next day might bring.

I awoke alive and ungassed, but with the gloomy recollection that we were at war, and also that I would be expected at work as usual.

I had taken an office job after passing my 'Higher' exams at school, with good grades in English and History but having failed to shine at Geography. I had taken that subject believing that I would learn all about the peoples and places of the world, but instead found that I was learning mostly about isobars and isotherms and suchlike.

University was not an option to me as it was only a choice for those who were wealthy enough—and my parents certainly could not have afforded such expense. The number of young Jersey people who went to university at that time could have been counted on the fingers of both hands. With my certificates freshly earned, I felt satisfied to gain the post of Office Boy at the General Accident, Fire and Life Assurance Corporation on Hill Street right in the centre of St Helier.

While my position at the Corporation was a lowly one, I would surely be missed had I not turned up and I found it was very much business as usual there, with everyone trying very hard to carry on as before. We were not encouraged to chatter about our impending deaths, or indeed talk about anything that was not directly related to our work. I was certainly expected to know my place, and the chief clerk, who was rather a martinet, made sure of it. Holidaymakers who had expected Jersey to live up to its pre-war promise of a peaceful sun-soaked paradise had realised the island could be vulnerable to attack and made plans to leave. That sent many of them to our door to make insurance arrangements, but still the feeling persisted that one should endeavour to continue as normal.

After a few days this became increasingly easy, as Europe sank into what would become known as the Phoney War. While we dutifully carried our gas masks with us everywhere, there was little sign that they would be necessary. The French after all had the much-vaunted Maginot Line, and somehow one expected that Hitler would not invade neutral territory such as Belgium and Holland in order to sweep around and attack France through the tradesman's door. Mercifully there was little likelihood of me being conscripted as Jersey's government (known as the States) had yet to implement fully the National Service Law they had agreed soon after the war began. We were all of the view that the war would take place 'over there'. However, Jersey has always been a patriotic island, and I became aware of an increasing number of my friends and acquaintances signing up for service. At that stage I was resolutely against any form of violent action against anyone after attending a Christian discussion group which debated how one should behave, and I hoped never to have that resolution tested. I distinctly recall questioning the intentions of a friend who had signed up for the RAF. How could you drop a bomb on a city, I wanted to know. Your bombs, like the biblical rain, will fall on the just and on the unjust, I told him, and probably kill far more women and children than any trainee stormtroopers. The Nazis, I was sure, wouldn't be sitting at home in their cities. He dismissed my arguments though, and prepared himself for battle.

Quite a few of us were pacifists. I had read about a strong movement on the mainland led by a dynamic priest that called for every citizen simply to defy the government and refuse any kind of military service, and with the idealism of youth I initially subscribed to that belief.

However, as the Nazi war machine started to smash its way through western Europe in early May, I began to wane in my determination to remain aloof from the conflict. On the wireless we heard of the invasion of France and the Low Countries, at the cinema we saw the Pathé newsreel footage of burning towns and floods of refugees. I had been devastated by the Nazi annexation of Czechoslovakia, a country I viewed as a model of progressive values. As the Panzers rolled westwards my outright pacifism gave way to a determination to help in some way.

My good friend Clifford du Feu was a member of the Quakers, a religious denomination which allowed its members to help tend the injured and dying on the battlefield. He intended to join the Friends Ambulance Unit which was run by that order, and wanted me to go with him. That, I decided, would fit the bill for my troubled conscience, and I was keen to go to England to start training.

Such a commitment was not to be taken lightly, however, and I encountered my first hurdle at work. My boss, Mr Barnes, pleaded with me not to go, given that the two other men in the office were already over the age of twenty and consequently likely to become eligible for military service once the conscription law was in place. 'I would be left alone with the women ...', he moaned. Women in those days were not expected to have a job of any consequence, let alone responsibility, and he held grave concerns for our business prospects should he have to rely solely on their efforts to keep the office running.

While my sense of duty to work argued with my humanitarian urge to do my bit, matters across the water in France were moving rather more quickly. The Germans swept the poorly equipped allied armies into the North Sea at Dunkirk and sped towards Paris even as the famous little ships carried the last of the evacuated soldiers homewards. On 14 June the capital fell, although the BBC didn't give the matter its highest priority. I remember their six o'clock broadcast that evening leading with the news that Pont l'Eveque had won the Derby. Nonetheless, people in Jersey were acutely aware of the imminent collapse of France, especially when a few days later the Bailiff, the leader of the States, was requested by the Admiralty to help. He asked members of the St Helier Yacht Club to aid in the evacuation of the harbour and beaches around St Malo, where some of the remnants of the British Expeditionary Force were holding out hoping for rescue. My pal Pat de Gruchy, who was to crew for his dad in their little boat, told me they set off with orders to pick up British troops first, then any fighting French, then any other English people. When they returned, he said that as well as sundry troops they had managed to pick up an English lord, his wife and their dog!

In the days that followed I could still see from my bedroom window British troop transports arriving in the harbour to garrison the island. The whole atmosphere was one of movement, constant questions and few answers. Some people, mainly those who weren't native islanders, started to leave. The news the following day turned the trickle of departures into a flood. The island newspaper the *Evening Post* announced blandly that Jersey would be demilitarised, and the garrison, together with any soldiers rescued from St Malo, would move out immediately. The news galvanised many islanders into making their own preparations to leave, as it seemed evident to most of us that the Germans would not stop at France when they could see our little island clearly from the western coast of the Cherbourg peninsula. One of the most agonising decisions faced by any Channel Islands family during the war was, 'Should we stay or should we go?'

For me and my family it was a very difficult debate, although I'm sure the conversations we had were similar to those in just about every household in the island. Should we stay and await an uncertain future at the hands of the enemy? Or go and leave our home and everything we loved behind? My father had many virtues, but a great love of work was not one of them. He was fifty-eight and owned our home and another property that was let. He also had shares in some utilities such as the gas and water companies, all of which were based in Jersey. After much discussion, he declared that at his age he was not going to be a 'penniless refugee' and have people telling him what to do. He was going to stay. I'm not sure my mother's opinion was requested or required. She was, in any case, concerned about how we might make our escape if we did decide to go. The Channel was known to be full of U-boats, and even the daily mailboat had been forced to sail at night.

Betty Ward Simpson, who worked in my office, brought news. Her father owned a pub at Gorey, and had met some French people there who had just come from France on a fishing boat. They reported seeing the first German reconnaissance motorcycles on the outskirts of Carteret, a small port just fifteen miles across the water from the island and easily visible from Jersey's east coast on a clear day. The tension rose further.

As a young man of military age, I worried what the Germans might do with me. Could I run the risk of staying only to be captured and perhaps turned into some kind of cog in the Nazi machine? I voiced my concerns at length to my parents, who finally agreed that I should try to leave—but without them. The following morning I would go to the Town Hall on my way to work and pick up the necessary paperwork which would enable my departure, as we had been told no-one would be allowed to sail from the island in any kind of boat without the correct forms. I could then ask permission of my firm to depart. Finally resolved to brave the sea crossing and face the war in freedom, I went to bed for an unquiet sleep. I don't suppose my parents were any more restful as they prepared to watch their only son sail away to an uncertain future.

The following morning I dressed especially carefully. After a scrupulous shave, I donned a clean shirt and my Burton's suit, all topped off with my brown pork pie hat of which I was immensely proud. Bicycle clips rounded off my natty ensemble, to ensure there were no tell-tale grease marks on the bottom of my trousers. I had standards to maintain, despite the imminent danger. My mother sent me off with a breakfast of porridge, toast and homemade marmalade served with a stiff upper lip before I pedalled off down The Avenue towards town, a bag full of my favourite ham sandwiches swinging from the handlebars, expecting to get to work in good time.

Upon arrival at Cheapside, however, it became clear that there would be no timely arrival for me that day, as hundreds of Jersey people appeared to have had the same idea and were queuing for their own paperwork to get away from the island. I could see that the line to get into the Town Hall filled the pavement on the south side of The Parade, and turned down into Gloucester Street. As I drew level, I could see it extended hundreds of metres all the way down past the Opera House, across Sand Street, onto The Esplanade and around the corner. More people were streaming to join the back of the queue and I realised that I had better join it myself jolly quickly. Some people were there alone, some had brought their whole family, others were queuing on behalf of eight or nine relatives. There was an atmosphere of contagious, but contained, hysteria. Trembling fingers held nervously smoked cigarettes to calm frayed nerves. Every now and then someone would try to push in, to be given short shrift from those already in the queue. Still, it was well behaved, a little like a queue for a cinema or big game. A hum of excited noise rose from all sides and I realised very quickly that I couldn't stay until it was my turn. The world may have been coming to an end, but still I could not be late for work …

My sense of duty got the better of me, and I resolved to ask permission from my boss to take some time off in order to join the queue. Much as I wanted to get away from Jersey I couldn't leave my work just like that. Reluctantly pushing my bicycle away from the ever-lengthening queue, I remounted and pedalled away in the direction of Hill Street. No. 37 was a large granite-clad building with its doorway set up a short flight of steps. I carried my machine up the steps to the double doors, which I had to wedge open carefully to allow it to pass. Woe betide me if I had scratched them with a careless pedal. Should the chief clerk have seen me even attempt the manoeuvre without wedging the door open first there would have been great trouble. As I pushed towards the little room where I kept my bike, I became aware of quite a hubbub coming from the main office on the right where people were already waiting to be served. All I could see was a row of backs, whose owners were facing the counter in some agitation, so I quickly parked my bicycle and went to see what assistance I might be able to offer them. An air of hysteria pervaded the office. The only other person to have made it to work that day was the youngest of the three typists, Mrs Phyllis du Feu, who was trying valiantly to remain calm while being assailed by distressed customers wanting her attention. It transpired that the chief clerk had arrived first thing, and simply handed her the keys to every lock in the building, from the safe to the lavatory. He had then disappeared to join the queue which I had so recently vacated, and wasn't seen again until he turned up in 1945 wearing the dashing hat of someone who had fought in Burma.

Pushing my way behind the counter I tried to address the most pressing needs of our clamouring clientele. One man, who was rushing to get to the great queue for a boat himself, wanted to insure a load of jewellery for the journey. He presented a valuation sheet for various pieces, which he assured me were packed and ready to travel with him. He was in his fifties, and gave off an aura of money and authority. Regretfully, however, I had to point out to him that he would need to prove to me that the jewels actually existed. Normally the boss, Mr Barnes, would have asked to see them, item by item, and checked them off against the valuation list. I knew as much, and told him that I could give him a travel insurance paper but it would only be valid on a licensed passenger boat—and, moreover, any war damage would be excluded from the cover.

My news was not welcomed. He blew up, shouting and hammering the counter with his fist. The phone was ringing constantly, and neither Mrs du Feu nor I could answer because all the other people in the office were shouting simultaneously at the tops of their voices with a rising sense of panic. Through the window I could see a rather beautiful young woman across the road in tears, who was shouting, 'Has anyone seen my little boy? He's only three!'

Gritting my teeth I tried to continue as best I could. There was a constant influx of people, most of whom were not thinking at all logically, and Mrs du Feu and I tried in vain to placate them. Surely, I thought, Mr Barnes will be here soon. Or perhaps our other colleagues, Mr Butterworth, Miss Locke, Miss Ward Simpson ...? But no, we were alone in the face of a rising storm. Whenever I could snatch a moment I tried to call the head office in Southampton, but the lines were permanently engaged. In those days the few lines to England were along a cable which ran from Plémont beach on the north coast via Guernsey across the Channel, and they were understandably inundated with callers wanting to contact their friends and relatives. In between arguing with clients and trying the phone, Mrs du Feu and I shared my sandwiches and wondered what on earth would happen next.

Finally the customers dropped away as the day grew late, and we were able to leave. Any chance of my joining the queue for evacuation that day had evaporated.

Three days passed before I finally managed to contact the branch office in Southampton. During that time the queue for boat permits became shorter, but I didn't succumb to the temptation of joining it. My basic sense of duty, inherited from my mother, compelled me to stay at work until the job was done. During this time, the mood for some became almost defiant. Some maintained loudly that Hitler wouldn't DARE approach our shores, and if he did then 'Our Boys' would soon send him packing. It was almost seen as traitorous to consider the possibility that the contemptible little corporal—as Hitler was derisively named—could hold any sway over His Majesty's subjects. Unfortunately I knew that those types weren't aware of the facts. The BBC news was always days or even weeks out of date. After Paris fell, we were still being told that the Germans had just reached the Seine. We had seen their aircraft in the skies overhead, and we knew they were just across the water from us in St Malo and Carteret. I became cynical about our chances.

My rather one-sided telephone conversation with the branch office did little to encourage me. The manager I spoke to was Colonel Thorpe, an ex-military man who I believe may have promoted himself somewhat from his original rank, although he always insisted on being addressed in that way. He rated a chauffeur-driven Humber in company livery, and was a most rarefied creature.

In a voice characterised many years later by Colonel Square from *Dad's Army*, he blew up at me for my preposterous effrontery in demanding of the girl on the switchboard that I should be put through to him. Did I not realise his position, he barked, or how great was the degree of his responsibility? He demanded in no uncertain terms that I should fetch Mr Barnes AT ONCE.

'But that's what I've been trying to tell you Sir,' I pleaded. 'We haven't seen him since Tuesday ...'

He then demanded an answer to the most pressing question of the day.

'Are you trying to tell me that His Majesty's Government is preparing to abandon British Territory without a shot being fired?'

Yes, I assured him diffidently, that did indeed seem to be the case.

'I cannot listen to such treasonable garbage any longer. If any of what you are saying is true then you and the girl had better stay right where you are. Should Mr Barnes appear at this office I will send him back to

Jersey IMMEDIATELY.'

I stayed as ordered.

For some days after the mass evacuation, there was a strange sense of forced normality in the island. More customers came and went, as did some of the furniture which was held in a storage warehouse upstairs from our offices. We got used to men lugging large chairs and tables through the doors, ''ere mind yer back mate ...', and tried to cope with the backlog of paperwork. We could regularly hear the sound of aircraft flying over the island, and could sometimes even see them, although they were usually too high to discern their markings clearly. We knew that we were no longer garrisoned and presumed that German intelligence would somehow know that there were no British soldiers here.

The mailboats continued to come, only three times a week, travelling at night because of the threat of U-boats. The potato exports even began again, and the usual queues of lorries laden with the produce of the fields began to form at the harbour. Life, after all, had to go on.

On 27 June we finally had news of the unfortunate Mr Barnes. He had arrived in Southampton with his wife and three children, no doubt to a rather warm reception from the Colonel. We were told he had been sent back to the island, undoubtedly in some disgrace. He was booked onto the mailboat on Sunday night, the 30th, to arrive on the Monday morning. Branch office clearly had no sense of the situation here, which was unsurprising as no announcement had been made of the Channel Islands' demilitarised status. Poor Mr Barnes had acted to protect himself and his family from the marauding Hun, but had received no sympathy whatsoever.

But if he was indeed to return, it meant that I could, with a clear conscience, prepare to leave the island myself. I went to the office of the Southern Railway, which owned the mail boat, in Bond Street and booked myself one of the last available tickets for the Monday night sailing, sitting on the deck. No doubt the business would be safe in Mr Barnes' capable hands, so yes, I wanted to go.

Unfortunately the Third Reich had other ideas, and my first glimpse of a German was through the plexiglass canopy of his aircraft, through which he was shooting up the island indiscriminately with a machine gun.

It happened the very day after I bought my ticket. I had cycled home after a long hot day at work, and resolved to have what could be my final swim in Jersey before leaving. It was a lovely evening, and the tide was halfway up. Living so close to the beach, I got changed at home and strolled across the road dressed in my swimming trunks and sandals. (I had persisted in wearing the new-fangled trunks, despite some baths in the UK insisting on the old-fashioned swimming costume.)

Paddling slowly out, I reflected that this could be one of my last opportunities for such relaxation for a very long time. I suppose I had gone about 150 yards out when above the sound of my splashes I heard the buzz of aircraft engines. These sounded a lot closer than those we had heard before. Then above the engine sounds I heard some muffled explosions. I stopped swimming, wiped the salt water from my eyes, and looked towards the direction of the intruders. They were indeed flying low over Fort Regent in St Helier a mile or so to the east, and as I watched something fell from one of them. It landed with a great splash, evidently in the harbour, then another crashed to the ground with a roar and a huge ball of fire. I quickly drew the conclusion that this wasn't the best place to be if the air raid was to continue, and made a very quick about turn towards the beach. I could hear the bombs falling as I swam, crashes and bangs echoing across the water from the direction of the docks. As I reached the shallows I put my feet down and began to run, but realised I would be a smaller target if I stayed as low as I could. There was a lot of sand to cover between myself and the apparent safety of home. Breathless and barefoot as I reached the slipway, I looked to the east and saw another aircraft flying over town heading in my direction, firing its machine guns in an angry rattle. It would be upon me in an instant.

There was little in the way of cover, but there were some large tamarisk bushes marking the division between the pavement and the road. Panting, I threw myself down underneath one of them in the vague hope that it might offer me some protection. Peering out from beneath the foliage I could clearly see the plane, and the shattered pieces of tarmac being thrown up from the ground as it was hit by the stream of bullets fired by the gunner, visible in the cockpit. Closer and closer they came, but strangely I don't think he was actually trying to kill me, rather using his weapon to inspire a feeling of terror. I lay there realising my shelter certainly wouldn't stop a bullet, but at least I would be hidden from view.

Luckily the plane flashed by over my head, and off towards St Aubin. As soon as it was gone I wasted no time in extricating myself from the bush, dusting myself off and running across the road to check on my family.

Bursting through the door, I could hear disembodied voices.

'We're in the cupboard under the stairs, Bobby,' called my mother. I was able to assure them of my wellbeing, and explain that the raiders seemed to have left us alone, for the moment at least.

(I was known to most people, including my mother, by the name Bobby. The one exception was my terribly correct Aunt Mabel. To her, I was always Robert. She was a governess in London with a wealthy family and looked after their young children through the worst nights of the Blitz with a phlegm that would have brought tears to Winston Churchill's eyes. On one occasion as the family sat down to tea there was a huge explosion very close by. 'What's that?' cried the children in alarm. 'Bombs, dear,' she said. 'Take your elbows off the table.')

Shortly after I discovered my mother and the neighbours under the stairs, we were joined by my father, who had spent the raid sheltering under a table in a building near the Weighbridge. He was followed by Auntie Ethel, who, together with my mother's brother Uncle Ernest, lived in a hotel on The Esplanade very close to where the bombing had been concentrated. They were a well-to-do couple, who would usually take their prized motor car if they wished to get around the island. But today there had been too much urgency to fetch it from its garage near the Gasworks on the other side of town, and they had instead pedalled the mile or so on their bikes to flee the explosions. Auntie Ethel was a rather rotund lady, and the journey had no doubt been rather difficult and uncomfortable for her. One of my abiding memories of that day was the sight of her enormous underpants hung out to dry on the line in our back yard. The air raid had had a disastrous effect on her …

My mother was most upset by what had happened. She expressed what many Jersey people were thinking at the time. 'Perhaps we should have gone after all! I suppose it's too late now.'

On the nine o'clock news that night, two hours after the raid, the BBC finally announced that the British Government had decided to withdraw the garrison from the Channel Islands, even though we knew the decision had actually been taken ten days earlier. The Germans would have been made aware of the fact through the American embassy. I remember feeling very cynical about this, that our own people were worse than the Germans when it came to denying disaster for their own ends. Rather than pretending to the world that all was well they should have made it clear to the Germans that we were undefended rather than risk the lives of islanders.

The following morning they announced that the Channel Islands had been bombed. It was transparent to me that we had effectively told the Germans that it was safe to attack us. Pictures of the destruction were in the newspaper the next day.

The whole island was on edge, but still people tried to continue their lives, perhaps in the hope that we would now be left alone.

On the Sunday, 30 June, relieved to have a day away from the office, I rode my bicycle west along the seafront to the beach at St Brelade to visit friends who lived in the bay. I was still wondering whether the mailboat might sail, despite the BBC having told the world that we were vulnerable. No further danger appeared that day, although we heard through the grapevine that German planes had been seen circling and landing in Guernsey.

The next morning I awoke to the sound of a German aircraft once more. Since there was glass on three sides of my second-storey dormer window, I was able to look out and watch it pass. There was no bombing or machine-gunning this time, but as it flew over Bel Royal a mile or so to the west, two parachutes came floating down from it. I thought for one excited moment that they were going to drop their men by parachute, but as they fell I realised they were not human bodies after all—they were long cylinders. They landed on the beach, since it was low tide, and their canopies collapsed gently around them as people approached gingerly to see what they might contain. The answer was bundles of official messages for the Commander-in-Chief of the Island of Jersey. That would usually be the Lieutenant-Governor, but he had already left, so the documents were passed instead to the Bailiff, Alexander Coutanche. We were lucky to have a Bailiff who, by a series of unlikely circumstances, had risen to the position before reaching the age of forty. He was known to be energetic and very able, and took up the unwelcome message from the Germans that he would have to share with us. As he could make no decisions without the States' authority, he called an emergency meeting.

I headed to work as usual, and news of the parachutes and the emergency meeting was already well known by people I met along the way. Mrs du Feu didn't come in that day, as she had given notice to leave at the end of June to have a baby. At this significant moment, I decided that the office could stay closed to customers for the time being, while I caught up with some essential tidying up. Gathering whatever important documents I could find, I took them to the filing rooms in careful order. The company's most sensitive documents I hid away in the safe, and put the key in my pocket to keep at home. I was still persisting in doing my duty by the company.

With everything organised, I headed the few short yards to the Royal Square to see if I could find out what had been concluded at the States' meeting.

Part of the square was already cordoned off, with workmen standing about as workmen do. I asked one of them what he was doing. With an air of enormous self-importance, he told me that he 'wasn't allowed to say, mate.'

I was only nineteen, but I felt instinctively that this was a critical moment. This man was enjoying the fact that he knew more about what was happening than the rest of us. He and his pals stood around in their working clothes clutching large paint brushes and paint pots, smug in their secret knowledge. It was information that we would find out soon enough though.

The square was full of people, all speculating with an edge of hysteria about what might happen to them. We had been told the Germans had swept through Belgium and France bayoneting babies and raping women, and many believed this to be true, so you can imagine the fear and apprehension running like waves through the hundreds of islanders waiting to hear their fate. I too was apprehensive, but I didn't believe the more lurid headlines. Perhaps there were one or two maniacs who had done such things, but there were maniacs in every country. Unfortunately, it seemed Nazi Germany now had a place for such people.

I was standing close to the golden statue of George II, who had surveyed the square from the top of his plinth for the past 200 years. In 1781 he had seen the Battle of Jersey in the very square itself, when the last invaders to attempt to seize our island had been repulsed. Two women were standing close to me, and I overheard one say to the other, 'The moment this is over we must hurry back home and barricade the doors. There are going to be a lot of women raped before nightfall.' That was the pervading atmosphere.

But just as it seemed panic might set in, Captain Benest with his pork pie hat strode to the fore to sort out the rabble. The Captain was a businessman with his finger in a lot of pies. Travel agent, furniture depository owner, and general 'man about town', he was very much a ladies' man and owned the building which housed our office. He insisted people used his military title, despite never having been a full-time soldier. He and his abrupt manner were well known in the island.

He was a natty dresser, and never without his well-brushed pork pie hat set at a rakish angle. He had one of those assertive army voices, accustomed to command, very much of the 'upper strata'. He strutted into the square from the direction of his offices in Mulcaster Street, took one look at the hoi-polloi milling about, and took it as his civic duty to call them to order. I heard his voice clearly.

'Now, will you stand in line! The Bailiff will be coming out shortly to make an important statement. He must have space to reach the statue! Not there madam, further back! You boy, you are on the wrong side, get lost!'

I did as I was told, for he would have recognised me as the squirt of a boy from the office.

Most regrettably for him, just as his diatribe was in full flow, a pigeon passed overhead and was evidently unimpressed with all the noise. With perfect aim it relieved itself copiously over the good Captain's immaculate hat, before swooping away to a convenient tree. With spluttering anger, Captain Benest shook the soiled piece of millinery and let loose a few choice words before marching off with as much dignity as he could muster. The unexpected drama pricked the bubble of tension, and gales of laughter echoed from the walls around the square, especially from the women who had feared a German attack on their chastity a few moments earlier. The tale was passed quickly around to those who hadn't seen it, and soon the whole crowd was abuzz with the downfall of the unfortunate Captain.

It was then that a door in the side of the States' Building opened, and the Bailiff came out looking very tense. Passing close to where I was standing, he waited for quiet before making an announcement from the foot of the statue.

He explained the demands of the Germans, as detailed in the documents which I had seen land by parachute. There was no choice, he said, but to surrender our island. Every property must display a white flag as a token of no resistance, before the troops arrived.

I heard his words without surprise. I had never expected 'Our Boys' to come back and had realised the inevitable some days before. No more than what I had anticipated was about to happen, and we would simply have to adjust.

The people in the crowd turned to each other for reassurance, muttering, and I saw the self-satisfied workmen begin the job they had been preparing for: the painting of an enormous white cross of surrender in the centre of the Royal Square.

By the time I got home, my mother had heard the news and was considering how best to make a white flag. She was fixing a beautifully ironed white sheet to a broom, to be flown from one of the dormer windows on the top floor. But as I watched, my father intervened. 'Take that down, and put it back where it belongs. One of my vests will be good enough.' He chose a garment that was full of holes, and fixed it contemptuously to the broom to hang out of the window. It was his little gesture of defiance, although I couldn't help thinking that perhaps some of Auntie Ethel's enormous bloomers might have done a better job: she was still living with us following the bombing, and I recall her saying that the RAF would be back to bomb us now!

Although I had effectively closed the office for the day there were still some duties to carry out, one of which took me to Grouville in the east of the island that afternoon. As I pedalled I reflected on my situation, and it dawned on me that I hadn't yet received my June salary and now seemed quite unlikely to do so. Technically I now had no job, no money, was living with my parents, was of military age, and therefore most vulnerable to any German impositions. It was not a happy thought. Struggling up Grouville Hill, I looked up to see a formation of aircraft heading west, towards the airport. I didn't know it at the time, but they held the first Germans who were to land in my island.

My business in Grouville completed, I coasted back down the hill and along the seafront home. While I had been busy, so had our new occupiers. At the airport, they had commandeered a bus that was usually used to shuttle passengers to and from the aircraft. On the front, in large letters, was the sign 'London', which it seemed they viewed as a good omen. In the quiet of the early evening we heard the engine of this old machine running along the Avenue towards our home, and naturally came out from our front door to see what was going on. Along came the bus, piled high with Germans, and it drew to a momentary halt right outside our house. We stood in the doorway nervously, wondering what to do. The doors opened and out they piled, soldiers in uniform, giddy with the excitement of conquest. At first I was shocked at just how simply normal they were: of a similar age to me, with two arms and two legs, and uniforms similar to those worn by our own servicemen. But these young men were full of swagger, shouting to each other, larking about, and waving at us. They were the conquerors, and had no doubt that the war was almost won. However, they seemed to hold no immediate threat; they didn't look as though they were about to embark on an orgy of rape and destruction. We stood and watched, unsure of ourselves, without responding, until they climbed back aboard their rickety bus and headed off towards town.

My mother was most upset, and particularly concerned that our home would be looted in short order. She begged my father to hide the expensive ormolu clock that stood in pride of place on the mantlepiece, visible through the living room window. 'But make sure you take the pendulum out before you move it,' she exhorted him, 'in case it gets damaged.'

Our Occupation had begun.

Chapter Two

OCCUPIED

There was no sign of our new friends the following morning, and I resolved to return to work despite my frustration with my superiors. I had obeyed instructions to stay put until Mr Barnes returned, and he had not done so, leaving me at the mercy of the mischievous Hun.

My first stop was to see the unfortunate Captain Benest, to ask him if our essential papers could be stored in his huge building for processing after the war. Mrs du Feu turned up as well but only out of curiosity to see the damage that had been caused in the air raid. She did, however, bring news; there was to be a meeting at the Pearl Insurance Company of those managers or their deputies who were still in the island and responsible for people's insurance matters. I reflected on my position that day, and resolved the following morning to attend in my new capacity as Acting Manager. Since there was no-one to disagree, I had promoted myself at a stroke.

The meeting was in an upstairs office, made intimidating by the rows and rows of expectant bentwood chairs. I took one at the back near the door, a little awed by the number of older men in expensive suits already seated around a large table in the middle. One or two turned to look at me, peered more carefully, and pointed me out to their colleagues. Some were as old as forty-five or even fifty, which seemed positively aged to a nineteen-year-old boy with a pimply face. Their discussions continued without me as I lacked the confidence to join in. Despite the war, they argued, insurance was important and should be maintained as a service. One representative, possibly from the Royal London, was very on the ball. He frightened us all by his understanding that under international law, we were all now effectively employees of companies which the Germans could consider enemy entities. They would therefore be justified in seizing our assets. He suggested we formed an Association in order to present a united front. Some demurred, and requested a day to consider the idea.

The following day we met again to thrash out a constitution, over the objections of some representatives who were still unsure, and we did what any group of Englishmen do when they take on responsibility; we elected a chairman, and a secretary who would take minutes.

By the third day it was all agreed, and I marvelled at how these matters had seemed far more pressing than the fact that our island was now under enemy occupation. Fortunately I had managed to keep our office open by appealing to Mrs du Feu's better nature. 'I have no money to pay you,' I said, 'but I have none for myself either. Can you at least come in for two weeks?' She agreed, despite having to cycle up the long and steep Trinity Hill to get home every day when six months pregnant. While I was away at those meetings, people still came in to pay their premiums, largely in cash. Over the door of our office was the elaborate sign of a lion and a unicorn, informing the world that we operated by appointment to His Majesty the King, so what could be safer? But as the money came in I was entirely unsure what to do with it. It was clear that we needed to keep the insurance money separate from the money required to run the office, and it would have to be safely deposited in a bank. I took myself, in my new capacity of Acting Manager, to Lloyds. When I got to the counter though, the clerk told me that the company account was in the company name in Southampton, and consequently he couldn't take the money. In desperation I asked if I could open a new account, with myself as signatory. That was above the capacity of the clerk, who made me an appointment with the manager, Mr Vaudin himself. In those days bank managers were pillars of the community, elevated individuals who would brook no messing about.

I was ushered into Mr Vaudin's office, where I beheld a man of great antiquity seated behind a grand wooden desk. Peering at me over the top of half-moon spectacles, he did not stand, nor invite me to sit.

'You want to open a bank account in the name of your company? That would be most irregular. Do you have power of attorney?'

I was awed by his words, and had no idea what the power of attorney might be. 'No, Sir,' I mumbled.

'Of course not. Why do you need a bank account? I am informed there is to be some kind of loose association between the insurance companies and that the companies are to run their own administration.'

At this point I must confess I was thinking purely of how on earth I was to pay the wages of Mrs du Feu and myself. I told him as much.

'I see. Well in that case there is only one thing that can be done. We will open an account in YOUR name, RE the General Accident Insurance Co.'

With that, he pressed a brass bell on his desk and almost instantly the door was opened by a suitably subservient flunkey. I was led away to fill in endless forms, and give a specimen signature. I was also given my very first cheque book. Fortunately in those days cheque books didn't have the details of the account holder on them, so on my way back to work I stopped in at a little shop beside the Royal Square. There, I asked them to prepare a rubber stamp, with a space for my signature above 'RE General Accident Insurance Co.' In a voice that had only just broken properly, I assured them that it was urgent, and required within the next two days. I was undoubtedly a rather timid young man who was not particularly self-assured; but I think we all had to grow up rather fast under the Occupation and I was prepared to stand up to my responsibilities. At nineteen, I was just beginning to assume command, together with acne and pimples.

When it arrived I took great delight in stamping out my name. With a flourish I wrote a cheque to 'Cash', went to the bank and withdrew what I needed to pay our wages. I was able to give Mrs du Feu her two weeks' salary, and after careful consideration allow myself a significant pay rise. From my modest forty pounds a year, I was gratified now to be earning three pounds a week, the maximum wage allowed by our new occupiers. To ensure we were capable of dealing with the more routine elements of our business I placed an advertisement in the *Evening Post* inviting applications from shorthand typists. Not wishing to divulge which company the job was for, I asked candidates to apply through a PO box. I needn't have worried about a shortage of suitable applicants, as I received 192 expressions of interest! The economy had collapsed and everyone wanted some kind of employment. Some applications were from women in their thirties with incredible shorthand typing speeds and much office experience which we really didn't need, and who frankly terrified me. At my tender age and experience they would have run rings around me, taking command in the way that only women can. Finally I took on a girl of my own age whose typing speeds were really most unimpressive, but whose personality struck a chord with me. She was serious, conscientious, and above all docile. She was known from the very start as Miss Hunt, and in all the five years we shared an office we never once progressed to first names. It simply would not have been right. I was Mr Le Sueur, and she was always Miss Hunt. It was not until she entered the Pinewood Residential Home in her eighties and I went to visit her that we finally allowed ourselves the informality of first names …

Although our Occupation had now begun, there was no immediate change or even perceived threat to our normal way of life.

But there was still the very awkward question of how one should behave towards our unwelcome visitors. To be friendly and polite would surely be anathema to any patriotic islander—yet they seemed to be unfailingly friendly and polite towards us. Two weeks after the Occupation began, my mother returned home from a shopping trip to St Helier. She was already very canny about spending ready money, and would regularly come home with parcels of things which she felt sure would be in short supply in later months. Of course there were no carrier bags then, and she would have to manage with brown paper parcels clasped precariously about her as she made her way back from town.

On this particular occasion she came through the front door greatly flustered and unsure of whether her behaviour on the homeward bus had been correct. She explained that the bus had been full, so she had been standing up with all her shopping in her arms until a bump in the road caused her to drop a parcel on the floor. A young German soldier got up, picked it up, offered her his seat, and handed her parcel back.

'But what should I have done?' she asked. 'I felt obliged to thank him, which meant looking him in the eye and being grateful to him, and surely that's not the right thing to do? I mean, what would Aunt Harriet have thought?'

Aunt Harriet lived in Bognor Regis with a husband who had been in the Indian Army.

'Aunt Harriet would not have had the good manners to thank him,' I said, 'but would have taken the seat anyway as her right. You did the right thing.'

The German was just a pleasant young man who had behaved perfectly correctly, and whose mother had brought him up properly. But all across the island people were asking themselves the same question—how should I behave to these polite young men? Was it really fraternising to return their good manners? As the first few weeks of the Occupation passed by, and the lurid tales of rape and pillage appeared increasingly baseless, we began rather to hope that perhaps it might not be so bad after all. With great ceremony, the ormolu clock was carefully replaced upon the mantlepiece.

I had my own moment of revelation. Standing at the corner of Broad Street after buying some stamps at the Post Office, I was chatting with some friends when a large car approached from the direction of Hill Street. It drew to a halt close to me, outside a printer's and stationery shop called Bigwood's. With little fuss, two German officers in green uniforms got out and headed inside. I watched through the doorway as they strode to the counter, the shop girls having fled to a back room as soon as the car had pulled up. Mr Hook, the manager, nervously asked them how he could help. With a salute, the officers presented him with a list of stationery articles which they required. As we watched, astonished, they then pulled out their wallets and PAID for the articles in advance. With another salute and a slight inclination of the head, they turned on their heels, returned to their car and drove away. My friends and I watched in amazement. They hadn't swooped in shouting and demanding this and that, there had been no threats or guns. They were just like normal shoppers.

Word soon got around. These were not the baby-killing, all-conquering Huns we had been expecting. They were considerate, well educated and well paid—and were happy to spend their wages in Jersey shops. Indeed, within a few short months the shelves of many St Helier shops were almost bare, as the souvenir-hungry soldiery bought up entire stocks of jewellery, silks, watches and trinkets. For a while there was profit to be made.

There were still those, however, who insisted that this would be a very short-term arrangement and that 'Our Boys' would soon return to beat off the ghastly Hun and send them packing. One such was Mr Rodd. Mr Rodd was my latest addition to our small staff. He had been a self-employed commercial traveller, who had come to the island on the very last sailing from Southampton a few weeks before. He had arrived on a Friday morning with a suitcase full of Christmas novelties. He went to his usual hotel to set up a stockroom and display ready to attract customers and perhaps arrange some early orders. While the establishment was patriotically called The British Hotel, the owners were rather more realistic about the island's impending fate. In no uncertain terms, they asked him what on earth he thought he was doing in Jersey, and persuaded him to go straight back to the ticket office, suitcase and all, and book a sailing back to England. He managed to get a ticket for the same Monday night as I did, with the same unfortunate outcome. I took him on about halfway through July, around three weeks into the Occupation, to undertake routine office work.

He had no doubts that the small German presence on the island was just a temporary inconvenience that would soon be resolved by our brave lads in khaki. He was a Wesleyan preacher at home, with a strong faith in what was right and proper. I can still picture him standing by the window of our office, heavily built with a pinstriped blue suit and white hair, as we heard the approach of marching feet and martial music. It was a large parade of soldiers, hundreds of them strutting behind a full military band down Hill Street and right outside our window. He gaped like a fish as the demonstration of might passed by, before giving vent to the strongest oath I ever heard him use. 'By Jehosephat!' he cried. It was so comic that Miss Hunt got up from her typewriter and ran to the back room to stifle her laughter. I found it hard to keep a straight face myself, but his confusion was typical of many other islanders. This Occupation was not to be a brief, unobtrusive inconvenience. We soon realised they were here to stay.

It wasn't long until I met my first German, as a result of my insurance work. We received a bill for repairs to a damaged car. It was a Standard Swallow—known, perhaps rather unfortunately, as an 'SS'. A beautiful vehicle with a huge long bonnet, it was typically owned by movie stars and other famous people. It really was the glamour car of its day. The car in question had been involved in a crash before the Germans arrived, and had been taken to an agency garage for repairs. When the Germans came, they had needed transport so they had gone around requisitioning as many cars as they could find—including those which were in garages being fixed.

We got the bill from the garage for this particular vehicle—and it was for hundreds of pounds. The invoice detailed a new radiator grille, new bonnet, new wing, new door, and many extra items. Aghast, I immediately called the establishment and asked to see the repairs for myself. 'You'll be lucky sonny,' the owner told me. 'The Huns have taken it.'

But I already knew that the Germans didn't just take things without a by your leave—at least not then. They always either bought them or left detailed and complicated paperwork explaining exactly what had been taken, who by, and from whom. I told him the car shouldn't have been repaired before I saw it. 'We didn't know you were still operating,' he told me. 'But you must have known,' I replied. 'You have been in contact with our office for weeks!'

'Don't get funny with me, boy ...'

I had to be careful how I responded. This was one of the largest companies in the island, and their business was very important to us. I decided to investigate before taking matters any further, although I had a very shrewd guess as to what had happened. A German would have seen the repaired car sitting in the garage, and requisitioned it for his own use. He would have examined the car for any defects, taken the chassis number, and completed all kinds of forms in triplicate before finally driving it away with a punctilious salute. My first stop, therefore, was to a States' office in St Helier which had been set up to deal with requisitioned property. The man in the Bond Street office told me that indeed, such a car had been taken, he believed by an officer who was staying at the Grand Hotel on the seafront on the western edge of town, not half a mile from my house.

I duly donned my bicycle clips, mounted my bike and set off on the short trip to the Grand, hoping the car might be parked outside without any grim-faced guards to protect it. Sure enough, as I turned up the adjacent Peirson Road, there it was. I put my bike against the wall, took out the garage bill, and began to look it over. It was certainly not sporting a new radiator grille, and while they had done a good panel-beating job on the wing and door, they were most certainly not new either. Crouched down low and engrossed in scribbling notes on the form I had brought with me, I suddenly became aware that I was not alone. On the pavement beside me was a highly polished pair of black jackboots. I looked up to see that they belonged to an immensely tall man in a dark German uniform. A cap soared like Shelley's skylark from his lofty brow, and to top it all off he wore a monocle. At that age I was awed by anyone who sported such an accoutrement; he was posh posh posh, far elevated above my middle-class family. He barked down at me from his enormous height.

'Vot are you doing?'

I felt my stomach drop into my lower bowel. Perhaps he thought I was trying to interfere with his brakes, or attempting some other kind of sabotage. Nervously, I began to explain, one–stuttering–word–at–a–time.

'I do speak English!' he shouted at me. He thought I was patronising him by assuming he didn't.

I carried on trying to explain what I was doing, but got a bit lost when it came to the intricacies of the insurance claim, which I felt sure was rather dodgy. He crouched down next to me and took from my hand the bill that had been presented by the garage. Had you passed by at that moment you would have wondered what on earth was happening. You would have seen a pimply young man in bicycle clips crouching alongside this elegant sports car, and squatting beside him an equally elegant German officer, calmly examining a by now rather grubby piece of paper. Slowly he raised himself to his full height once more. I had been told that the Germans had no sense of humour, and was prepared for the worst. He handed me back the bill and said, 'And so I see that the motor repairers in this island are no more honest than those in Germany ....'

He then lowered himself into the driving seat, took the wheel and with a twinkle visible through his monocle as he showed off his colloquial English, he spoke again. 'When you report to the motor repairers, I wish you the best of Jersey luck!'

When I returned to the office, I dictated a most carefully phrased letter to Miss Hunt, explaining what I had seen.

I addressed it to the car dealership's general manager, who oversaw the most important aspects of the company's work. I was telephoned in short order.

'Is that Le Sueur?' His tone was an attempt to put me firmly in my place. 'I understand you have been cosying up to the Germans!'

And I believe I had the cheek to reply, 'Perhaps just as well, because your accounting error in preparing the bill has been discovered.' I stopped short of accusing him of dishonesty.

The end result was that he said he would look into it. Behold, shortly afterwards, I received a grovelling letter saying that indeed the work had been carried out to the best of their ability but not with new materials as they would normally have used because they were not available. It had all been, he assured me, a mistake. I had in the meantime asked the opinion of another engineer as to the cost of the work they had carried out. I wrote back to the general manager and suggested he compromised by sending us a bill to that amount. He did so. It was my first real confrontation in business, and I felt proud that I had stood my ground. I was growing up fast.

Miss Hunt also congratulated me. Mr Rodd though was aghast. He could not believe that such a reputable firm could behave in such a dishonest manner. He was a survivor of a more honourable age.

In the months that followed, we all, by necessity, grew to accept the island's changed circumstances. The war was not over by Christmas, and showed no sign of being over by the following Christmas either. The Germans had imposed a curfew upon us so our hours of outdoor freedom were restricted, and little by little our supplies of food were cut back. Formal rationing was introduced just five days after they arrived, with controls on the amount of butter, sugar, meat and fat which we might take from our local shops. (By the time we were liberated, of course, we were surviving on the bare minimum to keep us alive.)

Some shopkeepers did very well out of the sudden rush of customers. The Germans were reasonably well paid and were keen to spend their money on luxuries unavailable in the austerity of Germany, which they could send back to wives and sweethearts at home. Within weeks the shelves of the jewellers and perfumiers along King Street were emptied by smiling, victorious young men who paid with ready cash—even if it was the newly imposed Occupation currency. I'm sure there was a veritable flood of Chanel No. 5 streaming its way from Jersey to Germany in the last few months of 1940. I remember going into Gallichan's in the Royal Square to buy a new watch in spring 1941 because I was sure there would soon be none left and, indeed, the choice was very limited.

While we resented the fact that we had no personal freedom or contact with the rest of the country, we did not for the most part feel personal oppression or undue individual hatred for the Germans. The average soldiers became known by the generic term of 'Greenfly', due to their standard grey-green uniforms.

My mother had a very close friend in France to whom she wrote regularly. In order for the letters to reach the required destination she was obliged to go to the German Post Office on Beresford Street in St Helier where she always dealt with the same helpful clerk. He would sell her the requisite stamps, which were all illustrated with Hitler's head. Knowing that it was highly frowned upon in our country as disrespectful to put the King's stamp on an envelope upside down, she was always very careful to lick Herr Hitler's image and stick it upside down on her letters to France. I often wondered if anyone noticed, but the significance of her gesture seemed to pass them by.

Life simply went on, in a way that did not significantly differ from our previous existence. I rarely had contact with a German, although I do remember one occasion when I had to make a decision about how I should conduct myself.

One hot afternoon I was walking up Mont Felard, a steep hill heading north up towards the village of St Lawrence, intent on some company business, when I was accosted by a perspiring young German in full uniform pushing a bike laboriously up the hill. In faulty English, he asked me if he was heading in the right direction for St Aubin—which he clearly was not. Many might have thought it a great joke to have answered in the affirmative, and sent him miles out of his way. Yet without hesitation I pointed out his mistake and informed him of the correct course. Why did I do that? Simply because there was no reason not to. There was no action, there was nothing to be gained for the war effort, and as one young man to another I felt sorry for him. In retrospect I still believe I did the right thing, although others may protest otherwise.

Some of those others were forced to confront their prejudices too. The grandson of a gentleman who lived near the seafront to the west of us at Bel Royal told me how his grandfather was an ardent anti-German, cut off from his family in England, with a visceral hatred of the Nazi regime. After fighting the Hun in the First World War, he was damned if he would have anything to do with them now they had occupied his island. One night he awoke to the smell of smoke coming from his property, and going downstairs realised his house was ablaze. Stumbling about in the smoke and flames with a bucket, he tried desperately to fight the fire—only to become soon aware that he was not alone. Two other men had joined him, working alongside to save his home and possessions while awaiting the arrival of the fire brigade. As they retired to let the professionals take over, he realised that his saviours were two German sailors who were billeted in a nearby house. They had smelled the smoke, understood what was happening, and done what any decent human being would have done; they went to help another person in distress.

Similar stories emerged of farmers being assisted by German agriculturalists when their cattle were having difficult births, of bicycles being fixed, of machines being mended. I, and most other islanders, settled cautiously back into the routine of work, social life—and even occasional relaxation—despite the presence of the enemy. In fact, as the months went on, we all became possessed of a deep, almost defiant psychological need to carry on as though things were normal. In recent years, I have come to realise that was exactly what the Germans wanted to happen. For the first two years of the Occupation I never felt as though I was being watched or followed, or under any kind of persecution from our occupiers, which allowed me to press on with my life.

Some activities were, however, limited by the curfew, which was introduced quite early on. From ten o'clock at night until six in the morning, we were expected to be safely at home. As you can imagine, for a young man of my years it somewhat curtailed my social life! My friends and I met often for house parties and get-togethers, but one always had to have one eye on the clock. The further away they lived, the earlier people would leave, to ensure they didn't run the risk of being caught by a patrol or sentry. It was particularly hard for me later in the Occupation, as the Germans set up a barrier across the road just two doors from my house, which came down without fail at nine o'clock on the dot. Soldiers who manned the defensive position on the sea wall were billeted in the house, and it was their job to prevent any latecomers from crossing over after the fateful hour. Many was the time I would pedal furiously around the corner breathless and apologetic before that barrier, having left things just a little too late at whatever entertainment I had been enjoying. I would dismount and stand there helplessly with my bicycle, until one of the guards came out to observe my plight with a grin. Luckily for me it was often the same fellow, and by pointing comically first at my head and then at my wristwatch I would give him to understand that I was no common law-breaker, simply a bit stupid. The grin didn't leave his face as he lifted the barrier for me to pass through, never once refusing.

Rather later in the Occupation, my mother softened her stance towards the enemy even further, thanks to a common kitchen utensil.

She was surprised by a ring at the front door, and opened it to find a middle-aged German soldier standing there. He could plainly speak no English, as he started to point down our hallway to the kitchen and made signs with his other hand as though he was stirring something. The next thing she knew, he had walked right past her into the house and through to the kitchen, where after some rummaging he found and took the largest saucepan we possessed, compete with lid.

He left still gesticulating and making signs which my mother was at a loss to understand, shaken as she was by the episode. By this point there were no saucepans left to be obtained in the shops, and the lost one was irreplaceable. When my father returned, there was a pointless argument, he telling her that she should not have allowed the soldier to take it, and she replying that he ought to have been in the house to stop him. We all thought the pan was gone forever, for the benefit of the Greater German Reich.

All ended happily however. About a week later the saucepan was returned by the smiling soldier, miraculously gleaming brightly, since the Germans had cleaning materials which we simply did not possess. Moreover, the saucepan contained a large, quivering piece of tripe. Thinking it unwise to ask too many questions, my mother thanked him, and set about making us some delicious *Tripes à la mode de Caen*, with whatever vegetables she had to hand.

About a week later the soldier was back at the door. I do not think my mother could get to the kitchen fast enough to fetch the saucepan for him. Tripe at that time was like manna from heaven. My mother, when doing the bedrooms, would watch from the upstairs window and take particular notice whenever the Germans washed something in a freshwater stream on the beach. This signalled another gift of tripe. The German never needed to enter the house again and would stand at the door whenever he visited, but a kind of relationship developed between him and my mother. He showed her photos of a little half-timbered house with pine trees, a woman and adolescent children which he indicated were his family. My father met him twice. It was approaching Christmas, and my father had bought several bottles of wine when supplies were still available, one of which was to be opened each Christmas Day. I could see that if the soldier was still in his billet he might have been invited in to have a glass of this precious festive treat. Unfortunately that crew was moved elsewhere, and their replacement did not seem to have any tripe contacts. We went without, but were perhaps spared from being labelled collaborators by jealous neighbours for our friendship.

I believe the perjorative term 'collaboration' can often be confused with the less serious charge of 'fraternisation'. There is an important difference. To me, collaboration is actively seeking to help the enemy to win the war. Fraternisation is informal contact with other individuals who happen to be wearing a different kind of clothing. While it may be frowned upon by some, there is no inherent harm in it, simply the expression of fellow human beings forced to share a similar existence, albeit on different sides. It would be preposterous, for example, to think that my mother advanced the Nazi war effort one iota by smiling at the officer with the saucepan, or accepting his gift of tripe. Hitler's tanks would not advance further because she accepted a seat on the bus offered by a German boy in uniform. I am sure that most of us had a moment in the Occupation when we thought 'not all Germans are bad'.

Common humanity was emerging from the idiocy of the war.

Alas, as is the nature of war, it was not to last.

Chapter Three

AN ESCAPE TO GUERNSEY

As the months went by I found myself working harder and harder at the insurance company, without a complete knowledge of precisely how the job should be done. I was after all simply an office boy, and felt a lack of guidance from any superior experience.

By the spring of 1941 I was finally able to communicate with the larger office on the mainland, albeit in a most circuitous way. The Germans allowed us to send Red Cross messages of up to twenty-five words to our loved ones in England, to inform them that we were well, despite our straitened circumstances. At this early stage, communication was only allowed with actual relatives, so I hatched what I thought to be an ingenious scheme. I knew that the manager to whom I should refer was called Colonel Eric Thorpe, and so I addressed myself to him as 'Dear Uncle Eric'. That took up three of my twenty-five words. I continued by saying that all was well, that I was very busy, and was working with some new staff. Fortunately for me, the censor passed my rather short epistle, and off it went on a journey of no small distance. From our island it was taken to the Red Cross in Berlin, then on to Geneva. From there it went on a sealed train south to Lisbon, until finally being put on a ship to England. When it finally arrived at 'Uncle' Eric's desk, it caused great consternation. They understood immediately what I was trying to tell them, but found it impossible to imagine that a mere boy of nineteen was able to run so complex an entity as an insurance office. They were also concerned that the 'bloody Germans' hadn't taken the whole lot over, and could be the new staff to whom I referred.

I discovered all this later, of course; at the time I had no idea whether the message had got through at all, and I remained in need of some practical guidance on the finer points of managing what for the time being was effectively my own business. Of particular concern to me was the question of re-insurance. To put it simply, if a big house in St Helier burned down, and my little office was required to pay the whole claim, it would be simply bankrupted—so who would cover our losses?

I did try to educate myself and was regularly seen at the library trying to learn whatever I could on the subject. I clearly remember one day a group of Germans coming in and informing the librarian that they were to search the shelves for any material that was thought hostile to German interests. While they were polite they were also very thorough, and climbed up to the highest alcoves in their quest to uncover literature to which the Reich might object. Their progress was marked by a series of thumps as books were flung to the floor, to be gathered up and disposed of. I'm sure there were many books there which were critical of the Nazi regime and it was hardly surprising that they were to be destroyed, but I found it very, very hurtful. It was a clear reminder that free information was something not to be countenanced.

I do remember thinking that any German soldier who was intellectually alive could not have done that job.

The search party returned frequently to scour the shelves. On one occasion when they were in mid-search a cleric from one of the northern parishes who I don't wish to name breezed in through the double doors with great commotion, against the library's strict rule of silence. At the top of his voice he bellowed 'Good news!!' and we froze. Was he about to give away the fact that he had been listening to the BBC on an illicit radio? He strode towards the librarian's desk and again bellowed 'Good news!!', just before realising that the Germans were in the library and climbing down from their ladders to see what the fuss was about. I thought, 'This stupid old fool is going to get himself arrested, and we might all be implicated.' He reached the desk, turned his back on the librarian, and at the top of his voice shouted, 'Good news! *Punch* is a hundred years old today!!!!!'

There was one place where I could find some solace. I happened to know a Jesuit priest from an order based in a building called Maison St

Louis that once housed the Imperial Hotel and later became the Hotel de France. He invited me to peruse their wonderful library which I don't think the Germans ever interfered with, despite taking it over as billets. Père Rey allowed me access, and I took an English-language edition of *Das Kapital* which would surely have been banned from the public library by then. I took it with the intention of educating myself, but I found it simply unreadable and abandoned it after perhaps twenty pages. What attracted me to it was that it was actually there and had not been confiscated, despite being in evident contradiction to Nazi ideology. The Jesuits were the intellectuals of Roman Catholicism. They were of the opinion that their priests should be aware of what the opposition was writing, and therefore there was no form of censorship in their library, which was very well stocked. Perhaps it was because Jersey had become an important centre for the Order of the Society of Jesus. In fact, when the States realised that they had no copy of the Haig Convention on countries' behaviour in wartime, it was the Jesuits who were able to provide one. It is ironic that at the time when atheism was starting to flourish within me I had access to such a fine theological library.

Fortunately for my insurance career I was able to make contact with my counterpart in our sister island of Guernsey, a man in his thirties who like me was trying hard to keep the business functioning as far as possible. Letters between the islands were permitted, but no phone calls, so we exchanged stories and he sent me very helpful details of a bookkeeping system that he had devised. I felt sure that we would both benefit enormously from a proper face-to-face meeting, but of course I couldn't simply hop on the mailboat to see him.

Taking a long shot, I went to see the German authorities who had based themselves at College House, a large building which had been used to house boarders for the nearby Victoria College and overlooked St Helier. I was determined to explain my problem. I was received courteously enough by a man on reception, who had enough English to understand what I wanted and assured me I would hear back from them.

To my surprise I did, and received an official letter inviting me to

College House to meet a German major who would hear my concerns. Encouragingly, he stood up when I entered his office, and listened attentively to what I had to say. It turned out that he had been in insurance before he was summoned into the army, and quite understood my problem. It would save me so much trouble, I told him, if only I could go to Guernsey to meet my colleague and discuss matters thoroughly. He promised to see what he could arrange, and I left feeling as though I had made rather an impression.

The days soon dragged by without any news, until one day two weeks later a rather shaken Miss Hunt came into my office. 'Mr Le Sueur,' she said, 'a German car has just pulled up outside. I think they are looking for you! I hope there is no trouble!' But no, they had come here on official business from the major I had met. They gave me notice to go to the Pomme d'Or Hotel to arrange travel details to allow me to go to Guernsey. The hotel, which overlooked St Helier's Harbour Building, had been taken over by the German Navy as its headquarters and also held the German Harbour Office. I went there immediately, only to be told there was no transport available and to come back the next day. This was repeated for several days, and I began to despair of ever getting away until finally I was told, 'You go tonight. At nine o'clock you must be at this hotel.'

Feeling none too sure of myself, being a lousy sailor, I reported promptly at the hotel carrying my briefcase, a suitcase, and a hessian sack full of provisions. I was to travel on a naval boat, together with a woman whose sick husband had been for medical treatment in Paris. We travellers were placed by the sailors up on the deck, and given some shelter behind the superstructure. They even provided a rug for the sick man and his wife. As a young man I clearly didn't rate a blanket ...

We sailed in the dark, as the blackout was strictly enforced. Bobbing about in the gloom, I could only see the wakes of our convoy of seven or eight boats and the vague dark outline of the island as we steered along the southwest coast past Corbière Point and headed north towards Guernsey just over twenty-five miles away. It took three long and nervous hours as the crew picked their way carefully to avoid not only the treacherous rocks all around the island, but also the mines which they believed had been sown in the area by the Royal Air Force. No-one had told me about that before I asked permission to travel or I might have thought twice! I was very happy to be heading off the island though. Part of my desire to go to Guernsey was a wish to be anywhere other than Jersey, even for a short time.

The island of Guernsey finally loomed up out of the darkness, the rocky heights around the harbour and main town of St Peter Port silhouetted against the night sky. We moored alongside two or three other boats and had to stumble across them until we reached a ladder which we were expected to scale with all our luggage. It was a struggle to manage with my various bags, but the Germans actually helped us all, as though they were paid porters. I followed one of the passengers, who was a Guernseyman of my age. He had suggested returning to his home to see out the curfew, as it was now about two o'clock in the morning. My original plan had been to try to find my aunt's house, but that could prove difficult in the darkness and I preferred to be off the streets. He took me through the darkened lanes. We were accosted three times by sentries and asked to produce the ID cards which we were now obliged to carry, and of course mine provoked some discussion as it was from Jersey. We were finally allowed to pass. I discovered as we entered his home that his mother and sister had evacuated to England before the Germans had arrived, but his father had not, and was even now asleep in bed—but not alone ...

The following morning I completed my journey to my aunt's house, where I was to stay for the duration of my trip. She lived on the middle floor of a three-storey building, and I traipsed up the stairs to find her. Here it was that I revealed the contents of my sack of provisions. I had heard through correspondence that they were already short of potatoes in Guernsey, because so much of their agricultural land was given over to the cultivation of tomatoes, in huge greenhouses which seemed to cover the whole island. In Jersey potatoes were rationed, certainly, but were still available. Much of the Jersey crop was bought up by the Germans and shipped to Guernsey to feed the hungry troops, who soon worked out a new way of making money out of the poor populace. The spuds were peeled by groups of soldiers under the command of NCOs who would have all the peelings scraped up and put into buckets. They would then be hawked to stallholders around the back doors of the market, to be sold to hungry islanders. I saw for myself two long lines of people waiting for the peelings to arrive, and was shocked to see them reduced to such measures when we were living in relative plenty.

Having prior warning of the situation, I had loaded the hessian sack with as many potatoes as I could carry before I left Jersey, and had succeeded in carrying it across the sea, through the darkened streets, and finally on to my aunt's house. She was delighted when I tipped them onto her kitchen table with a flourish, expecting her to make preparations to devour the lot. Instead, she very carefully divided them into three very equal piles. As was so often the way in those difficult times, the custom was to share in whatever good fortune might befall you, and so she sent my uncle upstairs with one pile, and then downstairs with another. The stairs were far less trouble to them than before, as they had both shrunk from grossly overweight to shadows of their former selves due to the wartime diet.

My business meetings with my Guernsey colleague proved very beneficial, if not for both of us then certainly for myself, and I prepared to leave with a far clearer picture of how to conduct myself and my business back in Hill Street.

But first I had to return. Our vessel for the journey was far smaller than the one which had taken me from St Helier, and she seemed to rise up and down violently with every small ripple. Several waves splashed over me, and it wasn't long before I began to feel distinctly unwell. I stood up, leant over the rail, and a kindly sailor brought me the necessary bucket.… At least it was daylight, and the sailors could keep a closer look out for any hazards.

Suddenly there was a shout, and a distant roar of an aircraft engine. The tension rose as the Germans realised it was not one of theirs. I remember feeling so unwell that I rather wished he might score a direct hit and put an end to my suffering, but he seemed to have no interest in our little craft and flew away. When I finally stumbled, exhausted, down the gangplank I could not have been more grateful to be back in my own island. Mind you, I still had to walk home, which took an hour with saltwater-logged clothes and heavy bags.

Despite my unpleasant experience at sea I had something else to occupy my thoughts, and it caused me great concern. My mind kept running back to the short time I had spent waiting for the boat to arrive and take me from Guernsey. I was waiting in the harbourmaster's office, which was on the ground floor of a hotel from whose upper floors I could clearly hear a radio, which was tuned to the BBC's one o'clock news. I was shocked and appalled to hear the announcer call for people in occupied territories to strike back at their occupiers, to commit acts of sabotage and insurgence and generally cause unrest. If it was expected that such acts were to be committed in our island, it was an unsuitable and irresponsible thing to say to people who were so unprepared and so vulnerable. The island was very small, with one German soldier to every four people and unlike France, there were no great forests or remote mountains in which to hide. I dreaded to think what would happen if islanders took them at their word and began an active resistance. The prospect was extremely unrealistic and I objected to the thought of it. Surely, I thought, this can't go on—surely the Germans can't allow us to hear this kind of thing?

I was right. Just a short time later, the order appeared in the pages of the *Evening Post* newspaper. All radios were to be confiscated. It was the first of some significant and unwelcome changes.

Chapter Four

IN TOUCH WITH
THE OUTSIDE WORLD

I grew up with a radio in the house, and its fretwork wooden casing with images of a beach and palm trees made a fitting centrepiece for our living-room table. Before the Occupation we listened to it nightly as a family in order to discover what was happening in the world, on the Home Service and the Light Programme. We purchased and studied the *Radio Times* every week, and would make an appointment to listen to a particular programme at a particular time. The six o'clock news was a regular feature. In the years before television became the entertainment of the masses, radio was an essential part of many people's lives.

The one drawback of this wonderful Pye machine was that it was powered by a large battery which was swiftly drained by our listening. Every week I would have to take the battery in a galvanised iron bucket to a nearby garage to be recharged. It was the size of a small car battery, and I would leave it with the garage and take a replacement home, until that in turn was drained and ready to be exchanged.

Finally, after many back-breaking trips to the garage, my father replaced that radio with a rather more modern Marconi appliance which ran from mains electricity. No more trips to the garage for me! The new one, a thing of Bakelite wonder, quickly replaced the older wooden Pye model in pride of place in the living room. I believe my father suggested the old model should be sold to a farmer or other deserving individual. Thus it disappeared, and I did not mourn the end of my battery-charging duties.

Then in June 1942 came a fateful order from the Germans. Advertisements in the *Evening Post* informed us that we were to hand in our radios, by taking them to a collecting point, correctly labelled so that they could be reclaimed at a later date, presumably when hostilities had come to an end.

My father was furious, distraught that the occupiers would deprive us of what he considered a family friend.

His rage was made ridiculous by my mother simply giggling at him. When he finally calmed down, she was able to explain what she found so funny. My mother, you see, was a natural hoarder. The battery radio had not found a new home with a farmer or been otherwise disposed of: instead it was secreted up in the loft under the roof, where she had somehow contrived to carry it herself. How she had managed to get the weight of it up through the narrow trap door I could not imagine. Her premise was that it was too good to be thrown away, and like anything else that had cost money, it 'might have a use one day'. As was so often the case, she was right.

Chortling to my father, she said, 'Take the steps to the top landing, push up the trap door, feel around on the right and you will find the Pye wireless.'

My father was delighted, and hastened immediately upstairs. Our heavy old fretwork radio was duly presented to the Germans all correctly labelled so that we had proof incontrovertible that our link with the outside world had been surrendered. In those days it would have been an enormous luxury to have possessed more than one radio. A few people might have had one in their bedroom or kitchen, but that was considered an almost insane extravagance, so by handing in our old radio, we were confident of being reasonably safe.

In the meantime, we had to ensure that we could listen in without exposing ourselves to risk. Casting about for a hiding place, my father first lighted on a loose floorboard under the carpet near the cupboard under the stairs, and this became the chosen spot for its secretion. To remove it from its new hiding place and listen, it required the labour of three people. First the curtains were closed. One of us would keep guard at the front door, while the others rolled back the carpet, prised up the floorboard, lifted out the heavy wireless and carried it to the living room where there was an electrical socket. We would turn it on very low, so there was absolutely no risk of the neighbours' hearing it. The wonderful thing, we discovered after the Liberation, was that our neighbours were doing exactly the same!

That system only lasted a couple of weeks as it became far too much trouble, so my mother found another solution. In one corner of our living room, near the window, there was a high-winged armchair. Crammed behind it was a great pile of old clothes which my mother had optimistically saved 'to be mended', in the sure knowledge that they never actually would be. The magnitude of the pile had rather overcome her, if the truth be told. But it seemed to be an ideal storage place for a radio—and so the clothes were pulled out of the way, the radio installed and plugged in, and the clothes stuffed back on top before the chair was jammed back against the whole lot. To listen, we simply pulled a few clothes out of the way, and tuned in. As ever, the six o'clock news was vital to us, but the Germans had forced us to adopt European time so we were always an hour ahead. Consequently every night at seven we made for the chair in the corner and huddled around to get the latest from around the world. When it was over, we would discuss it with quiet excitement. Early on our discussions were rather gloomy, as the Germans appeared to be advancing on all fronts, only to brighten considerably as details of their reverses in Russia became apparent—but only within our own house. We would NEVER give any clue that we had been listening to an illegal radio to ANYONE as we were by then all too aware that the Germans had eyes and ears everywhere.

Our system worked flawlessly until one night in late summer 1944, when the radio simply stopped working. To our dismay, we could not coax from it a single sound. What was to be done?

After some discreet inquiries, somebody told me that there was a young man who lived not far away who might be able to help us, working as he did for a firm in town called W. H. Cole which repaired radios for the Germans. I had it on authority that he was a very trustworthy individual, so I went to his house and knocked upon the door. My information was correct, and he came to visit the house to inspect our sickly appliance. The prognosis was both good and bad. Yes, it could be repaired, but it would have to be taken to the shop for the work to be carried out.

After some discussion, we decided upon a plan of action. I had by now acquired a trailer for my bicycle which was of ample size to accommodate the radio, together with some camouflage which would be necessary to hide my clandestine cargo. I wrapped it in a hessian sack, and placed it carefully in the trailer, before piling a load of firewood on the top. Smiling nervously as I left the house in case any Germans were watching, I mounted up and pedalled away in the direction of town rather more slowly than usual owing to the combined weight of wireless and wood.

The St Helier workshop had a back entrance off a narrow alley between Burrard Street and Waterloo Street, a fitting place for my surreptitious activities. Parking my bike and trailer outside, I quickly nipped up the stairs to be sure there were no Germans there. The essential thing was to look as natural as possible, and I was quite prepared with a cheerful *guten Tag* if there had been any hovering Greenfly. The workshop was dingy but busy, with a couple of men seated at desks covered with the coils and valves of broken radios. The coast was clear. Back on the street I pulled the firewood out of the trailer and threw it on the cobbles before lugging the radio through the door and up the stairs to where my friend awaited. All we had to do now was trust that he would do a discreet job.

'Be careful,' my mother and father had told me before I left the house. As I bundled the wood back into my trailer, I wondered if I was leaving myself open to scrutiny. It was, after all, slightly odd for someone to be coming FROM town with a load of firewood—usually it was the reverse. But as I pedalled there were no shouts or gunshots to call attention to my crime, and soon I was home and safe.

Of course ten days later I had to go to retrieve the radio. The technician came to our house to let us know it was ready, and I had to complete the journey again with the repaired wireless in the trailer. Before that we had to pay him, in cash, as it wouldn't do for the transaction to appear in the company's accounts where it could be scrutinised by the Germans.

Following more advice to 'be careful', I loaded up with extra firewood, put on my bicycle clips and sallied forth once again. The radio was indeed ready for me, wrapped in its hessian sack. After cautiously checking the coast was clear, I loaded it into the trailer, covered it with wood and began the final part of my journey feeling rather pleased with myself. I remember it being a lovely sunny September afternoon as I pedalled steadily home. Arriving at the house, the Germans from the gun position opposite and the nearby house were nowhere to be seen, so I propped my bike against the kerb and rummaged about to gather up the firewood which was then cast once more onto the floor. The pavement was far wider in those days. In preparation, I went through the gate to the front door and opened it, only to freeze in horror as I turned at the sight of a guard who had come up from the strongpoint and was leaning on the sea wall. I presumed he was keeping watch for non-existent British Commandos landing on Elizabeth Castle, which stood on a small islet at the mouth of the harbour, but crucially for the time being he was not actually looking at me. There was nothing for it but to carry on as normal. I lifted the wireless in its hessian wrapping, trying to make it seem as light as possible, turned, and made to go through the gate to the house.

But it refused to go through the front door. It was stuck on something. What on earth was wrong? Looking round, I saw to my dismay that the electrical flex from the radio had fallen loose from the sack and was trailing behind me. The plug had somehow managed to become jammed between the spokes of the trailer.

What to do? I darted a look at the guard across the road. He was still looking for non-existent Commandos. I succeeded with a wrench to pull the cable free, which caused a loud cracking sound as it broke several spokes. Bundling up the flex as quickly as I could, I hurried into the house and dumped my nefarious burden. As I came out to collect my bicycle, the guard had turned around and was looking directly at me. He was the one who often manned the barricade and let me through if I was late home from curfew. Looking me right in the eye he gave me a strange little wave and a very, very odd grin. On trembling legs I smiled cautiously back, went in and finally closed the door before breathing a sigh of relief.

The radio was well hidden for a few days until we were sure there was no trouble, and then it returned to its usual spot under the old clothes in the living room. I do not know to this day if that guard had seen what was going on and kept quiet to protect us, but nothing ever happened and we never had a knock on the door in the small hours to take us away.

Our radio listening resumed.

In fact, so many people were listening in too that occasionally there were wonderful moments of shared excitement.

By the middle of 1943, the Germans had taken over the house two doors away from ours to billet troops. Our next-door neighbours were separated from the Germans by just one wall, and yet they continued to listen to their radio at every opportunity. I used to see their son, who may have been fourteen or fifteen, chatting to the soldiers from the gun position outside their door. He never gave any sign that his family had an illegal wireless either and so we went on, listening quietly and discreetly and never giving any hint that we were in touch with the outside world.

Until one night when the news became simply too good to keep to ourselves.

I was visiting some people in town, in Grosvenor Square off Grosvenor Street, a small terrace on the outskirts of St Helier. I used to visit and play chess with Mrs Osborne, a widow whom I had met through some friends. She was a fascinating woman, very much into theatre and the arts, and who was to influence me greatly. Her father had been hairdresser to Sarah Bernhardt, and I think I craved her aura of exotic sophistication. She lived in No. 12, next door to No. 14 which had been abandoned when its owners evacuated just before the Occupation began.

All of a sudden, as I contemplated my next move, there came a series of cries, shouts, and the sound of something falling. We wondered what was going on, until there was a knock on the door. Mrs Osborne opened it, to be greeted by the smiling face of a neighbour. 'Haven't you heard the news?' he asked. 'Italy has collapsed! Mussolini is under arrest! We're going to the Royal Square!'

Is this wise? I wondered. Should we all be heading to such an obvious public place? It would only need one twit to start shouting and it could get very dangerous ... but we went, nonetheless. We walked down Grosvenor Street, and when we got to the bottom of St Saviour's Road we noticed several other groups of people all obviously heading as nonchalantly as they could in the same direction. From every street they came, all converging on the Royal Square. We all had the swing of elation in our walks. The Germans who saw us knew why we suddenly seemed so pleased. And they knew that we knew that they knew why—and still nobody said a thing. It was a beautiful warm day, and as we entered the square we saw many other people, some in little groups, others alone, had had the same idea. In very friendly terms we greeted relative strangers as though they were long-lost friends: 'Hello, how ARE you, what a WONDERFUL evening ...', until it was time to leave as naturally as we could. Every one of us had heard the news, by some nefarious or illegal method, but nobody was daft enough to shout about it or make a fuss which could have had serious consequences for all concerned. We behaved beautifully. A critic might say we were subservient, but in fact it was a wonderful demonstration of shared spirit and unity. Whenever any news of that kind came out, it was all over the island within the hour. Either by directly listening to an illicit wireless, or by cunning word of mouth, the news went around. It was a sort of double life. You never discussed the news directly, but somehow found a way to make sure people understood what was happening. The Royal Square became the place to which everyone gravitated to share and glory in the ever-improving news from the front. 'What a lovely day!' 'Yes, and apparently it will be even better tomorrow!' ... In fact, we were glad the Greenfly saw us there. They looked discomfited by our seemingly innocent humour, but couldn't point the finger directly at any wrongdoing. When El Alamein was won, when we landed on Sicily, after the German defeat at Stalingrad, we quietly exalted—together.

There were similar scenes when we heard about D-Day, late in the evening of 6 June 1944. The landings were just across the Cherbourg peninsula from the Channel Islands, and we could see the French coast clearly from the eastern side of Jersey. The following day, excited to see or hear for myself any progress from the landings, I pedalled all the way to Gorey on the east coast to look across the deceptively narrow strip of sea that divided us. I saw nothing unusual, and the sound of explosions I had expected failed to materialise. Nevertheless, the wireless assured us that the Allies were pushing their way inland and would soon liberate the rest of France. We, it seemed, would have to be patient, but it was surely the beginning of the end. I think our occupiers realised it too.

I remember well a visit to my grandmother, who was living with my aunt at the top of Wellington Road. Granny was a wonderful character who had so many tales to tell that visiting her was never a chore. One of her greatest concerns was to find out, when communications were restored, the fashionably correct length for a ladies' skirt. At the age of ninety-four, she did not want to become known as a frump by appearing in public with skirts that were inappropriately too short—or too long. In the later stages of the war she was bedridden and I used to sit beside her and hear the tales of her youth. She had fanned my young childhood curiosity with the world by taking me to a series of lectures at Springfield in town, the two of us catching the bus into St Helier and then walking the rest of the way. One was a discussion about whether there was anything to choose between Fascism and Communism, which we attended at the time that I was in my 'left-wing' phase. On the way back to the bus she asked my opinion of what I had heard, which I duly shared with her. 'I am glad you are growing up with some perception,' she told me. She was decades ahead of her time despite having raised nine children, the first of which had offspring of their own by the time the last was born.

She was a remarkable woman. Back in the spring of 1940, as the Germans were invading Denmark and Norway, she decided that she simply had to visit a cousin who lived in France. Their home was some distance from St Malo, the nearest port to Jersey, in a village beyond the city of Rennes. The family did their best to dissuade her, but there was to be no argument. 'If the Germans are coming then I had better get it done quickly!', she told them. Aged ninety-one she boarded the boat to St Malo, her plump figure well-dressed in the latest fashion with her white hair neatly arranged, from where she could catch a train to Rennes. Once there she would have to change to get to her cousin's house. Much to our relief she returned, on schedule, just as the Panzers rolled across the Low Countries and broke through the Ardennes onto French soil. She was horrified when they arrived in our island but would not let them interfere in the way she lived her life and continued to do whatever she had done before. She was an inspiration.

On this occasion, as I listened by her bedside, she began to get fidgety. I could see her twisting and turning under the covers and thought: my God, she needs to use her commode. Awkwardly I said that I would find someone to help her and made to get up. As I did so she grabbed my wrist, holding on with force beyond her years, and looked me right in the eye.

'I can trust you, can't I?' she asked. Oh, what have I let myself in for, I wondered, but assured her that yes, she could indeed trust me.

'Then take that off!'

She was pointing at the large tea cosy on the bedside table, which I had always naturally assumed to be covering a teapot. But no. I lifted it away, to find a gleaming wireless set tuned to the BBC which crackled quietly into life when I plugged in the cable. She then reached under the mattress and brought out a child's atlas of the continent which opened at the map of Russia. Upon the page was a series of pencil lines which marked out the advances and retreats of the Russian Front as described on the BBC news, which she had obviously been following for many months. As the time reached seven o'clock—six o'clock in Britain—we heard the announcer begin the latest bulletin. Like two conspirators we bent our ears to the set and listened to the latest broadcast. Afterwards we adjusted the pencil lines which were moving satisfactorily westwards.

She would not succumb to the Germans, but sadly she did succumb to old age in summer 1944—without seeing the Liberation she had longed for.

Chapter Five

THE SPANISH

Another unwelcome change to what had been a relationship of convenience with our occupiers came at the end of 1941 and beginning of 1942. Afraid the British might have the temerity to attempt to seize back the island by force, the Germans began a programme of building monstrous concrete bunkers all around the coast linked in many places by imposing stretches of anti-tank walls. Many other bunkers and installations were built inland also. The first we noticed was at Noirmont Point, a prominent headland clearly visible from my bedroom window, whose cliffs marked the southwestern tip of St Aubin's Bay. The road to the headland was blocked, the first such imposition the Germans had made upon us. Adverts began to appear in the newspaper, inviting local labour to come forward and help in the construction of their fortifications. Most islanders were horrified that some Jersey tradesmen actually took the German shilling; in fact more than just a shilling, because our occupiers cunningly offered a wage far higher than that which was allowed to be paid to anyone else at the time. Most of those who worked in that way were family men, with children who perhaps needed more food or medicines that they could otherwise afford. But still, to the average Jerseyman, it rankled.

Then one day in early 1943, the concrete mixers came far closer to our home. Right opposite it in fact, where there had been a defensive position since early in the Occupation. Early one morning a patrol came and installed a barricade across the slipway where I used to go down to the beach, then the gap in the beach wall was filled in, and they began to lay the foundations for a coastal defence bunker. All the granite setts from the slipway were pulled up and used for camouflage in some of their other defences, including Mont Orgueil Castle. No longer could I wander barefoot out of our front door, across the road and down the slipway to bathe. Now it required shoes. First I had to cross the recently installed narrow-gauge railway line which the Germans used to carry sand, stones and labourers from St Helier to St Aubin and on to Corbière for the western defences. Then I had to walk along the wall and down some granite steps further on, and finally step onto the sand. It is a common misconception that we were forbidden from going onto the beach; that was certainly not the case except for a few days after D-Day in 1944.

The view from our house changed from a beautiful maritime vista into a sprawling building site. We were dismayed, especially as I had just commissioned an artist to paint a picture of the view from my window. But in the spirit of the Occupation there was no point protesting, we had to accept it, and continue with our lives with as much dignity as we could muster. Thankfully, we were spared the ultimate imposition. Mr and Mrs Tregear, who lived two doors to our right at the junction with First Tower, were given a most unpleasant ultimatum. They were told, in no uncertain terms, that their house was to be requisitioned and that they and their unfortunate lodger were to be out within forty-eight hours. Whilst we felt very sorry for them, our immediate reaction was one of relief. Thank God it wasn't us! My father had been quite canny in this regard. He had realised that the Germans might be looking for somewhere to station their troops, so he had opened our doors to some lodgers who took over the middle floor of our house. He guessed that if there were more people in the building there was a lower likelihood of its being taken for billets. Whether he was right, or the Germans simply wanted the house next to the junction, we never knew. The Tregears moved out to be replaced by soldiers, one of whom was the officer who took my mother's pan and later returned it full of tripe.

When the crew took charge of the newly constructed bunker, and of the Tregears' house, our little area became a 'military zone', by official order. Parallel to our main seafront road, immediately behind it, was the Inner Road, and our neighbours were lucky enough to have back doors which led out onto it. We did not. Barbed wire and barricades prevented anyone from turning down the short road which led from there to the seafront—and our front door. If we left our house at night there were barricades to the left and right; we were effectively prisoners in our own home, which led to some unfortunate consequences. While the rest of the island was compelled to observe a curfew at ten o'clock in the evening, ours was an hour earlier because we had to cross through the barbed-wire barriers of the military zone to get to the front door. It cut into my social life drastically, as I had to leave any parties an hour early to get home on time! I had to be home by nine o'clock but frequently wasn't, and I had to ask the guard if he would mind lifting the heavy barricade up so that I could pass. He always did so, with a smile, and I always gave him a polite 'thank you' in return. I was often out of breath, having returned at a sprint after walking a girl home from whatever function I had been attending, out of courtesy. There was never a need to protect her virtue from the Germans, especially in the early days as they were so well disciplined. The lost hour was most irritating, although there was one way around it. Anyone who was involved in a piece of amateur theatre at the Opera House could apply for a special pass which would allow one to be out after the hours of curfew, not only for the dates of the performance but also for the rehearsal period. I made full use of this privilege, and enjoyed the convivial atmosphere of the stage—although I can't say I was very good.

Gradually our island became scabbed over with lumps of reinforced concrete. A chain of bunkers ran right around the coast, while above the cliffs and inland they housed heavy guns whose sound we tried to get used to as they fired in practice and then occasionally in anger as Allied planes and ships ventured closer. This overwhelming show of military force made us realise we were in for a long occupation, since Hitler would not be wasting such extensive resources if he meant to surrender the island cheaply. We felt claustrophobic, hemmed in by the miles of barbed wire and multitude of pillboxes, and the profusion of minefields with their skull and crossbones warning signs, 'Achtung Minen'. Signs proclaiming 'Kein

Eintritt' appeared everywhere, with the scarcely necessary translation of 'No Entry' printed below.

One of the consequences of the desire to fortify our island so extensively was the need to find enough labourers to carry out the work. While some Jersey people helped at the beginning, it was plain they would never be enough to achieve the scale of defences that our occupiers envisaged.

The first noticeable group to arrive to that end were Spanish. They lived in hastily built camps in the island, where wooden huts gave them sufficient shelter and facilities to make life tolerably comfortable. They were in no way prison camps, and indeed one was able to visit them and wander freely around. I decided to use their presence to my advantage. I had studied their language in school, but in truth my grasp of its finer points was woefully lacking. What better way to improve it than by speaking to some natives? In conversation, I discovered that they were refugees from the Spanish Civil War, who had gone to France to escape the fighting in the mid-1930s. Many had made the arduous trek over the Pyrenees, starving and impoverished, to start building a new life for themselves.

Of course when the Germans invaded and occupied France, that left them in rather a difficult position. The Germans had asked the Vichy government to send men for construction work overseas, and it was a very simple decision for the Pétainist state to send Spaniards instead of Frenchmen. The refugees were once again rounded up, and sent to Jersey. It was a bitter move for them, as General Franco might never have won the Civil War in Spain without the military aid of both Hitler and Mussolini.

They were relatively well treated however, and were allowed to go where they wished outside working hours. They also earned far more than the Jersey workers were allowed to earn. I remember them always having money in their pockets, and being able to buy up the food and clothes etc. that the average Jerseyman could not usually afford. It went some way towards compensating them for the unfairness of their situation.

Some of that money was of unexpected benefit to various gentlemen's outfitters who had run low on most of their essential stock, such as shirts and trousers. By the time the Spanish arrived they had little left in their windows except formal headgear, such as top hats and bowler hats. Who, after all, would have need of such attire during the Occupation, when there was no occasion to wear it? The answer was the Spanish workers, and soon the hats were selling like hot cakes to workers keen to protect their heads from the stone faces of the tunnels they were carving out of the Jersey rock. I understand bowlers were in particular demand—the tunnellers cut quite a dash on their way to work and they were immensely amused to consider themselves as an English *milord*.

The more I visited them, the more dramatically my Spanish improved. In my spare time, I would take my bike west along the seafront and then cycle up the hill at St Aubin towards La Route Orange, where the camp closest to us was located. I was even allowed to write to those with whom I became particularly friendly.

Unbeknown to me, my efforts had been noticed, and they led me into a conspiracy which could ultimately have ended with a general mutiny and the deaths of some prominent Jersey people.

One afternoon early in 1944, while walking through Parade Gardens in St Helier, I was approached by a man called Paul Casimir. He was an academic of Polish descent, who worked in a book dealer's called Berger's in The Parade nearby. Berger's was a strange little picture of Jersey intellectual life, where some odd people went to meet and hold serious discussions on philosophy, mathematics and literature. I had often seen intellectual German officers there, those who were not avid Nazi Party members, earnestly joining in conversations with the local intelligentsia. I myself had spent some hours conversing with people such as Dr McKinstry, the island's Medical Officer of Health who looked after the wellbeing of islanders throughout the Occupation.

Out of that melting pot of opinions, various little groups were formed of people with shared principles and beliefs. One, of which I was loosely a member, was the Jersey Democratic Movement. We were highly critical of our island's system of government, called the States, which allowed some people the automatic right to a seat and didn't seem to allow everybody's vote to have equal weight. Although not completely independent of Britain, Jersey had been proudly self-governing for centuries without any great overhaul of its democratic affairs.

We aspired to create a better system of government, where people could have a fair say in the way they were ruled. Ours was of necessity a secretive organisation for two important reasons. First the very fact that we were discussing it indicated our confidence that at the war's end the Nazis would be defeated and the island could govern itself once more. Second, we did not want the ruling figures of Jersey to know that we were planning to supplant them when we had the chance. The group's leader was Norman Le Brocq, whom I knew from my school days. There was also a right-wing parson, a stockbroker's son, and several women who held similar strong beliefs.

Our aim was not the overthrow of the Nazis, we were far too small— but we very much wanted to bring about change in the way Jersey was governed. Some even wanted the island to become a county of Great Britain, something to which I was strongly opposed. What we did all want was a change to the system to make it more democratic, so that no-one should be able to vote in the States without having been elected by the people of the island. That would mean an end to automatic seats for court officials called jurats and for rectors, both of whom were able to make decisions fundamental to our island simply by virtue of their appointments without any recourse to the people they were meant to represent. In fact many of our ideas were adopted after the war when the constitution was overhauled.

Naturally our little group had no formal constitution, no official meetings or minutes of what we intended and discussed, nothing that would provide evidence of treachery should we be discovered either by the Germans or by our own authorities.

Norman Le Brocq had had a very sad life, after finding his parents and sisters dead from gas poisoning in their house when he was only a small boy. He'd been brought up by relatives in the parish of St Peter, who paid his school fees at Victoria College, where I got to know him. He had been deeply affected by the loss of his family and left school at sixteen, his dark hair falling over a face that rarely smiled.

As the war progressed his beliefs grew stronger and moved sharply to the left until he felt compelled to join the fledgling Jersey Communist Party led by Leslie Huelin. The Nazis had ruthlessly stamped out any communist organisations in other countries they had occupied and I'm sure would have done the same if they had become aware of any threat from Jersey's nascent party. I was aware of this group, and in fact was asked to join it by Norman but I refused. He was a man with fervent Marxist views which I simply could not share, and I told him so. In the one country where communism had established itself, I told him, there was no political freedom and a strong government effort to suppress all opposing ideas. Our friendship survived, but he went on to recruit several members who were organised in cells so each was unaware of the other for security reasons. To Norman, the nascent party heralded a new dawn of social justice. To me it signalled the way to oppression and social backwardness. To describe it as a 'resistance group' is certainly an exaggeration, but history has proved time and again that a small bunch of determined individuals can have a major impact on matters of huge international importance.

I had already unwittingly helped them. During a visit to the bookshop I had been asked if I could get hold of some spare clothes for a Russian who was described as 'really hot', meaning he was on the run from the Germans.

I was keen to help someone in obvious need, but at a time when we were all wearing the backsides out of our trousers where could I find such a valuable thing as a suit? After much debate within myself, I went to visit the mother of an old school friend of mine called Victor Hamon. We had been very close while at Victoria College, but he had left the island before the Germans arrived to join the RAF. About two years later his poor parents had received a letter from the Red Cross to tell them that their only son had been shot down over Holland. It was not easy for me to knock on the door and ask his mother for help, but I hoped she might understand and still have some of his clothes. Not wishing to deceive her, I told her why I needed them.

She listened to me carefully before explaining that she had already given away most of Victor's clothing to people in need, but there was something left that I could have. Turning, she went up the stairs and returned a few moments later carrying a splendid blue suit on a hanger. It had been his best and she had simply been unable to part with it out of sentiment for her dear son. Handing it to me, she smiled tightly and told me that she was sure Victor would have wanted me to have it to save someone else's life. I took it. My God, we grew up quickly in those times.

Shortly afterwards I was asked, because of my acquaintance with Mrs Osborne, if I could get hold of some blonde hair dye from her hairdresser's shop. This was easy to procure, and I did so assuming it was going to help the same Russian. I remember thinking that it was wonderful that these different people were all helping the cause but were ignorant of each other's contributions.

That day in the Parade Gardens, after looking to see if he could be overheard, Paul casually asked me if I had seen the copied sheets that were being circulated around the island, written in German. They were very inflammatory pages, which told the average German that the war was certainly lost, that their leaders were not to be trusted, and that they should rise up against their Nazi masters. Indeed I had seen them, most of us had, they had achieved a remarkable circulation in the island. No one knew where they had come from, and many speculated that the RAF had dropped them in the night. Why, I asked him, did he want to know?

The answer was simple. Paul Casimir was one of the agitators behind the production of the pamphlets and wanted to expand their circulation to the Spanish labourers. The problem was that he spoke no Spanish ... The penny dropped. He asked me if I would take an English copy, and translate it for distribution among the camps to sow dissent among the workers. They, he claimed, were disaffected and bitter at their situation and should be persuaded to hinder, rather than help, the German war effort. Such an action would of course be highly illegal and risked severe punishment by the Germans. Would I help?

I accepted immediately. I was ready to do anything that would cause discomfort to any Nazi supporters in the occupying forces. Who could possibly know that they had been translated by me?

Casually, Paul passed me a handwritten sheet. I stuffed it into a pocket as nonchalantly as I could, and retired somewhere private where I could read it through. At no point did we behave in a furtive manner, or do anything that would seem the least suspicious. Cloak-and-dagger behaviour would have been far more noticeable than our natural way.

The text was a mixture of psychological propaganda, news of German surrenders, and tales of the desperate state of the German war effort. It was something to lift the hearts of anyone feeling disaffected or disillusioned with the Nazis.

After sending my staff home that evening, I drew the document from my pocket and began to translate it, finally typing out my efforts on my office typewriter.

I decided to get some help to ensure the wording was correct, and approached a Catalan friend of mine who had a law degree from Barcelona University. I trusted José Vila, whom I had known for months at the Route Orange camp.

He took my schoolboy efforts and reworded them into something that didn't sound like a poor translation from English or German.

After making arrangements for a meeting in Berger's, I passed the results to Paul Casimir. He seemed happy with them, and brought me more over the next few months. Our work was copied—I knew not where, how, or by whom—and distributed to workers across the island.

This continued for some time, and I congratulated myself on my clandestine efforts to subvert the German war effort in a way which was surely untraceable to me.

Until one day in August 1944, when I had a rude awakening.

A man called Mr Roberts was a regular visitor to our office. Every so often he came to service the typewriters. He would clean and oil them, straighten bent keys and replace ribbons so our epistolary efforts could proceed uninterrupted.

On this particular day, he asked to speak to me privately after performing his work. He looked at me very intently, and said in a low voice, 'Did you know that no two typewriters have exactly the same print? Each has its own distinctive variations in how the letters hit the paper and can be identified by its unique pattern.' I assured him that no, I didn't know that. He went on, all the while looking me right in the eyes, 'Have you seen, by any chance, any of those unpleasant anti-German pamphlets that are circulating in the island? They have even been translated into Spanish ... I hope no-one comes to ask me if I might recognise on which machines these Spanish translations might have been done ... anyway, good afternoon, Mr Le Sueur.'

His message was clear. If the Germans decided to try to find out who was behind our work, it would be simple for them to identify the signature of a typewriter in our office. At my next meeting with Paul Casimir, I told him of my decision to stop using it.

I would hear more from Paul Casimir later but very soon there was another man who needed my help rather more urgently, and he wasn't Spanish—but Russian.

Chapter Six

ANOTHER MOTHER'S SON … THE SLAVES AND BILL

The ordeal of the slave workers in Jersey had begun one Sunday morning in early 1942. I was at home with my mother and father when the doorbell rang. It was our neighbour, Mrs Carr. Visibly shaken, she urged us to 'come outside and see something horrible.' And horrible it was, indeed.

On the opposite side of the road to our front door was shuffling, in bedraggled columns of misery, a great grey mass of humanity. From their midst came a low muttering, moaning sound as each one struggled to keep up with the person in front. What really struck us was how several of them had no shoes; instead they had torn rags from their clothes to tie around their feet. The men were unshaven, dirty and unkempt, staring downwards, while the few women with them were scarcely discernible as such, being in a similar state of despair. These were people in the depths of exhaustion and anguish. Keeping them under control was an unfamiliar breed of German, wearing khaki instead of the usual green and armed with revolvers and batons which they used freely to hit their prisoners. Their armbands said 'Todt'.

Dismayed, we watched this pitiful column, fully five hundred yards long, pass us by heading west from the harbour. Where had these poor people come from? How and why had they become so dehumanised, by what right did these khaki-clad men lay into them with their sticks for seemingly minor infractions, what had turned these wretched people into such unfeeling automata? One neighbour saw a young woman among the crowd drop a little bag which must have contained her few pitiable possessions. She fell out of line to retrieve it, only to be beaten by the guard and forced to leave it behind.

For me, it was a defining moment in the Occupation. Up until that point the Germans we had met had seemed almost unfailingly reasonable, but as the news spread of these persecuted victims of Nazi savagery the realisation sank into everyone. This was a different kind of occupation. There is an underclass of thug that exists in every country, and I remember exclaiming that it is a sick society that finds a place for these people. It became apparent that what we had been told by the BBC about persecutions in occupied Europe was not simply government propaganda as some of us had believed, but could in fact be true. When the deportations came later, we thought, my God—will our people be treated like that?

A Russian told me more about their terrible journey later. He was a well-educated man, who had read a translation of Victor Hugo's *Toilers Of The Sea*, from which he had learned of the existence of some British islands in this far-off corner of Europe. He had rightly assumed that this is where they were being taken. They had travelled hundreds of terrible miles in railway trucks to get to the port of St Malo, where he had his most vivid memory. What upset him so much, he said, was the look of horror on the faces of people in that city who had seen him and his comrades shuffle past on their way to the boat that would bring them to Jersey.

The purpose of these wretched slaves soon became apparent. It had been decreed that the island should be fortified, and quickly; and the Spanish workers and local help were simply not progressing fast enough. Under the constant threat of beatings and even death, the slave workers were to dig the foundations, carry the stones and mix the concrete of the many gun emplacements, tunnels and walls the Germans thought necessary to protect them from any attempt to retake the island. Badly housed and hardly fed, many of them would die on our island, thousands of miles from their homes. My sense of common humanity was outraged, and when the time came for me to be able to help them in some little way I was ready to take action.

One day in early 1943, my work took me to one of the far-flung areas of the island, a remote part of St Ouen known as Millais. This was indeed rural Jersey, where the local patois called Jersey Norman French, or *Jerriais*, was still the language of choice for the farmers and labourers who eked out their existence among its fields and barns. Many of the children would start school without speaking English. More recently, its proximity to the northwest headland of the island meant that there were regular transports of Germans and labourers moving close by, heading for the defensive positions that were being gouged into the cliffs at Les Landes.

It was a long journey by bike, but the house was easy to find, being the only one in the area. La Fontaine was a typical Jersey mid-Victorian farmhouse of two storeys with a sloping roof and its stonework covered by a layer of grey render. Some time after its original construction, a second part had been added, slightly lower than the first. That was now serving as the local shop, run by the lady who owned the house: Mrs Louisa Gould. She had made an insurance claim with my company after an unfortunate fire on her hearthrug, and I felt it was my duty to inspect the damage before making a payment.

I noted Mrs Gould's name on a plaque above the doorway, a requirement which enabled her to sell alcohol as an off-licence, and the bell above the door rang as I entered.

It was a small shop, lined with wooden shelves bearing very little in the way of wares. Where once there would have been stocks of tins, packets, bottles and boxes, sacks of potatoes and bags full of flour, there was nothing but empty space. By that stage of the Occupation, nearly everything was rationed, and what little there was was held behind or under the counter of every establishment. Your ration cards allowed you to claim your supplies only from the shop to which you had registered, and casual browsing had become a thing of the past. Anything in tins had disappeared by the end of 1942.

A private door in the back of the shop opened, and Mrs Gould herself came through to answer the bell. She was a woman in late middle age, wearing glasses and clothes of a practical nature. For me the situation was wholly unremarkable, and we discussed her insurance claim in a direct and matter-of-fact way until the private door opened once more and a young man came through it. He was of medium height, with rather round features and dark hair, and seemed to be at ease and familiar with the shop. Mrs Gould broke off to introduce him to me as Bill, a Frenchman who was helping behind the counter. We greeted each other in English, and immediately my senses were alerted. I knew enough French and French people to recognise a genuine Gallic accent, and his was most certainly not one.

I presumed straightaway that he was an escaped Russian slave. The newspaper had printed several warnings detailing how some of these poor devils had escaped from their labour camps or working parties, and were roaming the island. Helping them was an offence punishable with the most severe sentences.

I was not shocked that Mrs Gould should be harbouring such a man, but I did think she was taking a big risk and certainly didn't think she should be allowing him to be wandering into the public area of the shop where he could be observed by anyone passing by. I said nothing to give away my suspicions, as this was plainly something I ought not to know, and I kept my thoughts to myself. I was a young man, perhaps thirty years her junior, while she was a customer of the company I sought to represent; therefore it was not down to me to give her a lecture on the nature of human behaviour. We finished our discussion on her insurance claim, and I pedalled away.

Two weeks later, the claim settled, I returned to La Fontaine to finalise my business with Mrs Gould. It was not unusual for me to visit clients in this way, and I had hundreds across the island whom I would visit on my bicycle with other forms and documents. This time, unasked, she shocked me with her indiscretion by confirming what I had suspected: that 'Bill' was the pseudonym for a Russian slave who had run away from captivity nearby and been passed to her for shelter. He was living above the shop! While I reflected on what a terrible risk she was taking, she continued with her revelations by describing to me how he came to be there.

His real name was Feodor Polycarpovitch Burriy. Captured by the

Germans during their Blitzkreig across Russia, he had been one of the hundreds of thousands of unfortunates destined for slave labour in the service of the Reich. While many of them starved and perished in the camps across Poland and eastern Europe, he and many others were bundled into railway carriages and sent on the interminable journey to St Malo before being shipped to Jersey to help build the new defences against Allied invasion.

He was taken to a camp at the bottom of Jubilee Hill, which runs down past the airport to the western coast of the island. The Kommandant of the camp was notoriously brutal and would march his starving charges to work every day with violence and harsh penalties for those who failed to keep up. Desperate, Bill had escaped, only to be swiftly recaptured. He was stripped naked and ordered to push a wheelbarrow full of stones at the double around the compound while all the other prisoners were made to watch. Every time he slowed or stumbled he was beaten with a stick, until he finally collapsed. Guards then lifted him bodily into a tank of cold water and left him to freeze there all night. Miraculously, given that this was in November, he survived, and the punishment he received did nothing to dampen his desire to escape. Realising that he was likely to die anyway, he resolved to try again just two days later. His work site was at the foot of the main hill which leads from St Ouen's Village down to the west coast at L'Etacq, known today as Mont Pinel. The quarry where slaves were expected to dig out granite boulders was on the south side of that road, while on the opposite side was the crushing plant where he worked. He arranged with some of his workmates that at a given moment he would walk over to the low wall separating the machinery from the road, ostensibly to relieve himself. When he did so, they were to create a diversion, by shouting and banging their tools to get the guard's attention. It worked, and he was able to slip over the wall and into the roadway. He was crawling on his hands and knees along the side of the wall, when a van came down the road towards him. Naturally he feared he was about to be captured once more but fortunately the vehicle wasn't German but a local delivery van with a big balloon of gas on top to power the engine. The driver, at great risk to himself, stopped and threw the back doors open, beckoning Bill to get in. He needed no second bidding and crouched in the back as the driver took him a few hundred yards along the road to where there were no Germans or other people. He was still some way from safety though, and realising it would be dangerous to stay on the road he set off straight up the hill through gorse and bracken until he reached the top at La Route de la Villaise. Knowing he had to get out of sight, he found a ruined hut with its door ajar, promising some kind of shelter.

Cautiously, he pushed the door. Nothing happened, but as he opened it far enough to hurry inside he felt a pair of hands close tightly around his throat. Purely through reflex, he gasped out in Russian and immediately the hands loosed their hold on him. In the darkness of the shed, his attacker revealed that he too was a slave who had escaped, and that a friendly farmer brought him food every evening. The farmer in question was a remarkable man named René Le Mottée. He was a tenant farmer with four children and little money who nonetheless had taken it upon himself to look after not just one escaper, but three. He had one in his house, another in an outbuilding, and this third whom Bill had met. René had contacts all over the island and looked after the Russians until they could be moved to safer houses elsewhere. One by one the others had been moved down this escape line, until eventually it was Bill's turn to live in the house. It was at that stage that René had asked Louisa if she could look after him for a while, 'just for a few days.' I don't know if René was aware that she had recently received notification that her son Edward, an Oxford graduate, had been killed in action. It was certainly the right psychological moment to ask her to shelter another young man, and her words to me as we stood there in her almost empty shop have stayed with me for decades since. 'I had to do something for another mother's son.'

As she finished the story of how Bill had come to be in her home, my mind was racing with all manner of thoughts. First how brave she, René, and the man with the van had been. But also dismay at the fact that she was telling me, a relative stranger, all the details. My God, if she was telling me, she must be telling all manner of other people too! Perhaps because her son had been at Victoria College, as I had been, she thought there might have been a connection between us, but the fact was that he had been several years older than me and would not have even glanced in my direction.

As soon as I left the shop I made my way to René Le Mottée's home, which was only a few fields away and known to me because he had a tractor insured with us. Mrs Gould had used his name so casually that I felt I should warn him she was being so indiscreet and could possibly betray their operations simply by telling too much to the wrong people. Mrs Le Mottée in particular was grateful for my intervention, especially as she had her own four children to be concerned about. René insisted that the intention had been for Bill to stay with Mrs Gould only for a short time.

Of course, it had quickly become far more than that. She was a very amiable, maternal and rather conventional lady who was intensely, even exaggeratedly, pro-British. Her husband had died, her two sons had been educated at public expense, and I'm sure she felt she owed the country in which she had been brought up a great deal. When those factors were combined with her very great humanity, she was the ideal person for Bill to have come to. The 'few days" stay at her home became months, and I too became friends with both of them, despite my misgivings about her lack of discretion.

Bill had his own identification card, without which it was dangerous to travel anywhere for fear of being stopped and questioned by the Germans. A young man who was a friend of Mrs Gould, Oscar Le Breuilly, 'lost' his card and went cap in hand to the Immigration Office in Hill Street to request a new one. This was duly granted, and the original passed to someone skilled in the art of forgery. They unstuck Oscar's photograph, had one which had been taken of Bill attached in its place, and very skilfully used a purple crayon to trace the lines of the rubber stamp which on every card extended over the document and the picture. It was highly successful. In fact, many cards were 'lost' for this purpose over the course of the war and naturally I was one of those apparently careless people. Unfortunately, just a short time after reporting my card as missing I genuinely lost my replacement card and was without one, which was terribly dangerous. It was about three weeks before I could summon up the courage to return to the Immigration Office and approach the man in charge, a Mr Clifford Orange. He was known to be a dedicated and very correct civil servant, who took a dim view of irresponsible people who lost such vital documents. In fact, I believe he suspected what we were doing and didn't like it. The receptionist at the counter said they couldn't deal with my case, and I was referred to the Head of Immigration. In a very terse interview, he made it clear that he found it very suspicious that I should have lost my card twice and more or less accused me of lying. If these cards fell into the wrong hands, he said, the people who found them could later try to claim British nationality. I told him I thought that was highly unlikely. Finally he relented, to my great relief.

About six weeks later a friend contacted me to say that she had found my card down the side of an armchair in her living room. Connie Gale knew all about Bill and returned it to me, leaving me in possession of two: one to keep and one to 'lose' again! So for some months of the Occupation there were three Robert Winter Le Sueurs wandering about the island. Each card was used to request the issue of ration books from different shops, and each holder was ultimately allotted a Red Cross parcel.

Mrs Gould became highly complacent about both her own safety and Bill's. She altered her dead son's clothing to fit him and began taking him with her to church. She took him into St Helier and to her friends' houses, and I was often one of the party. She had a wide circle of friends, to whom Bill was thrilled to be introduced. We came to trust a lot of people, and as the months passed I began to feel that my initial caution had been perhaps unwarranted. I learned that he had been an officer in the Russian forces, with a highly educated background. Curious to learn whatever I could about life in the Soviet Union, I asked him all about his culture, his background and his academic history. He had specialised in photography at the University of Tomsk, regarded as one of the most accomplished in the country. He also boasted about his amorous conquests, which I must confess I found hard to believe as he didn't seem good-looking enough for a Casanova. My dreams of a socialist workers' paradise were shattered when he explained to me how many of the female students had to 'work on the side' to pay for their education, as the state's funding was simply insufficient.

His skills with a camera were reflected in his skills as an artist, although he was not someone who could create masterpieces from within himself. Rather, he impressed by faithfully copying photographs using pen and ink, ruling the paper lightly with a pencil and making the copy with a mathematical exactitude. I still have the picture he made of me for my birthday in 1944.

His skills were later to prove most useful.

In the meantime, Bill and Mrs Gould's social life continued to expand, and they met some of my particular friends. The Brées, who lived on the hill above Beaumont, used to welcome me to play chess once a week and I introduced Bill to them as they were trusted friends. I had no fear they would betray us, although I didn't feel it would be wise to tell my family of our connection. I felt no fear because I believed that if one behaved sensibly there was nothing to worry about. Bill's English grew better by the day, he was accepted by many people as a friend, and to all intents and purposes was living a life as normal as it could possibly be, under the circumstances. It continued in this way until Easter 1944. Then came the warnings. Our secret was out.

One was from the acting headmaster of Victoria College, a Mr P. A. Tatum, known to all as Pat Tatum. The Germans had taken over the former boarding section of the school as a headquarters, since it had been vacated by the establishment. Every now and again letters from local people would arrive at the school, addressed to 'The German HQ, Victoria College, Mont Millais'. Fortunately for many, this address wasn't strictly accurate. The Germans were in a different building correctly known as Victoria College HOUSE, but often these letters arrived upon the school secretary's desk. She took them to Pat Tatum, who in turn took them home and steamed them open to read.

Sadly, the Occupation was seen by some as a chance to settle old scores or neighbourly disputes by denouncing one's enemy to the Germans. A hint of black marketeering, a suspicion of an illicit radio, even a suggestion that the Germans might find something interesting if they looked under the chicken coop of a St Ouen farmer, could potentially see their fellow islanders locked away or even deported. Their devious, anonymous letters hoped that our occupiers might make up for whatever slight they felt had been done to them.

If someone was being incriminated, Pat Tatum would endeavour to find a roundabout way of getting a warning to them. A day or two later, he would reseal the envelope and re-address it, 'Try Vic Coll Hse', and post it himself in a letter box near his home after the last collection of the day.

Inevitably the day came when one of these letters mentioned Mrs Gould—and the Russian she was hiding. It was written in very distinctive lettering. She was lucky that Pat Tatum was able to intercept it and send word to her.

I believe there was another warning. My understanding is that a St Ouen girl had acquired a German boyfriend who was attached to one of the gun crews in the parish. He told the girl that the other chaps in his crew knew that the widow woman who kept the shop had a Russian escapee. This German soldier thought that sooner or later one of them would report this to someone in authority, and perhaps she ought to go and warn the lady in question? She did so, but I don't think she was given a particularly pleasant welcome. I imagine Mrs Gould would not have hesitated to have told her to get out of the shop and would scarcely have listened to her warnings, which had nonetheless been delivered. I heard this explanation from close friends of the parents of the girl in question.

While unwelcome, Mrs Gould knew from the two warnings that the game was up, and she would have to act quickly. Without telling me, she and Bill sat up all night destroying any evidence of his presence, then at six o'clock in the morning, as soon as curfew was over, he left the shop and made his way to the house of Mrs Gould's sister Ivy Forster, in St Helier. I knew from Mrs Gould that she was already sheltering a Russian known as George, who had once been under the care of my cousin Francis.

I heard of Bill's move soon afterwards, on the Saturday of the Easter bank holiday. In those days, Saturdays were not considered as a day off, in fact it was court day which meant that St Helier offices could be very busy. I certainly couldn't leave my desk until the close of business, as my professional duty had to be carried out in the usual manner, but the hours dragged until I could lock up and pedal my way to the house near the Robin Hood junction. To my astonishment, when I got there I found not only George and Bill, but also Ivy Forster, Mrs Gould and their brother Harold Le Druillenec. I may have been young and still naive about many things, but after Louisa explained the warnings she had received I knew I had to persuade them that these two young Russians must be got out of the house within the hour. I assumed the Germans would be there very soon, possibly before nightfall. Ivy's husband Arthur would also be home shortly. Fortunately they appreciated my urgency, and George was taken to a certain women's dress shop and told to wait in the changing-room until someone came to take him elsewhere. I gave instructions that I was not to be told where. George turned out to be very different to Bill, always upbeat, outgoing and dynamic with a great love of life and later became quite a problem for his various hosts, as he sometimes came back late for curfew after going to look for girlfriends. Several times I had calls from people asking me to come and collect him. At various times he was sheltered by people all over the island, from a black-market butcher to the chief surgeon at the hospital....

While the Forsters made arrangements for George's first move, I decided that I would have to take responsibility for Bill. He still had the bicycle belonging to Mrs Gould's son so it was a simple matter for us both to pedal away from the flat as casually as possible, he following me at a distance of a hundred yards or so. There was only one place I could take him. Retracing my earlier route, I led him to the offices of the General Accident Insurance Co., No. 27 Hill Street.

Chapter Seven

ON THE MOVE

My supposition was that by leaving Bill in the office over a bank-holiday weekend it would give me an extra day to try to find more suitable accommodation. It was clear that he would have to be moved before Miss Hunt arrived on Tuesday morning, but at such short notice there was nowhere else I could reliably take him that would not incriminate other people. Once I had Bill and his bicycle up the stairs, through the door and inside, I laid down the rules for his stay. 'There is a lavatory upstairs. It opens with this key. You may use the wash basin to keep yourself clean and for drinking water. Apart from that, you must stay in this room, because no-one will be able to see you there.' But being an incautious and rather excitable man, he said loudly, 'No! I'll go into one of these other rooms, they have much bigger windows, they are far more cheerful!' I was most alarmed and tried to make him see sense. 'You must stay OUT of that room, and AWAY from the windows! On a bank holiday, if anyone looks up from the street and sees your face there they will wonder what's going on. They know the office is closed, they will think you are a thief! You must stay in THIS ROOM!' But he would not be persuaded. 'There will be no harm!' he cried. Finally I had to lock the internal doors to the rooms which faced the street, and take the keys with me. I had two days to get him out of there and to a place which would be safer for both of us. The question was, where?

I took my bicycle, locked the office behind me and rode home in my usual way. I couldn't be too late back or my parents would have worried, and neither did I tell them of the day's developments, as they were still completely unaware of Bill's existence. The less they knew, the better.

The following day, a Sunday, I had to get cracking to find a new place for Bill to live. Fortunately through my job I had a good knowledge of the island and some idea of the people who might be trusted with such a sensitive matter. I knew of a house on St Clement's Road which I thought might be admirable for the purpose, as it had a garden with a shed where Bill might able to remain undetected for a while. It was owned by a family called des Vergez, whom I knew reasonably well as I had long pined for their daughter who was very good-looking. They were of Norman-French stock, all blonde, and I hoped all ready to do something in the name of humanity.

The house was situated opposite a large garage that was frequently used by the Germans to have their vehicles serviced, but nonetheless I thought it might be suitable. It was a gabled house with a wall around the front garden enclosing the shed I hoped might be Bill's new temporary home.

I knew the des Vergez sufficiently to trust them, and I was not disappointed. They immediately said yes to my request and even agreed to share their rations with their visitor, no small matter when we were all feeling the effects of wartime shortages. The following day I picked him up from my office and we cycled slowly together to the new place. It could only be a temporary location, owing to its proximity to the Germans and confining nature of the shed, which I was sure would drive my charge mad with boredom.

I made some more discreet calls, visiting people who I thought might be able to help. His next stop was a lock-up garage in the west of St Clement, where the tenants of the property were happy to look after him for a short time. I seem to remember telling them that Bill was French and on the run from the Germans, and that no-one but they and I would know that he was there. I embellished my tale by claiming that he was connected to the legal firm that administered the property and needed somewhere safe for a couple of nights. Not wanting to upset the administrators, since they were living in a fully furnished flat for very little rent, they agreed.

I was constantly trying to think of a better, more permanent place for Bill to settle in, until I came up with the name of 'Bill' Williams. His real name was Stuart, and he was a fascinating man. He spoke Spanish very well after having worked for several years in South America representing an English export company, and had a flat at the top of Roseville Street above what is still a Post Office and pharmacy. He became the latest person to agree to take Bill in; just for a few days, although there would be a problem with food and space.

To my delight, a short time later he told me he had found a safer and more suitable place where our guest might able to stay a while longer. Dorothy Huelin lived in a large house on Trinity Hill together with her two sons—one whom was a bit of a scamp—and her two daughters, and he thought she would be happy to take on Bill as an addition to the family. Most conveniently this lady's husband was away in South Africa, with a lady friend as it happens, which gave her a little more room. I was worried about the children though, as they were all still at school and one never knew what they might say to their classmates about the strange man who had suddenly appeared in their home. Another bike ride, up Trinity Hill, confirmed that the house would be ideal, and that Bill would be living in opulence compared to some of the rickety places he had called home before. There was a sunken bath with gold taps, deep rich carpets and all modern luxuries. Bill was overjoyed to swap garden sheds and garages for such a refined abode.

Throughout this time, while it was proving something of a trial, I was pleased to feel that I was able to do something meaningful in this dreadful war. I had no desire to be a soldier and fire a gun, nor to be an armed resister pulling down telephone cables or sabotaging lorries. I felt that helping Bill was something that simply had to be done, and saw it as my welcome duty.

I was motivated almost entirely by simple humanity. I was not at all enthusiastic about dying for my country, but, my God, Bill and those like him needed help. They were the victims of a hideous philosophy of racist brutality and I simply could not stand idly by while such cruelty was perpetrated on my own island.

At around this time, I heard from Mrs Gould's family that she wanted to get something to him. Thank goodness she had no idea where he now was, and I was able to lie and say that while he had been in my office he had now moved and I did not know where. I knew that his movements had to be kept a secret from as many people as possible, and unfortunately my prudence was soon to be rewarded. Just a short time after Bill's move to Trinity Hill, Mrs Gould, Ivy Forster and Harold Le Druillenec were arrested. Also taken by the Germans were their friends Dora Hacquoil and Berthe Pitolet, together with Mrs Gould's maid Alice Gavey. People who were aware that I knew them passed the news on to me, but I had to be careful how I reacted so they didn't guess there was anything more to it. It transpired that the warnings had been correct, and the Germans had somehow been tipped off about the possible presence of an escapee. Although Mrs Gould and Bill had spent a busy night removing all traces of his stay before he left, they had missed one or two vital pieces of incriminating evidence, including a Russian–English dictionary. Fatally, being a sentimental woman, she had also kept a single photo of him, a copy of which had been displayed in the German military police headquarters captioned, 'Have You Seen This Man?'. Somehow, during their questioning, they had avoided all mention of me.

Jersey authorities were uncertain of how to proceed against Mrs Gould and her brother and sister. There seemed to be nothing in the laws of the island detailing how to prosecute someone who acted against the interests of an occupying power. It seemed highly unlikely that such a law could be passed, as the section of the British government responsible for island affairs would never advise the King to sanction it. Even during the so-called French Occupation at the end of the Wars of the Roses there had been no such thing.

The Germans charged my friends with their various crimes and handed down sentences accordingly.

Louisa was sent to prison for two years primarily for failing to surrender her wireless and sharing the BBC news, but also for 'abetting breaching the working peace and unauthorised removal'.

Ivy Forster was sentenced to five months and fifteen days on similar charges.

Harold was sentenced to five months simply for listening to the radio.

The delightfully French Berthe Pitolet was given four months and fifteen days, Alice Gavey three months and Dora Hacquoil two months. But for Mrs Gould's insistence in court that Dora had always arrived late and never listened to the wireless, she could have fared far worse.

Ivy was lucky as she was able to serve her time in the German section of Jersey's own prison, thanks to some clever intervention by the Medical Officer of Health, Dr McKinstry. He told the Germans she had tuberculosis and they moved her to a specialist ward before a German doctor later pronounced her able to move into the prison. By that time it was too late to deport her. She got civilian rations, her family was able to visit and bring her food, and when they arrived she was allocated Red Cross parcels. She survived in reasonable health until the Liberation. Alice Gavey and Dora Hacquoil also survived in Jersey.

For Mrs Gould, her brother and Berthe Pitolet it was a very different story. I heard that they had been taken away, then nothing. I would not discover their awful fate until after the war.

Bill, an emotional man, was shocked and upset when he heard his friends had been taken, which added to his restlessness and frustration at being cooped up for most of the day despite the richness of his surroundings. I had always understood that this would be a temporary arrangement, but it came to an abrupt end when a very angry Bill Williams strode into my office and told me in no uncertain terms that the Russian would have to go that very day. Out of earshot of my customers and staff, he explained how he'd discovered that Bill had approached the milkman, about whom he knew nothing, and asked him to cycle out to Mrs Gould's house at Millais to fetch some of his art materials after letting himself in with a key which was hidden outside the premises. Such a request put all of us at enormous risk of being compromised and showed just how little Bill understood the need for security. He was proving to be a danger to everyone, but we couldn't simply put him out on the streets because he would be picked up by the first passing German. I thought he had fallen into a state of complacency and I would have a real job on my hands to find someone who would take him after being told, of necessity, of his total irresponsibility. I felt ultimately responsible for him, and could not allow him just to wander the streets after curfew. He had to be put somewhere, and whoever took him in would have to know the full story. I could not go back to the des Vergez family, as Mr des Vergez would quite rightly be unwilling to expose his young family to such a risk. Under pressure of time, I decided to call on the remaining two people who I thought might be willing to harbour my renegade Russian.

Michael Frowd and René Franoux lived in a flat in Grosvenor Terrace, but I knew that René was at that moment in hospital having his appendix out. He was a real character, born in London during a Zeppelin raid in the First World War of a father who was a French chef and a Swiss mother. Growing up long and lean, he had moved to Jersey in 1940 to work on the farms as a conscientious objector and progressed to giving lessons in French and German from the flat. Some of his students were German soldiers keen to better themselves. That night though, I knew his bed would be empty and I was desperate. Straight after work, on a balmy summer's evening, I went to the flat. Upon entering I found Mike lying stretched and thin on his back on the living room floor, typing on a typewriter precariously balanced on his midriff. He had been injured in a fall while working as a tree feller, and had permanently damaged his spine which made it more comfortable for him to work in this recumbent position. He had also left England as a conscientious objector, and had met René while working in the fields in the north of Jersey. The farmer had never told them that the island was under threat in the spring of 1940, nor that they could have evacuated if they had wished, and they were both now stuck in the island. Mike was now the editor, and main contributor, of a magazine called *The Jersey Forum* which he was working on when I came in. We later knew that publication, rather irreverently, as *The Jersey Bore'em*.

He asked me to what he owed the pleasure.... Unsure how to approach my subject, I took a deep breath, and came at it in a very roundabout way. I had a quandary involving someone who was rather irresponsible and dangerous, I told him, and needed some help. Finally I felt obliged to tell him the whole story until he turned to me abruptly and said, 'Bob, for heaven's sake get to the point! You want to know if he can have René's bed until René is discharged from hospital? Of course he can, and then we shall discuss it again. It sounds as though it's high time he had males looking after him instead of a succession of sentimental women!' While he was a few months younger than me, he had an air of confidence that was a result of his upbringing in English boarding schools. That confidence, however, was tempered by cool good judgement, a quality which he was sure to need in dealing with Bill. Had Mrs Gould known that Bill was to be housed with them she would have been outraged. How could her favourite young man be housed with *conchies*, people who hadn't dared to pick up a gun to defend their country?

And that was how I found Bill his final and most successful home. I went straightaway to pick him up and escorted him to Grosvenor Terrace, where he stayed until July 1945. These two young men, Mike and René, would never pick up a gun under any circumstances but were ready to risk their lives to save another's. They knew what had happened to Mrs Gould, Ivy Forster and Harold Le Druillenec, but were prepared to hide Bill in their attic without a second thought. Bravery is not only found on the battlefield.

Of course bravery can be eroded by hunger, and these two young men were faced with the challenge of having to make their already meagre rations stretch to accommodate a third hungry mouth. I recognised the problem and paid another visit to René Le Mottée in St Ouen. Without going into too much detail, I told him that Bill was in town in a household which was very short of money and food. They had nowhere to plant anything, I told him, apart from a little window box with some lettuce in! After that René would cycle to town every Saturday with his handlebars laden with two large bags full of potatoes, vegetables and sometimes a little pork. He couldn't take the main roads because they would be full of Germans, and anyone riding towards St Helier with such a load would almost certainly be suspected. Instead he took the little back lanes which he knew well as a true Jerseyman, and approached St Helier from the north. He would come to my office and lug the bags up the steps and through the doors, turning his head every few seconds to make sure no-one pinched his bike, which would have been catastrophic for him. I took the bags openly, having told Miss Hunt that Mr Le Mottée was helping some friends of mine who found it hard to get hold of enough food. That was true enough and managed to allay any suspicions she may have had. René would then casually walk back out of the door and down the steps to collect his bike before pedalling away. Nothing we did was furtive or really illegal, the goods he brought to me were not rationed and so the whole process was quite safe to that point. That was as far as René needed to go and we never burdened him with the knowledge of where or to whom the food was going. He did not need to know and it was safer for all concerned if he did not, so either myself or Mike would take the bags onwards to the flat.

René Le Mottée did that every week until Liberation, and should have been decorated for his courage and generosity of spirit which defied the Nazi philosophy of persecution so completely. Without his efforts, René, Mike and Bill could have spent a very hungry Occupation.

Although ...

As he became more settled, Bill took to leaving the flat and disappearing around town on his own. He wore what he regarded as a foolproof disguise of a calf-length raincoat and a trilby hat pulled down low over his eyes, which his hosts believed made him look like a failed Chicago gangster but seemed somehow to be effective. He wore this getup regardless of the summer heat. After he had spent some time living at the flat and had gathered enough confidence to perambulate further he would occasionally return and boast that he had just eaten a wonderful steak dinner with all the trimmings and a glass of wine whose provenance he kept a strict secret. He flatly refused to tell Mike and René where he had been for such a feast for reasons of security. They were understandably intrigued and guessed that it must have been within walking distance of the flat, but never found out the truth until after the Germans had left.

Close to Grosvenor Terrace was, and still is, the Mayfair Hotel. It belonged to a man named Woodhall who had left for England in 1940 with his family, but his brother Fred had an Austrian wife and had decided to stay on and manage the hotel in his place. They moved into his brother's accommodation on the first floor and attempted to run the business as before, only to be rudely interrupted by the Germans deciding to turn it into a *Soldatenheim*, the German equivalent of the English NAAFI. Possibly because Mrs Woodhall was technically German they were not moved out and remained at the hotel for the duration. Naturally they socialised and became most friendly with some of the German soldiers who graced the hotel, listening to their descriptions of the fortifications and fights they had been involved with. What the soldiers didn't know was that Mrs Woodhall was an intensely patriotic Austrian, who resented the fact that her country had been forcibly taken over by the Germans before the war. Moreover, her father had been a member of the Austrian parliament only to be arrested with her brother after the 1938 Anschluss as political suspects, together with thousands more of her countrymen; her father was eventually released in gibbering madness because of his treatment in the prison in which he had been held. Her brother had been less fortunate and became one of the millions who simply disappeared under the Nazis, whom she now had every reason to hate. Her revenge was sweet. In their flat at the Mayfair Hotel, she and her husband hid not one but two Russian escapees, right under the very noses of the Germans enjoying the facilities they offered. It was the very last place the Germans would have thought of looking for them.

There were two doors to the flat. One led downstairs and outside into the street, while the other led directly into the *Soldatenheim*. When the Russians were inside they kept that door locked. German soldiers were intrigued, and asked Mrs Woodhall why. Her explanation was that she had returned home one day to find a Greenfly poking about in the drawer of her dressing table and wished to make sure that they could not gain access to her personal belongings again. The punctilious soldiers quite understood.

When her charges were hungry she was able simply to go down to a sympathetic chef in the kitchens and with a long face describe how she had no meat to give to her husband, and could he help her.... He would go to find her some scraps while she swept whatever else she could find into her bag, and that was how she fed the Russians.

Somehow Bill had got wind of this arrangement—maybe he had met one of the escapees on a foray into town—and Mrs Woodhall had been pleased to add him occasionally to her roster of grateful hungry guests.

Ostracised by Jersey people for her apparently cosy relationship with the Germans who used her hotel, Mrs Woodhall was one of many islanders who led secretive, furtive lives of risk and doubt in order to save the lives of strangers. Like René Le Mottée her efforts went unrecognised, as unlike some others she chose not to make a fuss about it once the war was over. All through the Occupation while I was trying to find places for these poor young men I took the elementary precaution of never even trying to place one with the kind of people who would boast about how brave they were. There were known to be loudmouths who could be most indiscreet about who was living in their spare room, simply to gain short-lived local glory. Those who truly made a difference, the bravest and most laudable, were those such as Mike Frowd and René Franoux, who took the risks without a fuss and then melted quietly back into everyday life.

When René came back from hospital he naturally wanted his bed back, so the two young men cleared and prepared the attic for Bill to occupy. He was quite comfortable there and even used to wait, in the company of a galvanised bucket, while René gave language lessons to German soldiers in the room below. Once they had gone, he was able to descend to sleep in a sleeping bag on a rubber airbed. This was not in the best condition and would frequently deflate to leave him lying on a thin Kapok mattress, the discomfort of which I had personally experienced when I slept there myself on one or two occasions. They had frequent recourse to their bicycle repair kit to try to keep some air pressure, but I fear it was a losing battle.

He was also able to take more time to enjoy his passion for drawing, which led to a most lucrative arrangement with a local shop. Having seen one of his drawings and been impressed by it I asked Victor Hamon's mother if I could borrow a photo of her son. She had given me Victor's best suit despite suffering terrible grief from his death and I wanted to give her something she could use to treasure his memory. She gave me a photo of him in uniform and I later surprised her by returning it with a framed pen and ink copy made by Bill. She admired it greatly, and wanted to know more about the artist who had managed to capture her son's likeness so well. It was a sad story, I told her. The young man who had wielded his pen and ink so cleverly was very frail and terminally ill, unable even to come down the stairs. Perhaps I laid it on a bit thick as she then asked me if the young man in question was short of money. Knowing of the perpetual financial crisis at Grosvenor Terrace, I said that yes, that was indeed the case. Mrs Hamon suggested I should try to find someone with a shop who would put the artwork and the original photograph side by side in the window with a sign saying 'Orders Accepted'.

Seizing the idea with alacrity I went to see two friends of mine, a Mr Leader and Mrs Osborne, who traded as Leo's on Colomberie. Theirs was a very classy ladies' beauty and hair salon, whose patrons were just the type to be moved by the sad story of both Victor and the frail young artist. Within days commissions started to come in and at a fiver a time Bill soon had an income much in excess of his two young hosts!

Although because of his communist upbringing he had no Christian belief, one of his most sought-after specialities was making drawings of Jesus Christ. These were sold at the religious bookshop in Waterloo Street, the manageress of which was very touched that a young invalid could produce work of such spiritual feeling. I could not tell her that from time to time the artist in question would walk past her shop in a slouched hat and long mackintosh to admire his genius on display in her window.... The amount of cash coming in meant that as his effective agent I had to open a bank account for him in my name so that his hard-won loot could be held safely.

Mike and René had a circle of close friends whom they trusted, and a very active social life. Despite the oppression of the Occupation they held many parties which they and their girlfriends would always host with the same infallible strategy. They knew very well that the way to ensure a party went with a swing was to take a bunch of like-minded people who hadn't had a square meal for at least twelve months and then serve them with liberal amounts of Calvados! It never failed and we had some wonderful times at their flat. Bill was introduced to everyone as a Pole who had come to the island before the war to study the Jersey cattle breed only to become trapped when the Germans invaded.

I remember one party at Grosvenor Street in particular. It was at the end of September 1944, when we had been warned that the gas supply was to be cut off. For most people in town this was not a reason to celebrate, but we were young and resilient. Somebody had got hold of a rabbit, others had brought various contributions of root vegetables, cider and Calvados. Two huge pans were simmering on the stove as we prepared to mark the moment with a wonderful blow-out. Sadly, on this occasion, Bill found the Calvados before the evening officially began and made free with it while we busied ourselves with the rabbit. We suddenly became aware that he was ready, in no uncertain terms, to start the celebrations right away. He sank down on his haunches, folded his arms, and bellowing Cossack songs at the top of his voice began to kick his legs in and out like Thomas the Tank Engine's pistons.

Being a lovely warm September evening the sash windows were open wide and right at that moment a squad of Germans were crashing in their hobnailed boots down the street outside. Fortunately for us they too were in full song. I distinctly recollect two quick-thinking people slamming down the windows while someone else ran into the kitchen and came back with a revolting dishcloth soaked in water. Bill, blissfully unaware of the furore he had caused, was abruptly and unpleasantly gagged with the forceful insertion of the dishcloth into his mouth. As he struggled the Germans marched on by, blissfully unaware of the scene being played out just above their heads. As the danger subsided, we realised the game was up, as no Pole would sing Cossack songs and dance in that way. How lucky we were that Mike and René's friends were as trustworthy as they appeared.

Other parties followed, with or without gas but never without Calvados. The limits of the curfew were a source of frustration, and several of us began to turn up with sleeping bags as well as food and drink so that we could simply stay for the night until the hours of darkness had passed. One night I was trying to sleep top to tail with René in his bed next to Bill when the Russian started talking in his sleep; not in Russian but in English. I was fascinated to hear what he was saying … 'Bugger this bloody world' was the general theme. Neither Michael nor René ever swore, as they were well educated and had a sufficiently good command of English not to need to, and I wondered where Bill could have picked up this interesting vernacular!

He certainly enjoyed getting out of the flat and making the most of his relative freedom, although it had not always been plain sailing. Mike and René used to like to tell the story of the first time they allowed him to make a small excursion. By then he had grown a moustache and was sporting by way of disguise a pair of plain-glass spectacles which I had managed to liberate from the Green Room amateur dramatic club. They told him he was not to go into town, but instead could go up College Hill towards the countryside where he could enjoy the twists and turns of the Jersey lanes. Unfortunately as Bill came to the junction with Mont Millais a German car pulled up alongside, a soldier got out and marched straight towards him waving a piece of paper. The soldier started gesticulating and asking Bill questions, not a word of which he could understand. He feared he had been recognised and that his hard-won freedom was about to come to a bitter end, until a middle-aged woman came out of a house nearby. She asked if she could help, and from Bill's anguished looks realised that he was possibly in a very difficult situation. Things did indeed look bleak, until the woman managed to translate what the German was saying. The piece of paper in his hand had written upon it the address of a house that he was looking for, he had become lost and frustrated, and he had simply been asking Bill for directions. The woman was able to point the German in the right direction, while Bill returned immediately to the flat where he was most regrettably forced to change his trousers.

This moment of excitement hadn't been enough to satisfy his yearnings for freedom though, and before long he would take regular outings to town and beyond. He often took risks that his hosts were unaware of, even going to the cinema which was regularly full of soldiers. After all, he had his trusty trilby and rain-coat ... He even managed to have an affair with a certain young lady to whom I had introduced him. Ultimately she married a liberating British soldier, but Bill did tell me that in their brief time together she had taken him 'to heaven and back'!

I tried to include Bill if we were going on outings with a group of friends; after all with several of us it was easier to keep an eye on what he might get up to. Periodically a number of us would walk from St Helier to Archirondel on the southeast coast where a place sold meals which usually contained some kind of protein for which you were not required to provide clippings from your ration book. The place, run by the Ferey family, offered a boarding service too, for which you had to book in advance in writing. We would often go there on a Sunday, taking the back lanes and footpaths we knew well. We walked casually and normally, not at all on our tiptoes or in any way furtively which might have raised suspicions, looking to all the world exactly what we were—a group of friends out for a stroll.

We were all determined that our lives should go on as normally as possible despite the curfew and rationing and hunger, and also determined that Bill should have every right to that enjoyment too.

We held debates on the world situation in the flat, not just a free-for-all argument but structured in a truly democratic way. Often friends of ours would come to join us, and sometimes there would be up to twenty people crammed into the living room. Someone would propose a motion which would then be seconded, resulting in a debate led by a chairman. Of course, this democratic exercise could never have happened in the Soviet Union, and our discussions gave Bill a glimpse of intellectual freedom which he might otherwise never have had, and a chance to exercise his right to agree or disagree with whomever he chose. We discussed religion, philosophy, politics and social matters, wide-ranging topics which affected us all. I remember how astonished he was that Mike and René had been allowed to register formally as conscientious objectors, to refuse to fight for their country. In his homeland, that would simply not have been countenanced.

But by now Bill was not the only escapee I was helping, and my accommodation problems had started once more.

It began through my association with two Russian women who lived in the island. Mrs Metcalfe was married to a former British naval officer, while Miss Demetrieva had been naturalised as British. They now lived in a flat just up from my office on Hill Street above a second-hand shop that they ran, but their journey to Jersey had been an eventful one. After the Russian revolution in 1917 the British had sent help to anti-Bolshevik forces known as White Russians in the far north of that country, and many who opposed the new regime were able to escape. Mrs Metcalfe and Miss Demetrieva were two of them.

They had been smuggled out of Archangel in the north of Russia by Mrs Metcalfe's husband onto a British warship, before finally coming to settle in our island in an attempt to avoid civil war in their home country and any further fighting in western Europe. These women were refugees from Communism, but the concept of Mother Russia overcame that and they were keen to help their fellow countrymen to escape the clutches of another oppressive regime. Word somehow went around the slave camps that there were two Russian women who would help you if you could manage to escape. They were both well-educated, middle-class women who spoke not only perfect English but also French and German, and had been allowed to live unmolested by the Germans.

The two women knew that I knew people who might be able to help them with any slaves who made their way to them, and one day Miss Demetrieva came to see me in my office. Perhaps they had been tipped off somehow by Bill, but they were aware that through my business contacts I might know where 'certain people' might be able to find a safe place to stay at short notice. If I received someone from them, she told me, they didn't wish to know where that person might go to afterwards. That was a sensible and secure approach, and I agreed to do what I could to help.

One of the escaped slaves they were helping wanted an English–Russian dictionary. After consulting my mental list of people who might have such a thing in our little island, I went to see an elderly Englishman who I knew had worked in Manchuria, a city full of Russian refugees from the civil war. Yes, he had a Russian dictionary, which he was prepared to sell me without asking why I would need such a thing. I split the cost of the book with a group of friends and we proudly presented it to the escapee, who was called Sergei. Much to my dismay instead of being overcome with gratitude he became furious because the dictionary was all written in the old-fashioned spellings which were no longer used, rendering it obsolete. So much for gratitude!

Despite their caution and security the Germans finally caught up with Mrs Metcalfe and Miss Demetrieva. Two plain-clothes policemen turned up at their second-hand shop while Miss Demetrieva was working, and most politely told her that they suspected she was hiding a Russian worker. They were going to search the premises for him. One went upstairs, while the other stayed in the shop to question her. Unfortunately their suspicions were quite correct.

Mrs Metcalfe encountered the officer who came up the stairs, and he made it clear that he was going to go through her rooms until he found his quarry. She later recounted to me how she was sitting in the corner opposite the door, alongside the windows which looked out over Hill Street with the officer in front of her asking questions. To her horror, over his shoulder she saw her Russian guest creeping down the stairs from the second floor carrying his boots, but she had the presence of mind not to look his way or give any sign that she had seen him. As the Russian crept past the doorway, she told the German that of course he must do his duty, but really, with four children living in the house, how on earth did they think they could accommodate a single person more? Just go ahead and search, she said, turning her head away from him and looking out of the window with a dismissive shrug. All the while she was thinking of the one stair which always creaked when you put any weight on it, praying that the young Russian would manage to miss it. She waited for the creak but luckily he must have discovered which stair to avoid, and in moments Mrs Metcalfe was able to watch him emerge into the street and escape. The German went through her rooms with a fine-tooth comb before heading down the stairs to summon his colleague who had been peering suspiciously behind everything in the shop. They left empty-handed, thanks to the coolheadedness of the women and the dexterity of their guest. While they were later arrested, the Germans realised they didn't have enough evidence to court-martial them and they were finally released, only to continue to pass further escapees on to me.

I must have been acquiring a reputation for my clandestine work, for I was soon approached by more people in need of help. But how to find dwelling places for more ragged men on the run? I would have to take a series of calculated risks, and trust to my judgement of islanders who I thought might be suitable.

Most of the people whom I approached I already knew, often from my insurance work. I had now become quite adept at spotting those who had an attitude of defiance to our occupiers that was not just empty verbiage. While not all of them said yes, I was never afraid that any of them would actually denounce me, and I cycled from one end of the island to the other knocking on doors and in a roundabout way asking whether the inhabitants might perhaps have room for a guest who unexpectedly needed a place to stay. I usually found that it was best to speak to the man of the house, and sometimes went out into the fields to find him. Between myself and the two Russian women I should think I managed to house perhaps ten or twelve men in this way. The moment I found somewhere I would recommend strongly they keep their visitor for perhaps two months and then pass them on to someone they knew as trustworthy, and not to tell me or anyone else where they had gone. I didn't feel as though I was doing something particularly brave because I thought I was covering my tracks pretty well and wasn't exposing myself to too much risk—and besides, I believed that I had a duty to humanity to do what I was doing. I was aware that some others were acting in a similar way, but perhaps with slightly different motives. Norman Le Brocq, for example, was acting for idealistic reasons as a dedicated communist, while others were simply determined to defy 'the bloody Germans'.

One effect of my work was to make me realise the essence of the individual. When they arrived from the boat the slave workers had shuffled and marched down the island's roads in a kind of amorphous mass, one scarcely distinguishable from the other with their downcast eyes, ragged clothes and unwashed bodies. But of course among them were all kinds of people. Officers, privates, shoemakers, farmers, men who were proud, men who were desperate. Fathers, sons, husbands, thieves and vagabonds, educated men and paupers. Some had been captured while serving in uniform and were technically prisoners of war. Others, a very few of them women, had been simply rounded up from their home villages by German squads sent to help feed the Reich's insatiable demand for manpower. They had been dragged from their homes, their fields, or even their prison cells, to help build the fortifications that would defend the very regime that oppressed them. Every one of them had his or her own unique story, their own personality, their own reasons for wanting to survive and live in freedom.

Yet when the first of these poor people were brought against their will to our island, little did we imagine that it would not be long until some of our very own people were to be taken away from it.

Chapter Eight

WOMEN AND CHILDREN

Our first warning of the approaching calamity appeared quite suddenly. It was 15 September 1942 when the notice, signed by the German Feldkommandant Oberst Knackfuss, appeared in the newspaper as an Official Announcement. I read it when I got home from work. By order of 'Higher Authorities', British people who weren't native islanders, AND all men who were not born in the Channel Islands *together with their families* were to be 'evacuated and transferred to Germany'. Oh, my God.

Who were those 'Higher Authorities' pushing the local commanders into such action?

Maybe I could understand the reasoning behind the first category. People from the mainland who had been caught here by the outbreak of war could perhaps be plants for British intelligence and I did have my suspicions about a couple of people that I knew.

But the second category of those to be deported, men with their families—what possible reason could there be for that? My heart pounded as I thought of all the people I knew who might fit into that group. One family in particular gave me great cause for alarm. The Dunns were very close friends of ours with four lovely children, three girls and a boy, ranging in age from fifteen right down to three. How on earth would they cope? I knew that the newspaper would have been delivered to their house already, but it was unlikely that Mrs Dunn would have had time to read it as she would be too busy preparing food and looking after the children. Her husband was an electrician and often worked late. I very much wanted to make sure that she heard about it from someone sympathetic rather than reading it in the newspaper, so I resolved to get to her before she could open the paper. Jumping on my bike, I pedalled and pushed my way up the steep hill of Mont Cochon in the centre of the island. They were renting a house in a nice estate that had been built in the 1930s with a view out over the bay and large garden, which the owners were quite happy to let them have for fifteen shillings a week. Empty properties were vulnerable after all, and many had already been ransacked for firewood.

As I approached the door I hesitated. How could I possibly tell someone that they were in danger of being shipped away to heaven knew where, simply for being British? How could I explain it kindly without causing them undue alarm? How could we possibly explain to the children?

But there was no time to debate these questions for long, and I knocked. Mrs Dunn came to the door, a kindly woman in middle age with light brown hair and spectacles. She had married a widower and enjoyed a very happy family life. The smile on her face told me she was unaware of the awful news I was bringing. 'Eunice, I must speak to you,' I said. 'Have you seen the *Evening Post*? There's something we must talk about before Billy comes home.' She hadn't read it, but it had been delivered and was sitting there on the kitchen table. I showed her the notice and she went pale. 'My God, that's us! Billy was born in Dundee! What will they do to us?' Then, in a reaction which was common right across the island in so many homes, she said, 'We mustn't alarm the children. We must pretend everything is all right, that everything is normal. They mustn't be frightened.' Even as we considered this dreadful scenario there was a knocking at the door. Standing on the doorstep was a Jersey Honorary Police officer with a German soldier, both looking rather apologetic. 'I'm terribly sorry,' said the officer, 'but you are on the list and you are to be on the boat *tomorrow*.'

Yes, the Germans used Jersey's own voluntary police officers to facilitate the deportation of her own people, but in my mind I am glad they did. In the rural parishes the constables even made arrangements to transport the affected families to the harbour. After the war many of them were vilified for helping the Germans to implement this hideously cruel policy, but one must remember that they had very little choice in the matter. In these terrible circumstances the Jersey authorities got involved to try to make things as easy as possible for the islanders who were being forced to leave—these orders were from the Führer himself and could not be simply ignored. If it had to happen, the constables thought, we must make it as painless as possible. It was surely better to have the knock on the door and a sympathetic explanation from someone you knew and trusted, than a faceless German soldier issuing a cold-hearted order. Did their critics really think that the constables could sit back in their own houses and watch from the window as people living at La Corbière, L'Etacq or Rozel struggled to make it to the harbour with small children? How otherwise would a pregnant woman get from a far-flung part of the island lugging her suitcases in time for the boat which she had been told she must be aboard?

The Dunns had to be at the harbour in the late afternoon, something which we had to explain to the distraught Billy when he arrived home from work. What a situation to be placed in, to be told you had to leave your own home with less than twenty-four hours' notice and taking no more than you could carry! What should be taken, what should be left, what would become of the house, of your possessions, of your friends to whom you might not even have the chance to say goodbye? These were just some of the questions which greeted the unsuspecting Billy. He completely agreed with Eunice that the children should be protected as far as possible, and they concocted a tale that they were going off on an exciting holiday, to have great fun in the German mountains where there would be snow in the winter! The children listened bravely to what they were told and appeared to be taken in. Years later, however, the two eldest told me separately that they knew it was all a lie and that their parents were trying to put a gloss on something unpleasant. But at the time they'd decided, with extraordinary maturity, to go along with the lie in order not to upset their younger siblings. They knew this was something serious, but they had to attempt to put on a carefree façade. It was a heartbreaking scene that was being played out all over the island as families got the fateful knock on the door and orders to prepare themselves for the journey into the unknown.

Of course I stayed to help them, rushing about to find things they thought they might need in the days ahead. Mrs Dunn prepared to dress her children in two of everything so they would be able to carry more in their suitcases. It was a dreadful, heart-rending time as they made decisions about what treasured possessions would have to be left behind, and whether they would ever see them again. There were very tearful scenes when three-year-old Jean couldn't find her teddy from which she was almost inseparable, and without which she found it very hard to sleep. Billy and Eunice knew that she would be far happier and would sleep regardless of what was going on around her if only she were able to clutch this teddy. We searched the house to no avail and the following afternoon the family had to leave without it. It was only weeks later as I prepared a trunk of things to send to them in Germany that I found it, in the place where the little girl had hidden it to 'save it from the Germans'. To my great satisfaction I was able to send it to her.

I arranged transport for the Dunns to the harbour through a farmer I knew, and he refused to take any money for the job. He'd already taken another family when he turned up at the house with his horse and cart and I went along with them as far as the assembly point near the harbour. I remember bumping along The Avenue and being passed by a group of people in a truck heading to the same place who shouted and waved at us, 'See you there, we'll be off together, don't be late....' And this is what I can never forget. Whatever emotions there may have been at home, whatever desperate tears may have been shed, whatever frantic and rushed goodbyes, it had all been in private. When we got to the meeting point, in a building opposite the Pomme d'Or Hotel where the bus station is now, hundreds of our fellow islanders were milling around waiting to be called to the boat.

There was no hysteria, no sobbing, people in their warmest clothes because they would be facing a German winter created the atmosphere of Victoria Station on a bank-holiday weekend in an extraordinary collective defiance of any German who may have expected to see broken spirits. As they stood there waiting for instructions they chatted and laughed with the greatest of British pluck. 'Hello, how are you? What a coincidence, we may be on the same boat…. Oh, you just finished school, now you're just off on another holiday, lucky you….' These people had seen what the Germans did to people they took from their homes, they had seen the treatment meted out to the slave workers and must surely have wondered if the same fate awaited them in some far-off corner of the Reich. Were they destined for labour in the arms factories of the Ruhr, to drudge on the land to feed the German people, or simply to be locked behind barbed wire and left to starve? Would they be beaten, chained, or even killed away from the watching eyes of their fellow countrymen as a warning to the world? Somehow, collectively and without any need for discussion, not a single person gave in to their feelings of fright or injustice. It was extraordinary. Even the youngest children stood quietly, holding their mother's and father's hands and watching the bustle with wide eyes.

I had been inclined to laugh at the expression 'a stiff upper lip', a relic of the old days of the Raj and the British Empire, but by God I saw it that day and I cannot think of it now without great emotion.

There was a lady who was probably in her early sixties with an obviously frail husband, who was trying and failing to lift the suitcase which carried all they had left in the world. A young German soldier, perhaps nineteen years old, in a gesture surely rooted in common decency, approached and tried to help her. She held on to the handle tightly, glaring defiance into his face and refusing to let him have anything to do with it. He was mortified and looked as though he was about to burst into tears. If I live to be two hundred years old I will never be able to forget that image.

The future Occupation historian Michael Ginns and his family were on this boat. His father had to be carried on board on a stretcher after collapsing on the quayside. As he was passing, a German naval officer whispered to his wife, 'I hope you know that the officers of the German Navy do not approve of this.' Michael never forgot those words, and they helped to form his determination that the people of Jersey should be reconciled with their former enemies.

He was not the first German to voice these opinions. I heard later of dozens of incidents where German soldiers knocked on people's doors to tell them they were not happy at what was being done in their names.

The older people, the infirm, and those with children were encouraged to get on board first by the volunteers of St John Ambulance, as they said it was more likely they would be able to travel under cover and protected from the elements.

The terribly plummy retired army officer, Major Butterworth, whom I knew as a client of the insurance company, was standing near to me with his suitcase all ready to go—but seemed in no hurry to join the queue pushing past the barrier to the quay. He was probably in his late sixties. I asked him if he didn't want to take advantage of the early boarding to ensure he had some shelter. 'Dear boy,' he said, which term of familiarity I'm sure I did not like, 'as far as I am concerned that barrier there could mark the end. As long as I am on this side of it, there is hope. My motto today is "women and children first!"'

After a last goodbye my friends the Dunns walked slowly through the barrier, with everything they now owned either on their backs or in the overstuffed suitcases they lugged along with them. The eldest children made sure the younger ones had their little bundles of clothes and did their best to cheer them along on their 'wonderful adventure'. All around me friends were saying similar last goodbyes, with lingering handshakes and final kisses until the fateful barrier separated them for good. Still that extraordinary spirit held strong until the Germans announced that the boat was now full and would take no more passengers, leaving many who had been called still waiting their turn to go through. They were simply told to go home and return for the next boat. Those poor souls had abandoned everything to make it to the harbour and yet now they had to struggle with all their luggage back to a home which might be many miles away. When some of them arrived they found that their not-so-friendly neighbours had already helped themselves to the furniture.

Major Butterworth was one of those sent home, and in fact never was deported despite being called for several further sailings. His determination to stay on the right side of the barrier had served him well.

As the ship prepared to sail I felt a rising surge of anger and despair that what had been until now a relatively benign occupation had become something so sinister and overbearing. The boat would sail out from the harbour to head south, and I heard many of those who were not required to be on the boat planning to wave it off from the wall above Mount Bingham where there would be a clear view out over the harbour. I resolved to go with them. Hundreds of Jersey people streamed down the road together in a resentful crowd, climbing up the hill to stand with a view looking onto the quay where the ship was moored. There was waving and people called out as they spotted friends moving about on the deck who waved back with their handkerchiefs until finally the ropes were cast off and she set sail. As the vessel withdrew from the quay everyone on the deck moved as one body to the Mount Bingham side to be as close to their friends and family as possible for the last time, to the extent that one could clearly see the deck of the boat tilting over towards us.

Then the singing began.

I don't know who started it but suddenly from the land and from the sea people joined in with patriotic songs, popular songs that we could only have known by listening to our illegal radios. One I remember in particular was Vera Lynn's 'White Cliffs of Dover', a moving and emotional song at any time. Our voices made a bridge between the steamer and the island and broadcast an almost electric defiance to any German who may have heard it, in contempt of this abject inhumanity. The voices faded as the ship drew slowly away towards the horizon and we were left standing in powerless frustration. The tears in our eyes were those of anger and helplessness, and some of the young men were prepared to take physical action against the Germans who would surely come to disperse what had become an unruly crowd. Indeed, as I pedalled away a patrol was heading to do just that. I heard later that there had been some disturbance, that a few German helmets were thrown over the wall into Pier Road and some young men were arrested.

Still struggling to contain my emotions I made my way down to the centre of town and onto Queen Street. As I pushed my bicycle I noticed ahead of me a small knot of Germans fussing around a rather silly young Jerseywoman who was giggling and flirting with no apparent sense of shame. For what I think was the first and only time in the entire Occupation my temper got the better of me and I could not help but express how I felt. Ignoring the soldiers I confronted her. 'Don't you have more sense on a day like this when people have been sent away perhaps to their deaths? To be laughing with your German boyfriends when just a few hundred yards away Jersey people are going to misery?!' I must have been very angry indeed to take such a step, but I remember thinking that if one of the soldiers reacted, what the hell did it matter? They may not have understood exactly what I said to her but they must have understood the sense of it, and yet they stood back and did nothing. For her part, I must at least give her the credit of appearing rather ashamed and contrite.

The Jersey grapevine spread the news of the deportations very quickly, and I'm sure there wasn't a person in the island who didn't know what had happened that day. Most of them would have known someone who had been sent away.

It was a critical turning point in the Occupation. This vindictive uprooting of hitherto peaceful and passive islanders had exactly the effect the German top brass had hoped to avoid when they had ignored the order some months before. The mood in the island changed that day from one of a sullen acceptance of the modus vivendi to one of intransigence and non-cooperation, of resentment and ridicule. Until then the Germans had been proud of the 'model Occupation' they had created, only for that to be thrown away by Hitler's act of spite.

There were further deportations in the following weeks and each time there was a stronger German presence to deter a repeat performance of our show of defiance. To our dismay, Mr Rodd from the office was one of those called up to leave. Unfortunately for him he fell into the first category of people to be taken away, as he had arrived in Jersey on the very last boat to come from the mainland before the Occupation began. People in that category were naturally suspected of being involved with British intelligence. But in fact Mr Rodd was the very last person who would have been of any use at all as a spy. Not because he was dim in any way, but he was simply incapable of telling a lie and far too honest to be involved in intelligence work.

He received his summons to be at the harbour the following day and came into the office to see me with the news. I rather think that he also came because he wanted to explain why he would not be coming to work the next day, and possibly also to return any pens or minor pieces of stationery he had which might otherwise have preyed on his mind. He was an upright, honest and straightforward man who went to his fate in Germany with a straight back and a clear conscience. I'm sure there were many other Mr Rodds in the island, of no threat to anyone, who were taken hundreds of miles away from home on the Führer's whim.

Another friend of mine called for deportation was a tea-planter who worked largely in Assam, but happened to be at home in Jersey when the Germans arrived. He and his wife together with their fourteen-year-old son who was at Victoria College were on the second or third list to be drawn up. I met them when they arrived at the meeting point and stayed with them as they queued. As they approached the barrier which would cut them off from their island, a German was counting people through in groups of five in order to keep a tally of how many had embarked. My friends ushered their son through and were about to pass through themselves when the German's hand came down to prevent them from moving. There can be no more, he said, the number is correct, the ship is full. Can you imagine the effect this had on my friends? The mother tried to explain to the soldier but he didn't understand and on the other side of the barrier the passengers were being ushered towards the boat. Finally, after some pleading with the soldier a single man came from further back in the queue and offered to take the boy's place. He was duly passed back through the barrier and the whole family was allowed to go home in the back of a farmer's horse-drawn cart.

On the way home, along the seafront past my house, they passed a horse-drawn van belonging to Le Gallais, a local firm specialising in removals, going in the opposite direction. When they had first been called for deportation they had arranged with that company that all their furniture would be taken away and held in storage against their hoped-for return to the island. As they passed the van on the other side of the road the mother said jokingly, 'I hope that isn't our furniture in there or we'll have nothing to sit on!' Lo and behold, when they arrived back at their home at the top of St Brelade there was not a light bulb left.

They had learned their lesson. The next time they were called they loitered discreetly at the back of the queue until the German's arm came down to indicate that the boat was full, and returned home once more. They reclaimed their furniture from Le Gallais, sent their son back to school, and never left.

I didn't go again to Mount Bingham to watch the ships sail, but I did go to the assembly point on two further occasions with good friends of mine who had been called upon to leave. Both times saw a repeat per-formance of the one I had witnessed previously, with tight smiles and firm handshakes the only signs of emotion from those who were destined to be taken away. There was no fear, no hysteria, only a sullen show of determination which inspired and made me so proud of my people. It set me an example of how to behave in my clandestine work which had already been influenced by my mother's assertion that one should never betray one's emotions in public. I'm sure that more islanders became willing to help frustrate the Germans as a result of the deportations.

After some weeks we were informed that we could write to any friends we may have had on those forlorn little boats. They had been taken, we were told, to a castle in Germany in a town called Wurzach, just north of the border with Switzerland. We were even allowed to send them parcels, and thus I was able to reunite the Dunn's little daughter with her favourite teddy. The detainees themselves were allowed to write back, and also to write to their relatives in England—which gave me a cunning idea. I still very much wanted to get in touch with the branch office on the mainland

and so I wrote to a friend of mine in the camp asking him to pass on a message to Colonel Eric Thorpe, 14 Cumberland Place, Southampton. I explained that the office was still open and operating, and was able to describe to him far more than I could on the standard Red Cross messages to England from Jersey, which were limited to twenty-five words. My message to the office went from Jersey, all the way to Wurzach and then by some hugely convoluted route all the way back up north and across the sea to Britain. Despite being left open for the censors to read, it got through.

Chapter Nine

THE YELLOW STAR

My father had a very good friend called Willie Leopold. They were of the same age, both having been born in 1882, and met often during the Occupation to drink a cup of terrible acorn coffee while they put the world to rights. Willie used to come to our house and sit in the front room, chatting and catching up on all the latest news and remembering old times with my father. When he'd drained the last of his ersatz brew he would take leave of us, walk out of the front gate and head home, appearing to all as if he didn't have a care in the world. But he did. Because Willie Leopold was a Jew.

Very soon after the Germans arrived, they required all Jews to be registered. In all honesty I was surprised that any had been so naive as to remain in Jersey when it became obvious that invasion was imminent. Anyone with any grasp of world affairs would have been under no illusion what fate was likely to befall any Jewish people in occupied countries and I had anticipated that anyone of that race would have left at the earliest opportunity. Alas many decided not to leave but hoped the Germans might approach what the Nazis described as the 'Jewish Question' with a little more leniency here. Only a handful of them registered. The rest, with varying degrees of success, kept their heads down and most, like Willie Leopold, survived the war. 'Why didn't you get on the boat?' my father would ask him over and over again as the Occupation ground on. Willie was a popular and well-known man who was discreet about his descent and trusted that the hundreds of people who knew him would be equally so. He was right to do so; he was never denounced and lived right through to the Liberation.

I can well remember the sense of outrage I felt when the first restrictions on Jewish people came into place. They were restricted in when they could be outdoors, they were not allowed to go into the cinemas, and their properties and shops were daubed with the Star of David as a warning to us all that this was a 'Jewish Undertaking' and to stay away. For me it had the opposite effect. One day I was walking down French Lane, the little street behind the market and the site of a clothing shop called Krichefski's, which had the Star of David painted crudely but clearly on the window. Coming down the lane towards me was a platoon of German soldiers, marching with noisy hobnailed boots over the cobbles. On the spur of the moment I decided to make a point. Straining to make my voice heard above the crashing of their boots I said loudly in my terrible German, '*Ich gehe in diese Kommerz!*'—'I am going into this shop!' Turning my back to the soldiers I did just that. I don't suppose they even heard my outburst but I was so sickened by the Nazi persecution of the Jews that I had felt compelled to give voice to my sense of disgust.

The shop sold various goods and seemed to have a reasonable supply of shirts, but perhaps people had been put off by the oppressive signs outside. The manager was known to me as a client of the insurance company and when I asked him how he was coping his response showed some of the ingenious ways in which Jersey people and the island's government succeeded in frustrating the Nazis' attempts to drive the Jews out of business. He, the manager, was shortly to buy the shop from its Jewish owner for a very reasonable price with the whole deal facilitated by the States. Sure enough, a few weeks after my visit the offensive daubing was scrubbed from the windows and the shop was able to return to its previous prosperity, at least as far as wartime austerity allowed. The clever part was that as soon as the Occupation ended the previous owner was permitted to buy the property back at minimal loss to themselves and resume business as before.

I knew of at least one other shop that did the same, a furrier's called Peretz in New Street which was popular with wealthy islanders and the higher German officers until the dreadful yellow star was painted crudely across its windows. The owners' agents quickly came to a deal with the manageress who 'bought' the shop for the duration and 'sold' it back to them as soon as the Germans were sent on their way.

I knew of several Jewish people who managed to survive the Occupation through a combination of good luck and careful judgement. Bill Benjamin, for example, was a conscientious objector who had come to the island to work on a farm digging potatoes when the war broke out to avoid having to take up arms. While he was not a practising Jew, he was widely thought to be of Jewish background but nobody denounced him and he was never picked up. I remember people saying 'He'd better be careful with a name like that ...', but he never registered and worked through the war as a fisherman.

Two Jewish women in St Brelade, Claude Cahun and Marcel Moore, made no attempt to hide themselves, in fact quite the opposite. They were flamboyant artists and would stride out along the beach together as lovers without caring who saw them. I knew them well enough to say hello, or actually '*Bonjour*', and was usually rewarded with a nod of the head. While their Jewish origins may have been undetected by the Nazis, they were eventually arrested for helping to spread the mutinous propaganda for which I was at least partly responsible. Sentenced to death, they served a year in prison before being released to continue their exotic and eccentric lives together.

Not every Jewish person was so confident or brave about their background. One old couple I knew in Vallée des Vaux were terrified into staying indoors the whole time with the curtains drawn and windows shut. If they ever went out it was only during the short time permitted by the Nazis before they scurried back to their blacked-out flat. People tried to encourage them to open the curtains, come out into the air and go into town or even into their garden, but they would not hear of it and maintained their self-imposed exile in their own home. But the pressures of this dreadful existence were too great, and finally too much for the husband, who was committed to St Saviour's Hospital.

The artist Edmund Blampied had a Dutch-Jewish wife named Marianne who made no particular effort to disguise her lineage and had registered at the outset. I would often see them walking their dog across the beach. Wonderfully, he was responsible for designing the Jersey stamps and banknotes which were printed when the pre-war supply ran out, and he did a super job of it.

The Nazi authorities did attempt to make all remaining Jews wear the yellow star as they had in many other countries across Europe, but I'm very glad to say that the Bailiff categorically refused. He was forced into making some very delicate compromises on so many other matters but on this question he was not to be budged and thank goodness that law was never enforced. I did see some poor souls wearing the star though, when a crowd of slaves was brought to the island from Alderney in June 1944 after the Allied landings in Normandy. I saw them shuffling to and from their camps with the star sewn roughly onto their ragged clothes and remember the feeling of dread and revulsion it gave me. My anger almost pushed me to go to them and start ripping the yellow patches from their clothes, but reason prevailed as I realised that it would only get myself and them into deeper trouble. We had heard of the yellow patches, which had been inflicted on people elsewhere, but it needed the actual sight of them to inflame my anger.

Willie Leopold and many of the other Jewish people in the island were lucky to come through the Occupation either undetected or without being badly persecuted, thanks to both the careful equivocation of the island's authorities and the willingness of the Jersey people to keep their mouths shut. My friend Max was not so lucky.

Max Finkelstein was a grey-haired Romanian, who had retired from his work as a chartered engineer to live in Britain. He'd worked on the Suez Canal project, only to fall in love, like so many others, with the beauty of Jersey and decide to live there, despite the growing clamour of war across the Continent. He'd also fallen in love with the wife of a British Army officer who had stayed in the island. His country was neutral, he assured us, and he felt quite safe, even registering as a Jew when the Germans first arrived in the island because he didn't want to get into trouble with the Jersey authorities. I knew him because he held insurance with my company.

For two years he was safe and unmolested by the Germans even as Romania was taken over in a military coup by fascists who turned the country into another dictatorship under Hitler's influence.

Perhaps inevitably his luck finally changed when in 1943 the second wave of deportations from the island happened. He was sixty years old when he was arrested and for some reason sent to the camp for male Jersey deportees without families in Laufen. He wasn't allowed to linger there for long and within weeks was sent in a cattle truck to the hell of Buchenwald concentration camp. He survived, spent some time recovering, and strode one day into the office some months after the war finished to set his affairs in order and to insure a new bicycle which was leaning against the office wall outside. He told me some of what had happened to him, which was more than enough to make me believe that what we had seen on the newsreels was, if anything, a slightly sanitised representation of what people like him had been through.

One night at Buchenwald he had been attempting to sleep in the freezing, louse-infested and overcrowded barrack hut, where bunks were stacked up high with scarcely room to breathe. All of a sudden the door was kicked open and three guards swaggered in before grabbing Max and two of his companions out of their bunk. The guard for their section ordered them to stand, naked, against the wall of the hut. He was roaring drunk. As they stood petrified to attention he bawled out that he was going to kill them all, and lunged forward plunging his bayonet into the belly of the man standing next to Max, who collapsed bleeding to death onto the ground. As Max, appalled, prepared to meet his maker the guard finally collapsed himself from the effects of the drink. As his fellow guards went to help him, Max and his friend took advantage of the confusion and threw themselves back through the door and into their bunks. They knew the man responsible had been in prison for violence before the war and they simply had to get as far away from him as possible. He was a clear example of a sick society making use of its most callous individuals for its own ends. Luckily for Max, he was left undisturbed to live another day.

As the Americans approached Buchenwald from the west, the

Germans evacuated the camp and Max was jammed with thousands of others into a boxcar and sent east. Many of them died on the way before they arrived at what had been the Theresienstadt ghetto, whose Jewish inmates had been sent to the gas chambers at Auschwitz. Finally he was freed by the advancing US Army, having survived treatment that would have killed many men younger than himself, to return to Jersey and his beloved officer's wife. Seldom have I seen such an example of physical and mental toughness and his story had a lasting impact upon me. He was not only physically untouched by his ordeal, but appeared to be mentally unharmed also and I'm sure he must have had great reserves of strength to come through the concentration camps without being scarred by the experience. He died, well into his eighties, at the Little Sisters of the Poor.

There were other Jewish people in Jersey who went into hiding aided by some brave islanders whose sense of humanity compelled them to offer help to those who needed it. Typically, those who were most effective at doing so made the least fuss about it, as I was to discover.

Chapter Ten

LEAPS OF FAITH

A woman living in Bagatelle Road had looked out of her kitchen window one day to see a man dressed in rags pulling a rotting vegetable out of the ground of a neighbouring field. As she watched, he spat on it, wiped it on his filthy clothes, scraped some soil off and took a large desperate bite from it. The man's plight and hunger moved her so much that after checking there were no neighbours watching, she waved to get his attention and signalled that he should come to the hedge which separated her garden from the field. Checking once more that the coast was clear, she then beckoned him into the house to give him some food. Once he had eaten his fill, she hid him away in a lock-up garage which opened onto the pavement of Bagatelle Road just a few feet away, and sat down to wait until her husband came home.

When he heard the story he was happy to try to help the escapee, but was worried that his young children might give the story away to their friends at primary school. The Russian would have to be moved elsewhere. After asking discreetly among his friends one of them suggested he should come to see me, and so I received yet another nervous-looking individual asking for a discussion of a private nature at my office. I think it was generally known that I had been acquainted with Louisa Gould, and I must have had a reputation of being trustworthy with such matters. While that could have exposed me to great risk, I was not prepared to refuse help to these poor devils who were in such need of food and shelter.

My search for a hiding place for my latest charge led me to the masseur and physiotherapist Albert Bedane, who had a practice at a large house in Roseville Street just down the road from a German headquarters. I had heard on the island grapevine that this former soldier, a native of France, was sympathetic to people in trouble with the Germans who came to him for help—but it was to be my first and most forthright refusal.

I walked from my office up through the bus station to the surgery after making an appointment, and waited to be seen. When my turn came I was ushered through the door into his well-appointed room.

I was cute enough to begin with flattery. Sitting in his patient's chair, I told him that someone whose opinion I valued very highly had recommended his help to deal with the rather personal problem that confronted me. 'They tell me you are a person of great understanding,' I told him, 'even though you are a physiotherapist, not a psychologist. I do hope you might be able to help …'.

As delicately as possible I explained the situation, only for him to blow up completely when he realised what I was getting at. He didn't raise his voice for fear of being overheard, but he was very forceful. 'You've got a cheek!', he told me through gritted teeth. 'Why on earth do you think I would involve myself in anything so silly? The Kommandant's office is just up the road, guarded by sentries, I have German officers here as patients and lots of other people passing through. It would be foolish and irresponsible to do any such thing. Get out, and don't trouble me with this nonsense ever again.'

Surprised and taken aback, I did as he asked, finding myself back on the pavement in short order. I was unused to such a strong response, and as an impressionable young man was easily cowed by an older man in position of influence. I remember crossing the road and looking up at the windows of the upper floor, reflecting on how frightened some people were, without cause. I felt his reputation as a respectable man of integrity was all a bit hollow, and had to hope that his anger wouldn't prompt him to betray me. The person who had recommended him to me had obviously misjudged his worth. With such dismal thoughts I slunk back to my office with my tail between my legs.

It wasn't until after the war that I discovered that at the very time I was in his surgery, he had hiding in his cellar a distant maverick cousin of mine called Francis Le Sueur who had escaped from the German section of the prison and was now on the run, a Mrs Richardson who was a Jewess, and not one but two escaped Russian slaves. Perhaps he believed I was a stool pigeon setting out to trap him, and wanted to convince the Germans that he was a trustworthy individual; he certainly convinced me in no uncertain terms that there was no room at the inn. I remember thinking that if he had put a card in the window saying 'No Vacancies' it would have saved us both a lot of trouble! Years later his bravery was recognised by the State of Israel when he was named as Righteous Among the Nations at Yad Vashem.

A few days after he turned me away I managed to house my latest charge at a farm in Maufant.

While some people have described me and my group of friends as a 'network', I would hesitate to use such a term as it implies a far more formal organisation than was actually the case. In fact, had I felt at any time that I was part of a wide 'resistance' group I would have had nothing further to do with it, because it would have been easily detected due to the very high proportion of Germans in the island. This was not France, where the *Maquis* could move out of the cities and into hiding places in swathes of forests or mountain caves. Jersey is an island measuring nine miles by five, and if you had a group of people in a shop or on a bus, one in five was a German soldier. You simply could not avoid some kind of contact with them. They were in the pubs, on the streets, billeted in people's homes and sunbathing on the beach. They strolled down the High Street, they rode their bicycles on the roads, and marched down the streets behind their military bands. I was simply one link in a chain in which people knew as little as possible about each other.

I did know little groups of perhaps two or three young fellows who would go out and cut German telephone wires under the impression perhaps that they were striking a blow for liberty. In my eyes it was simply a foolish and dangerous exercise which had very little effect on the German war effort. Jersey was such a small place that the break could be traced and repaired, often within an hour, in no way justifying the risk to themselves and their families that these young men had taken. The Germans would round up perhaps twelve heads of local families and hold them until the culprits were found and then suitably punished. I made myself rather unpopular with some people and remember telling one chap in particular that what he was doing was brave but ultimately a waste of time and potentially harmful to many innocent people. The transitory benefits of a cut telephone wire simply did not justify the risk. He wasn't convinced. 'You don't do anything like that because you're scared!', he told me. I told him that in a way he was right, I would be afraid of being found out, but I was more afraid of what might happen to others. It was all very well being urged on to action through the BBC but I felt strongly that petty sabotage was pointless.

Others were involved in what became known as the 'V' campaign. They would creep about at night with a tin of paint or tar, and daub 'V' for 'Victory' on street signs, walls, and in particular the houses of any woman suspected of having a relationship with a German. These unfortunate women were known universally as Jerrybags. The Germans struck back with ingenuity, daubing their own 'V' signs across everywhere in the island, sometimes on the houses of the most respectable of citizens. I thought all such acts were a waste of time and effort, especially when I was involved with something altogether bigger.

Later in the war some young men decided that rather than demonstrate their opposition by taking action in the island itself, they would risk everything by trying to escape from it altogether. This became particularly popular after the Cherbourg Peninsula fell into Allied hands after the invasion of Normandy, but Denis Vibert was one of those who went early, in autumn 1941. I had grown up with Denis and had always regarded him as a daredevil, someone who rather frightened me with his bravery, especially in the sea. While I was learning my first faltering doggy-paddle strokes he was already a confident swimmer and egged me on to increasingly dangerous escapades, forcing me to swim in eddying currents among the rocks where I couldn't touch the bottom. He climbed walls with impossible footholds, and trees with impossible branches. Oddly it required more courage to refuse a dare from Denis than to attempt the dare itself. He had a spark of splendid madness in him.

I knew he was going to attempt an escape and I thought it reckless and unlikely to succeed, but he was not to be dissuaded. His first attempt was in a little boat that we used to play in, but it was far too small for his plans. He intended to head southwest for the Roches Douvres, then relaunch the next day and make for Start Point. Inevitably the escapade failed, and he found himself stuck on the rocks for a week, eating limpets and drinking out of puddles before managing to struggle back to the island. Soaking wet, he made his way up the beach between Ouaisne and Portelet on the southwest coast before laying up for the day in the bracken. When it got dark he made his way across country, dodging German patrols before knocking on the door of his friends the Sarre family in St Lawrence, who took him in and warmed him up. Fortunately for him the Germans hadn't missed him and he was able to recover from a mild bout of pneumonia before trying again.

He was tough, resourceful and had the good sense to keep his plans to himself. We only found out later that he had lurked about the harbour until he found a suitable boat, one which had been damaged in the air raid, and bought it from a grateful owner. I knew he had rented a wooden hut at the end of Bel Royal, and that's where he set off from. After dodging German sentries and an inquisitive E-Boat, he had to row for three days after his petrol tanks got swamped with water before arriving finally at Portland Bill and being picked up by a Royal Navy destroyer. In his pocket was a waterproof pouch weighted with shot which contained details of all the German positions on the island he had been able to observe, valuable intelligence for the British. What he did not expect was to be told that he had to pay import duty on his boat!

Back in Jersey we all knew that he had gone and hoped that he had succeeded in reaching friendly shores. A notice appeared in the newspaper. 'By Order of the Feldgendarmerie. Any information in relation to the whereabouts of Denis Vibert, when last seen, etc., is to be communicated to the Police Station.'

By then it was too late, and Denis went on to fly in the RAF.

While I admired Denis' bravery and resourcefulness in getting away in such challenging circumstances, I was never tempted to make an escape myself. Aside from the fact that I had no navigational skills, I had a clear duty to my job—both in the office and for my Russian and Spanish friends.

Fortunately the average German was not always particularly keen to act on any suspicions he might have about possible wrongdoing. Like the soldier who apparently told his girlfriend that he knew about the existence of Bill, many perhaps wished to avoid getting involved in something that did not directly affect them because that could involve more work and duty in taking statements and perhaps even going to a court-martial. Unless they stumbled across something that was plainly dangerous to German interests, it would take a keen party member to run the risk of reporting something and then have to follow it through. Most soldiers in any army want to avoid being noticed, unless there is a sniff of promotion on offer.

I don't like to use the word 'resistance' in the context of what we were doing. I wasn't resisting anything. My principle motive was not to oppose the Germans. I was working to help my fellow man, and I believe the difference is crucial.

Others of course had a different motivation. The few communists in Jersey had a small but dedicated membership, and were doing all they could to annoy the Germans and help the Russians on purely ideological grounds. They made the rather naive assumption that all Russians were communists, while I knew for a fact that was far from the truth. I remember clearly a conversation I had with my friend Norman Le Brocq, who tried very hard to recruit me to the Party. 'Norman,' I said, 'you must realise that I will never submit to any kind of order which will decide for me what books are fit for me to read.'

As the Germans revealed their true nature, with deportations and the arrival and treatment of the slave labourers, people's attitudes to them began to harden. Where once islanders may have been charmed by their manners, impressed by their uniforms and swayed by their assurances that they did not want war with our country, they began to be prepared to take some kind of action against their occupiers. The Germans had now become Enemies. Even though people had some little private relationships with individuals, it was now realised that the Nazi system and all it stood for would have its malevolent effect here on our island.

Chapter Eleven

A LIGHTER SIDE

The Occupation was not without its lighter moments, often due to some of the characters who seemed determined to make the best of the bad situation into which we had been thrust.

Barney Quinn was one such. Dressed in a frock coat, formal trousers and bowler hat all in an advanced state of disintegration, he would push a handcart up and down the main streets of town advertising whatever wares he had for sale at that particular moment. I would often see him huffing and puffing up the hill with his cart as I ate my lunchtime sandwiches in the public garden up on Mount Bingham. After pausing to gather his breath after what was undeniably a hard push, he would begin to pick the daffodils which grew in profusion around the park before returning down the hill into town, where he would sell them to passers-by at Snow Hill.

Flowers were not his only commodity, however. Bright signs on the side of his cart proudly offered 'Jersey Wonders' for sale. Most Jersey folk recognise the eponymous Wonder as a deliciously sweet, fried delicacy similar in ingredients and texture to a doughnut, which is twisted into a knotted shape before being doused liberally with sugar.

With a shortage of all the necessary ingredients we were sure that the entrepreneurial Mr Quinn was unable to sell any such thing; and we were proved right when it was revealed that rather than tasty sweet comestibles, his Jersey Wonders were in fact French Letters.

He had been given something he called his 'housewife' but which was actually an *Ausweis*, a German-issued pass allowing access to certain areas which might otherwise be off-limits; his allowed him to go onto the Albert Pier. It had evidently been issued to him by a German with a sense of humour, as it permitted him to meet the French sailors who came across on the barges from Granville. They sold him the prophylactics, which were in short supply in Jersey, and he was then able to sell them on to soldiers and islanders alike from his cart.

I also remember him displaying a sign one day well into the Occupation which read 'Top Quality Coffee'. Of course we had seen no such thing since 1940 and had made do instead with roasted acorns or dried parsnips to make a vaguely tolerable brew, so we all assumed that was in fact what Barney Quinn was selling. Unfortunately some busybody reported him to the Food Office, which was on the top floor of Burton's in St Helier. Now it was reported, something had to be done and the unfortunate merchant was duly summoned. Two policemen went to his pitch at Snow Hill and led him shouting and blasting at the top of his voice all the way down Queen Street to the office. 'Wouldn't they let an honest trader continue with his work, they were taking the bread out of the mouths of honest workmen, it was a liberty', etc., etc. Still shouting the odds, he was led up the stairs into the large open-plan office at the top of the building. A patient food officer spoke to him. 'Now look, Mr Quinn. We know this cannot be genuine coffee, it's no use pretending it is. Be honest. It's substitute, isn't it?' 'Yes', was the surly reply. 'Well, in that case, it is perfectly acceptable to sell it,' said the officer, 'but your sign must say so!' The disgruntled hawker took the moth-eaten bowler off his head and cried, 'And how the bloody hell do you think am I supposed to spell substitute??!'

As Barney Quinn pushed his barrow up and down he would often have passed George Le Sueur up a ladder. George was a painter who was employed by some of the High Street shopkeepers to smarten up their shop fronts and he was always a popular sight with island folk. Shellshocked during World War One, he seemed to have little fear of upsetting the Germans—or anyone else, for that matter. I particularly remember him stuck like a fly at the top of his ladder painting the walls of Hettich the Jeweller's near the Royal Square. Reaching across dangerously he would look to see if anyone was watching then dip his brush in the paint and flip some over whichever unlucky soul happened to be walking below—

whether they were in uniform or not. Often an insult would accompany the gesture, or even a well-mimed fart. The Germans tolerated his antics because they knew of his background, and he was allowed to brighten up St Helier throughout the war.

Aside from the hill above Mount Bingham, another favourite place of mine to take my sandwiches in the summertime was an area on the beach at La Colette which was usually peaceful, despite being known as a place where men would gather to sunbathe and swim. I was keen to keep my swimming up and would go there for a dip and then eat my lunch. Some of the men who went there would swim and bathe naked and trusted that their modesty would not be disturbed, although on one occasion their little haven was violated in unwonted fashion.

Colonel Fawcett was one of the regular bathers there who liked to dispense with a costume, despite his terribly upper-class reputation which he worked hard to cultivate. He did however consider it impolite to appear in public without a hat and was never seen without it on.... On one particular summer's day I was sitting nearby finishing my food when there was something of a commotion. The Colonel, it appeared, had gone to answer the call of nature behind some rocks only to be greeted by a most unwelcome sight. I looked over and saw him, silhouetted against the sky, his raised hat in one hand and his private parts clutched in the other. 'Help!' he cried, 'There are women here!' Casting his panic-stricken gaze around, he lighted on me. 'Le Sueur! I believe these women are French! Can you help?!' Chuckling inwardly I went to investigate and found he was absolutely right. There they were, all lying on the rocks laughing and giggling—and completely naked. As some of the other more prudish men nearby scurried back to their clothes and began to dress, the women's laughter only increased. I explained to them that they were in an area usually frequented by naked men and they replied that *oui*, that was why they had come here! I later discovered that they had been brought to the island by the Germans to work in their field brothel at Grève d'Azette nearby.

Most of my swimming was closer to home on the beach opposite the house, despite it being under the watchful eye of the German defensive position. I tried to stay in the habit of immersing myself as often as possible, even in the winter months when the cold made my teeth chatter before I even got in. On one chilly occasion I remember disrobing on the beach at Millbrook just down the road before wading briskly in and swimming for ten strokes out, and ten strokes back to shore. That was quite enough, but as I emerged I was greeted by a round of applause. Looking up I saw a bunch of German soldiers above me on the sea wall clapping and cheering my performance, much to my embarrassment. I hadn't done it to show off and I hadn't noticed them as I went in but I'm sure their applause was meant in good spirits.

Looking back, I'm astonished that I managed to find the time for everything I packed into my life apart from working and helping my Russian and Spanish friends. I even managed to fit in another theatrical effort at the Opera House, this time in a Terrance Rattigan piece called *French Without Tears*. I was not a major character, having been told I was not sufficiently passionate to play a lover, and was mainly used to grace the background, but I enjoyed the play because of its humour and entertaining use of bad French. Many of the costumes were threadbare, and I tried not to allow my acting to be as wooden as the stage, but it was wonderful to be able to leave behind the stresses of my double life and pretend to be someone entirely different. I remember the liberating feeling of moving across the stage confident of being that other person, and it gave me a sense of freedom from all of my day to day concerns. The parties, of course, were exciting even though we had little to eat or drink and our shared experience gave us a happy bond that allowed us to ignore the Germans for a little longer.

Other islanders took their drama rather more seriously and even managed to make a political statement though it. There was a performance of *The Merchant of Venice*, a play approved by the German authorities no doubt because they considered it carried a fine anti-Semitic message. Richard Winnereh played Shylock, and gave such a sensitive performance that the anonymous reviewer in the *Evening Post* declared that he made the audience understand that the Jew's unpleasant characteristics were a direct result of his inhuman treatment by those who persecuted him. Somehow that got past the German censor and was printed. Very soon afterwards some unpleasant men visited the editor of the paper, Arthur Harrison, and demanded to know the name of the reviewer, who was always published under a pseudonym. Harrison quite rightly refused. In Jersey, he told them, everyone knows each other and it would be completely unfair to expose their real name as they would be unable to continue providing objective reviews. Facing down their demands, he said that his reviewer's life would be unendurable if their identity was to be exposed. Remarkably he got away with it. The Germans knew that his cooperation was essential if they were to get their notices and propaganda into his newspaper, which was virtually the only way to disseminate news to the general population. He had been playing a very clever game with them throughout the Occupation. Whenever the Germans wanted to insert what was essentially propaganda dressed up as a news story Harrison always made sure that it appeared as a poor translation which any Jersey person would immediately recognise for what it was.

He won the argument over the theatre reviewer and the anonymous writer was spared persecution for his seditious article. Thank goodness for that. He was Mike Frowd.

My young self with my mother.

And with my father!

Our house Horizon View, taken with my back to the sea wall.
My bedroom window is at the very top.

The slipway immediately opposite our house, demolished to
make way for a German gun emplacement. It was up this slipway
that I ran as the bombs fell on St Helier.

Our darkest hour; workmen, to whom I had spoken just moments before, paint the white cross of surrender on the Royal Square. I am somewhere in this crowd.

Soon one person in every five in Jersey was German.

A shop window in St Helier with a German sign intended to deter customers and instil racial hatred.

The photo used on my identity card.

The staff of the General Accident Insurance Corporation outside the Hill Street office in summer 1942. From left to right, Mr R H Le Prevost from Guernsey, Miss Myra Hunt, myself, Mr Howard Rodd.

My aunt and uncle in Guernsey who appreciated my gift of potatoes.

My wig appeared more natural on stage than I did! Wartime theatricals with my girlfriend Ruth.

A photograph of my friend the Spanish worker José Vila relaxing in 1942.

He kindly gave it to me and and on the reverse of the photo it says
'To my friend Bobbie with gratitude and friendship.'

The Dunn family, who were given less than twenty-four hours to be deported.
Note the little girl's teddy bear in the wheelbarrow!

René at his typewriter in the Grosvenor Street flat.

Louisa Gould: a heroic, warm-hearted and loving woman.

Sketch drawing of myself, drawn by Bill and given to me for my birthday in 1944.

Looking down from our vantage point onto the Royal Square,
the day before Liberation.

Our view of the Bailiff addressing the crowds in the Royal Square
on that wonderful day.

Three friends: René Franoux, Bill and me, taken immediately after Liberation.

The Russian Major Gruzdev (Left) and Bill (Right) in Jersey immediately after Liberation.

René with Bill at the Russian transit camp in Guildford.

Bill and I with his wife Nadia in Siberia.

A very moving moment, Bill at the unveiling of the commemorative plaque at
Mrs Gould's former home in St Ouen where he was once a fugitive.

In This House
Mrs Louisa Mary Gould,
née Le Druillenec,
Sheltered An Escaped Russian P.O.W.
During The German Occupation
From October 1942 Until May 1944.
After Her Arrest She Was
Deported To The Concentration
Camp At Ravensbruck
Where She Perished
In The Gas Chamber.

'Nazi racists ranked their Russian
slave workers as sub-human.
Any racial prejudices we personally
may harbour are first steps on
that same viciously slippery slope'

Bob Le Sueur
Islander and Occupation veteran recognised
by Russia for assisting slave workers

I am honoured that my thoughts are preserved in a St Helier paving stone.

In conversation with Prince Charles while receiving my MBE. We talked about the celebrations which had marked the 50th anniversary of Jersey's Liberation, which he remembered very clearly.

Chapter Twelve

NOT ENOUGH HOURS IN THE DAY

It is a well-known fact that the Occupation was a time of shortage; but for me time was the commodity whose lack I felt most keenly.

Every little task seemed to take on a magnitude unprecedented in happier times, and I simply never had enough time in my day to get everything done. My bicycle was a case in point. I was very proud of its racing shape, with semi-dropped handlebars and three speeds. In the early days of the Occupation I could climb aboard and pedal myself to wherever I needed to go, either on business or to visit friends. The wheels were true, the tyres were strong and the all-important inner tubes devoid of holes. It lasted for twelve months until the unwelcome news that the Germans intended to confiscate many of the islanders' bikes for their own use and, unluckily for me, mine was one of those chosen. On the appointed day two of the parish's unpaid police officers came to our door and claimed it. In vain I protested that I needed my bike for work, that I wouldn't be able to do my job effectively if I couldn't visit my far-flung clients across Jersey, it was an essential not a luxury. You are young and fit, they told me, and we have to fulfil our quota of bikes for the Germans. Tough. Why not ask your employer to buy you a second-hand one at an auction sale? It was easy, as my own employer, to agree to the need for a replacement, but finding one was not so simple. A decent bike, even after just twelve months of occupation, was not an easy thing to find. When I had bought it, before the war, my lovely departed Raleigh had cost me about five hard-earned pounds. With the company budget weighing heavily on my mind, I waited for the next auction at Le Gallais.

In the meantime life had to go on, which meant getting up earlier to go to work and arriving home later, walking to see any clients nearby and limiting myself to corresponding by letter to those in more far-flung places. Of course I had less time to spend socialising as it took far longer to get to and from my friends' homes. It complicated my love life too. At the time I was seeing a girl who lived at Clubley Estate, up a steep hill from St Helier. While in possession of my bike I could walk her home up St John's Road, and then speed down Tower Road to get home. When reduced to two feet I had to leave her far earlier, and this was often the cause of me arriving rather late at the checkpoint outside my home.... I changed girlfriend soon afterwards. (In fact I changed them as often as I changed my library books at this point!)

When the next auction at Le Gallais came around I headed there (on foot!) to see if I could find myself a serviceable bike at a reasonable price. I was to be disappointed on both counts. Dreading the impending drain on the company's resources I found myself bidding on the only machine on offer, an old-fashioned sit-up-and-beg affair with raised handlebars and three clunky gears. To my dismay I soon discovered that I was not the only one who wanted a new set of wheels. The bidding very soon went past the five pounds I had spent on my brand-new bike before the war. Ten pounds went past in a flash, fifteen, twenty ... and still I held on, feeling I simply had to have it. It was finally mine for the extortionate price of fifty pounds and I remember wondering how on earth I was going to justify that expense to my employers after the Occupation was over. As I pedalled away on my new steed the chain fell off, something which was to become a regular occurrence, as my oil-stained fingers would show. The inner tubes were perished and I was often to be found trying to fix punctures with a dwindling supply of glue and patches. The poor tubes had no protection to speak of from the tyres, which were themselves completely threadbare. It was not long until both tyres and tubes gave up the ghost, and I had to adopt a last-ditch remedy which was becoming prevalent among the island's cyclists. All I needed was a piece of garden hose ...

It was surely proof that necessity is truly the mother of invention. Across the island people's hoses were becoming progressively shorter as they were pilfered to replace worn-out bicycle tyres. I took advice from friends on how to measure and cut it to the right length, wrap it tightly around the rim of the wheel and then, in the trickiest part of the operation, take a specially shaped piece of metal and fasten it around the two cut ends to keep it tightly in place. This last stage needed a special skill which I simply could not master, but luckily my father worked out the technique and was able to do it for me, keeping me on the road. These improvised tyres gave none of the comfort associated with pneumatic tyres, and fairly rattled your teeth out over cobbles or rough roads. Even on smooth tarmac there was the regular clunk, clunk, clunk of the metal joining-pieces hitting the ground on every rotation. Of course with such use they could not last forever, and if the metal piece failed the resulting noise sounded like a pistol shot. The first time it happened to me was just outside Barclays Bank on Library Place, when I was going rather fast. I had come down from Mulcaster Street and Church Street which was a two-way road, when there was a sudden explosive Bang! and the bike shuddered to a halt, mercifully without dislodging me from the saddle. By now I was getting used to pushing my bicycle home.

The second time it happened to me was on Liberation Day itself, and it could have cost me my life.

Still, having two wheels again was a great relief to me, and both my business life and my love life were able to regain their previous efficiency. I was also able to use it for more practical purposes, when I bought myself a trailer that would fix to the back and allow me to carry far more. It was made out of a wooden box with pram wheels and allowed me to cart about all kinds of essentials, or even illicit gear such as our radio when it needed to be fixed. I could ride out in search of wood, vegetables, apples, whatever I could find—you never knew what might turn up from one day to the next. Needless to say the whole contraption became very heavy, especially if I had managed to get lucky with some supplies, and I'm sure I spent a lot of time pushing when the gradient became too severe.

Even when I did have a bike, it always seemed as though time was in short supply. Something as simple as getting in touch with someone in another parish, for business or for pleasure, could be a very lengthy process, particularly if the telephone system was out of order, as it so often was. The alternative would be either to pedal all the way to see them on the off chance that they might be in, or to write them a letter which would of course take a couple of days to get to them and then another couple for their answer to return. Laundry had to be done by hand, often without soap or warm water, one had to repair one's own clothes or take them to a mender's, and the finding and preparation of food could take up large parts of the day.

My poor battered shoes were taken to a cobbler's in Sion after our usual shop in town refused to have anything more to do with them, requiring another journey on my bike. There were very few delivery vans, and the few that were in operation were used in the more distant parishes. They all carried great big balloon-like structures on top, which contained the gas used to power the engine in the absence of any petrol, and found some of the steeper hills as challenging as I did on my bike.

So much of the day was taken up with the mundane requirements of simply maintaining your existence that I find it extraordinary that I was able to hold down my busy job, let alone any of my extracurricular activities. I certainly wouldn't have held down my job in peacetime if my bosses had seen the state of me when the shortages really started to bite. At the outbreak of war in 1939 I was the proud owner of two suits. One was a school uniform suit bought for me by my parents for my attendance at Victoria College. Unfortunately I had managed to roughen it considerably by the time I left school. That didn't deter my mother, who managed to sell it to the parents of a boy who was still at College. This left me with one dark blue outfit which I had bought at Burton's in St Helier, until I bought myself another for a friend's wedding from the fifty-shilling tailor. That was a lovely suit, light blue with a stripe, including waistcoat, and it was to be kept for best.

The rest of my wardrobe was remarkable only for its limitations. I had perhaps two pairs of grey flannel trousers, one sports jacket and a handful of shirts, plus a few scraps of other clothing which I could use for roughing it. Two pairs of shoes and a pair of iron-shod cadet corps boots were the extent of my footwear, combined with socks which became increasingly threadbare as the weeks passed.

As the Occupation wore on my clothes wore out. My working clothes in particular became less and less suitable, and I'm sure I would have been sent home by my previous manager if he had seen me turn up, as I was compelled to by the end of the war, in my patched flannels and sports jacket combined with the cadet corps boots which were often used to wade about in the sea when fishing. A colleague of mine in the Prudential was able to buy respectable working clothes on the approval of his superiors from the local auction. Fortunately both of my parents had grown up in frugal households with the habit of making do and getting the best use out of things before they would be thrown away. The pile of ragged clothing in our living room wasn't just to hide the radio.

My shirts were washed and mended over and over again. All of my trousers gave way either at the knees or backside, and in common with many other people I looked sometimes a little like a patchwork quilt. While I learned to sew on buttons and make minor repairs from my mother, some jobs required more expertise and I'm sure the island's tailors enjoyed a very profitable time. It was no longer a sign of poverty to have patches on the elbows of your jacket or the seat of your trousers; one friend in particular used to wear his socks upside down on his feet when the soles wore out. I learned to darn mine, although the wool available was often a completely different colour to the socks themselves. Many people used up hours of time unpicking old clothes that could then be re-fashioned into something more practical, as there was very little spare cloth. On the bus nearly every woman would get out their bag of knitting, not as a hobby but out of simple necessity. We were all in the same boat, and as I discovered one night rank and title were no guarantee against the want we all felt.

Charles Edward Malet de Carteret had been the Bailiff of Jersey, a position enjoyed by many of his ancestors. By 1942 his health was failing and he took lodgings with Mr and Mrs Carr in the house next door to us. One night, during the curfew, Mrs Carr came banging on our door asking for help. 'Mr Malet de Carteret has fallen out of bed! He's not well! What can I do?' I and my father went next door and upstairs to where the great man lay and helped him onto the bed while awaiting the ambulance, which was still allowed to operate during the curfew. As it drove away, my overriding impression was one of dismay that even such an elevated individual should have patched pyjamas ...

It meant, of course, that any stray garment that one could pick up became highly desirable. The houses of those who had left the island before the Occupation were often ransacked, not for the more usual valuables but for any clothing they had left behind. It could be worn if necessary, or sold at vastly inflated prices on the black market—or at auction. On one occasion I went to one of these sales out of curiosity, and watched from the back as people bid for an old suit. At a time when the maximum wage was three pounds a week, this rather threadbare garment reached the ludicrous price of seven pounds, upon which I stood up to get a better view of who might have the money to make such an offer. Unfortunately the auctioneer mistook my curiosity for a bid—'Going at seven pounds to the gentleman at the back!'—and I didn't have the courage to deny that I wanted to buy. Fortunately someone else must have wanted the suit very badly and my accidental bid was allowed to fall away.

I did manage to acquire some clothes, as I had little else to spend my money on. I remember a very stylish light blue raglan jacket of which I was very proud, also an overcoat and a scarf, which was necessary to keep out the cold during the times when there was no heating. My pride and joy was a Harris tweed jacket, rough and indestructible, so strong that it never needed patching. Quite where I got these garments from I don't recall, although it could have been during my brief trip to Guernsey. My aunt and uncle there ran a lodging house on the same street as Victor Hugo's house, but several of their tenants had made a sharp exit when the arrival of the Germans was imminent. They had left a lot of clothes behind, and my aunt and uncle certainly weren't going to let them go to waste. 'Take what you want,' they said, 'and we will write out a receipt for it. If they ever come back we will agree a price for whatever you have taken and settle with them.' I don't know if they ever did come back.

I do remember making one of the very few investments of my life at this time, which turned out to be well worth while. I was concerned that the money I was making could be discounted after the war because we were all effectively earning in Reichsmarks, and I didn't know how far they would be honoured once peace had returned. I wondered if I might be able to put some of my savings into something which would perhaps increase in value over time and provide me with a little nest egg should I ever need it. The answer was there on my desk, staring me in the face.

As the Occupation had dragged on and telephone communication became increasingly unreliable, we were forced to carry out a significant amount of our correspondence by letter and eventually the pre-war supply of stamps ran out. In 1941 the first Occupation stamps were printed, a fairly straightforward design into which the designer had managed to incorporate an almost unnoticeable anti-Hitler message. Then in 1943 the artist Edmund Blampied was commissioned to produce new ones which represented some scenes of Jersey, for example Elizabeth Castle. I recognised that these might just be the things I was looking for as an investment. During a brief break away from my desk I managed to find a shop that still had some tissue paper and bought several pieces before heading to the post office where I asked the lady at the counter for several pages of the best-looking Jersey stamps. She handed them over without much surprise, as I gather I was not the first to have such a creative money-making idea. Back at home I wrapped each sheet of stamps as carefully as possible in the tissue paper so they wouldn't stick together and stored them away in a nice dry cupboard where they stayed until the end of the Occupation.

Naturally our office ran on paper, which was required for letters, receipts, bills and all kinds of other correspondence. This is one of the few times when I managed to plan ahead and very early in the Occupation I bought stacks of it, assuming rightly that it could soon be in short supply. Likewise with envelopes, which I hoarded and used only as necessary. Any sheet of paper with a blank side was turned over and re-used, often pinned into a pad with other sheets. My foresight was well rewarded, because later in the Occupation paper did indeed run out, and children in some schools were reduced to writing on the back of cast-off wallpaper or even slates.

Other business establishments didn't manage to plan quite so well, and I remember the Midland Bank in particular used to issue cheques that were printed on the back of papers which had been used to cover boxes of produce before the war. On the reverse side of your cheque to a customer would be all sorts of bright writing all about Jersey tomatoes! Lloyds, where I banked, printed its cheques on some brightly coloured material which was evidently left over from a pre-war stock of decorative paper. I remember handing a cheque over to my bosses in England at the end of the war for £12,000, a huge sum which would have bought three houses at the time. I sent it to the Southampton branch only to see it again a year later when I visited head office at Perth in Scotland where they had put it in a museum after having it cleared.

While I might have congratulated myself on my foresight at buying up supplies of stationery, there was one item I had forgotten which, while mundane, was nonetheless indispensable to our office. So it was that I took out an advert in the paper, to be placed in a section simply known as 'For What?' This was a simple and effective way of helping people to trade their belongings without resorting to the black market. You could advertise what you had—a pair of children's shoes, a pair of men's trousers, 32' waist, good condition, a piece of furniture—and ask what someone might give you in return. Or, as I did, you could ask for something you needed before negotiating with whoever might be able to supply it.

What we needed most was typewriter ribbons which would fit the brand of machines we had in the office. Our letters were becoming increasingly hard to read as the keys of Miss Hunt's typewriter smacked onto ribbons that were almost bone dry and left little more than a faint impression on the paper. Such ribbons were a simple stationery item, but without them our company would effectively grind to a halt as we would have to resort to writing everything by hand. Even placing the ad took up more time, as I had to cycle to the *Evening Post*'s offices and fill out the requisite form before it could be approved and printed in the next edition.

The request was duly published and I awaited any response, regularly checking the company's Post Office box to see if anyone might by some miracle have what we were looking for. I must have had luck on my side because shortly afterwards a letter arrived from a woman to say that yes, she had some ribbons and we should meet up to make a suitable exchange. Her telephone number was enclosed. I called and asked her to bring them to the office but for some reason she began to play very coy, refusing to walk into an office she had never visited before. Finally she told me, 'I am going to my hairdresser in Colomberie to have my hair tinted, and afterwards I will meet you at Snow Hill.'

I told the office girls and they were most amused that I was going to meet some old dear who was trying hard to preserve her youth with the artifices of our local hairdresser. They watched from the window as I walked the short distance up the street to meet the woman concerned and were surprised to see me greet her warmly and enthusiastically. In fact, she was none other than Connie Gale, a friend of mine who had put on a funny voice on the telephone and deceived me utterly, having known it was me all along! It was in her house that I was to lose my ID card down the side of a chair, and her quick lively sense of humour gave me a wonderful lift. She did indeed have some typewriter ribbons for me which were quickly pressed into service, and although they were well used they were a great improvement on what we had been utilising.

The effects of such enforced parsimony have stayed with me for decades, both comic and ineradicable. To this day I keep any papers that have only been used on one side and staple them together for future re-use, cannot bear to throw away food unless it has become green with rot, and I cannot part with any garment which is still capable of being worn.

I also, like many of us who survived the Occupation, make use of every possible scrap of food....

Chapter Thirteen

A MOUTH FULL OF KLIM

Perhaps unsurprisingly, the first thing many people remember about the Occupation is hunger. While the island had always been known for producing large amounts of potatoes and other crops, as well as high-quality milk, it still relied on imports of wheat and flour to make bread. Many other staples which were not produced here also had to be brought over the sea, and given that need for foreign supplies it was far too much to expect that the island could be self-sufficient in wartime. Thousands of German soldiers billeted here simply added to that burden, which was made worse when some of the island's scanty stocks were exported to feed the hungry occupying army in France.

A degree of rationing had been implemented before the Occupation began, organised by a States department. It did a pretty good job with what was available, but once the Germans arrived our allowances were steadily reduced; and as the war continued they dwindled further with supply diminishing and demand steadily increasing as more Germans were imposed upon us.

Of course my mother, like all mothers, put more than she should have on my plate and went without herself—and I'm sure that was the same across the island.

We were all issued with ration books, containing little coupons which would entitle you to just so much meat, fat and bread. I never did the shopping. My mother, ever frugal, would do that, taking our books with her and gathering what she could to feed us. Every morsel was carefully weighed by scrupulous shopkeepers, who had meticulously cut each coupon from the books before serving what was due. Families guarded their provisions very carefully to prevent any sneak thievery or waste, even to the extent of individuals in the same family cutting up their butter and labelling it carefully so everyone had their precise share. I had my own shelf in the kitchen.

Shelves in the shops steadily emptied until all that was left was what was on the ration books, although from time to time there was what you might describe as 'under the counter' stuff, un-rationed goods that had come into the island goodness knows how. It was usually found by the Jersey Purchasing Commission and sent to a shop to be distributed. The word would go out on the ever-active underground grapevine. 'They've got some Camembert at Le Riche's!' And there would be a rush from all parts of the island to get there. If you were known to the shop assistant, and my mother made sure to be friends with as many as possible, then you might get a little furtive wink ... 'Pssst ... Mrs Le Sueur ... we've got a little cheese, would you like some?'

The greatest challenge was to get some protein, which was like gold to acquire. With meat severely rationed, everyone looked to the sea to try to supplement their diets. Fish wasn't rationed, but it was very expensive. Some fishermen were allowed to set their nets, but only under German supervision. That of course meant that when the catch was landed the Germans had first choice—although they did pay for it—and then those of us who were able to afford it could buy fish on the open market. My family could not. As hunger gnawed at us, I became friendly with some fishermen who allowed me to take one of their nets to go draw-netting when the tides were right. I would dress up in layers and layers of old clothes to protect me from the cold water—a singlet, a sweater and a battered old jacket—and then wade out into the sea with a net at low tide. As the tide rose, my hope was that some kindly fish would allow themselves to be trapped in it. Contrary to myth you could still go down onto the beaches, except for Plémont on the northwest coast, and the shore in front of our house became a fishing ground for me. While I could endure that in the summer and autumn, once winter set in and the temperatures dropped it became simply impossible, except for the true professionals and the very dedicated. I certainly saw some people wading up to their waists even in the month of January. Our clothes line was frequently hung with revolting salt-stained rags of old clothes which I had worn to try to supplement our food stock, but I was forgiven as I rarely returned from an expedition empty-handed.

Like most people, we attempted to provide for ourselves as far as we could. In our small backyard we had some bantam hens, kept for their eggs as well as their meat. Small and agile, they were kept under control by a cockerel called Uncle. He looked down his nose at Mrs Hatchwell, a rather unattractive hen who nonetheless was as productive as her name implies. Uncle would peck and harass her even when she was sitting on her eggs prior to them hatching, but it never prevented her from bringing up her chicks. In time Uncle became a part of the family, and we couldn't bring ourselves to eat him. He died, stringy and tough, of old age.

Sadly, the same could not be said for our pet rabbit, who lived in a hutch in the midst of Uncle's harem. Fluffy ate what few vegetable scraps we could feed him, and grew sufficiently robust to be ready for the stewpot. But starving as we were, neither my mother, father nor I could bring ourselves to kill or eat a creature to which we had all become attached. Fluffy looked complacently out from behind the wire of his hutch for days, nostrils twitching, as we tried to summon the necessary sangfroid to turn him into a tasty dinner, but we simply could not do it.

It seemed as though Fluffy would defy the odds and survive until the war's end, until my parents discovered quite by chance that our neighbours, the Carrs, were having exactly the same dilemma with their own rabbit! Some dark dealing was done, and the rabbits changed hands. Having no attachment to the neighbour's much-loved pet ourselves, it was duly despatched and consumed with relish. No doubt Fluffy suffered the same fate next door.

Such luxuries were few and far between, however. My overriding memories of Occupation meals are those of vegetables. Root vegetables became the mainstay of every meal, and I believe I have eaten swedes and turnips served in every possible way. They were on the menu two or three times a DAY, along with endless servings of carrots and greens. Towards the end, when the gas was cut off, one got used to eating them raw. Hunger can reduce even the fussiest eater to desperate measures after all, and in an island full of starving people, none could claim they were constipated. The vitamins in such a diet were very important to us and we were so full of vitamin C that it had an inadvertent effect on the population. Couples who had resigned themselves to being childless, women in their forties, found themselves expectant parents because of diets which, while not generous, were in many ways very healthy.

After a long day at the office, followed perhaps by some difficult negotiations with someone who might take in one of the itinerant escapees, I was frequently welcomed home by the smell of my mother's vegetable stew. A few potatoes, a lot of swede and perhaps a couple of beans floated around in a thin soup. If I was lucky there would be a very small piece of bread with which to soak up every last morsel. Any peelings, of course, went to feed our little menagerie out the back. You learned never to ask what was for dessert, although when they were in season we sometimes had a morsel of fruit from the small trees that mother kept up with careful applications of bug spray. Any berries, apples or pears were wonderfully sweet to palates which had become jaded with the same bland menu.

My father had his own priorities. Often he would don my cadet corps boots and a rough old coat and take himself off to the rocks at low water armed with a screwdriver or similar sharp instrument. There he would chip away at the limpets until they gave up and could be prised off and into his bucket. They were very rubbery and needed a lot of bashing to make them edible, but all his efforts were not to provide for his starving family. No—the limpets so painstakingly gathered were for Moumoutte. Moumoutte was my father's pride and joy, a small brown cat with no tail which he had inherited when her previous owners, who were French, had died. He could not countenance the thought of her starving, and went out of his way to make sure she was kept supplied with her favourite seafood delicacies. He became butler, valet and secretary to this demanding creature, often sacrificing the larger part of his relaxing armchair to her comfort.

He was an avid reader, and would always try to finish a chapter or two in that chair before coming upstairs to bed at night. Moumoutte would become impatient and jump on his lap, trying to worm her way in between his legs and the side of the chair. On one memorable occasion, which I scarcely believed could be true, my father managed to ignore her despite some most insistent badgering. Disgusted, the cat jumped down and went to the door which led outside and began making the most pitiable noises of distress. My father, assuming she was going to be sick, jumped up and opened the back door to let her out. As he did so, as quick as a flash she ran behind him and jumped up onto his chair, twisting herself well and truly into place before sitting there and gazing at him defiantly. He could not win.

Of course there were many in the island who sought to supplement their diet on the black market. We hardly ever did. The fact was that it was simply far too expensive and largely the preserve of the lucky ones who could afford it. I think it's true to say that most people could not afford black-market prices, and if you hear someone say 'of course my grandparents would never have survived without it' then what they are actually telling you is that their grandparents had more disposable cash than others.

I do believe that most black marketeers were operating for the wrong reasons. Many painted themselves as patriots, doing their bit to defy the shortages imposed by the Germans and help out their own people, but in fact they were simply in it for personal greed. While I was earning the maximum wage allowed by the Germans of three pounds a week I was not tempted to use it to line the pockets of those who were out to make a fast buck.

There was one aspect to the black market to which I had a very strong objection. A Catalan contact of mine, an intelligent man with a law degree, worked at a desk job for the Germans who administered the camps. He told me he had come across documents detailing the rations which were meant to be allocated to workers to keep them in relative health as they toiled. No doubt these had been carefully worked out by someone in the food ministry in Berlin to contain the requisite number of calories to obtain a full day's work from a labourer. It is likely that with the usual German efficiency exactly the correct amount of rations would be sent from Europe to Jersey to feed the correct amount of registered workers here, but the simple fact was that only a small proportion of it actually reached their hungry mouths. The rest was pilfered and pinched between the warehouses in Germany and the bowls of the men wielding picks and shovels at Val de la Mare. Much of it was sold on the black market by those who had stolen it. It disgusted me that by participating in such deals at any stage one could effectively be depriving those poor souls of whatever little nourishment they may have had, and I remember saying so quite forcefully to a man who would regularly boast that he was able to 'source' meat from the canteen of an OT camp. Certainly, the uniformed guards who found themselves working for that organisation were well placed to supplement both their rations and their incomes in this way.

I remember feeling constantly hungry. To fill ourselves up we simply drank water—or in my parents' case, endless cups of awful coffee made from acorns or parsnip shavings. What else was there to drink? Milk was rationed or ridiculously expensive on the black market, and there were no such things as fizzy drinks. Tea was tightly rationed until it ran out. The Lyons tea factory at First Tower began the Occupation with a reasonable stock, all of which the States would have bought up to ration out carefully. Sometimes it became available on the black market at prohibitive prices. It was said that a packet of tea could fetch up to twenty-five pounds—at a time when the maximum wage was three pounds a week—and the result was that those desperate for their daily cuppa spent hours experimenting with alternatives. Blackberry leaves were a popular but time-consuming option and I watched people snipping them carefully from bushes then grinding them in a pestle and mortar in an attempt to make a palatable drink. I was simply not interested and contented myself with Adam's Ale.

My father's cousin was the Dean of Jersey, Canon Matthew Le Marinel. He was an obese man who very much enjoyed the pleasures of the table while at the same time holding very strong Christian and moral principles. The Occupation was truly a time of trial for him as he simply refused to eat anything that was illegal or ill-gotten. While they kept hens and rabbits and grew vegetables in the back garden of the deanery, he still deflated steadily as the months wore on until he became almost skeletal, a shadow of his former large self. I watched how he became ever smaller and his suits ever larger each time he came to visit. A man in his position had enough influence not to need to be frugal but he was, to the extent that he refused to throw away any of his old clothes. Neither did he have any of his clothes altered to fit his reduced waistline, arguing that he hoped to be able to fill them again one day.

Shortly before the deportations began in 1942, some friends of mine were keen to be married quickly so that the wife would not have to be taken to Germany with the rest of her family. Afterwards they described how at the ceremony at the deanery office it was just as well that neither of them suffered from vertigo, because anyone who did would have been overcome by the deep chasm between the Dean's dog collar and his chest.... Sure enough, not long after the war, it fitted snugly once more.

One common way for us to find extra food was by gleaning. This ancient practice involves going onto a farmer's field just after the harvest and picking up any stray ears of corn or missed potatoes which could still reasonably be eaten. It had gone on for centuries in rural areas everywhere, and it certainly proved popular as hunger really started to bite us.

It became a major family pastime in the latter stages of the Occupation not just for us, but for many families in town who would make the excursion to the countryside just to see what the harvesters might have left behind. While the farmer might not miss the odd barley stalk, to the people starving in St Helier it could make all the difference. I was in the fortunate position of knowing many farmers across the island thanks to my work, and they would sometimes tip me the wink that there were gleaning opportunities to be had. My mother would often accompany me to the field in question where we would cram into our bags whatever we could find on fields which had already been subject to the sickle and possibly other people following on behind, but even one bag of neglected corn was considered a bonus for us.

On one occasion at harvest time in 1943 I obtained permission to glean in the fields of a Mr du Feu, who had land in St Ouen near the church which overlooks the sea on the northwest coast. It was a long ride on my heavy bike with its trailer, but I was sure it would be worth my while after such a useful tip-off. My mother was equally excited about our chances, to the extent that she took her bicycle and pedalled along with me. Our first stop was above Beaumont to pick up Phyllis Brée who was in just as much need as ourselves, and together we half-pushed, half-rode all the way out to St Ouen.

Unfortunately by the time we arrived word had got around that there was gleaning to be had, and we were greeted by the sight of a field half of which had been picked clean by others who had got there before us. The reason the other half had not been touched was that it was right next to a German gun battery, and a line of barbed wire ran right across the middle of it. The accessible part was simply barren—but on the other side of the wire I could see ears of corn lying around everywhere, missed by the farmer and left on the earth simply to rot away. And we had come all that distance! In our present state it seemed to be a terrible waste and I resolved to make it ours if I could.

'This is crazy,' I said to my mother and Mrs Brée. 'The Germans aren't hungry enough to collect it themselves and we could fill all of our bags in ten minutes with what is lying right in front of us. I'm going to go across.' I knew that Mr du Feu's workmen were allowed to go through there, but the Germans were always watching. My mother and Mrs Brée were against it, telling me it was too risky and that we should look elsewhere but I simply could not walk away and leave all that food to go to waste. 'I'm going, and will ask a soldier politely to stand nearby and observe what I do so they can see we are only looking for ears of corn and nothing else,' I said.

I could see a sentry standing at the corner of one of the bunkers, so I lifted the barrier, crossed onto the other side of the field and walked straight up to him to explain what we wanted. It became immediately apparent that he spoke no English and despite my increasingly inventive sign language he could not understand what I was asking of him. He summoned another soldier, and before I knew it I was being brusquely marched through the gun position with a soldier on both sides of me. All around were things I'm sure I should not have been allowed to see and had I been a spy it may have proved most useful information but in moments I was being pushed down some steps into an area underground. 'Stand here! Remove your boots!', they ordered me. As I stood there barefoot they also took my belt away. Humiliated, I had to stand with one hand holding my trousers up or they would have fallen down due to the weight I had lost over the recent months, a sure way of making certain I could not run away.

I must have stood there in misery for thirty-five or forty minutes. What had I done? Was I to be arrested, imprisoned, deported, simply for trying to find something to eat? What about my mother? She would have seen me being marched away and would certainly be worried sick. And my Russian friends, who depended on me? Soldiers came and went without giving me any information about what was to happen. My youthful confidence of before had quite evaporated.

At last the guards ushered in with some deference two men dressed in civilian clothes, who had evidently been summoned to deal with me. One of them spoke English with a pronounced North American accent. He asked what I had been doing on the wrong side of the wire, and seemed to be an articulate and intelligent man who could perhaps be reasoned with. I used all the charm I could muster. I tried to communicate with him as one human being to another, explaining our hunger and the fact we had come all the way from First Tower just to find some ears of corn. We certainly intended no harm to you, I said, nor to your bunkers or your guns. We just wanted some food. He seemed to listen with a sympathetic ear, and I hoped he might even forgive my trespass and allow me to gather some of the wasted crops. But no. Quite affably, but quite forcefully at the same time, he told me to get back on my bike—and clear off. While the Germans looked on in amusement I threaded my belt back into my trousers and replaced my boots, burning with the shame of it. They escorted me back to the fence, past all the discarded corn, and saw me through the barrier before turning back to the gun position. My mother and Mrs Brée were nowhere to be seen. Where were they? Pedalling off, I cursed my impetuosity at taking such a risk. I could have been arrested, and who knows what might have happened as a result? I was, after all, responsible for hiding an escaped Russian at the time and what might the Germans have found out if they had questioned me more closely? I worried all the way to Mrs Brée's house, where I stopped to find out if there had been any sign of her or my mother. Thank goodness, her husband informed me that they had both come to the house to tell him what had happened, and then continued on to my house. He called my parents immediately to let them know I was all right, and I sped off down the hill as fast as I could. My mother was at first hugely relieved to see me back in one piece, but naturally the recriminations followed soon after. What had I been thinking? I'd asked for trouble by crossing over to the German side of the field, she told me, what did I expect? I should never have opened that barrier, never do anything like that again ... she was right, of course, but the temptation of all that food had really been too much. My empty belly reminded me of all the effort we had expended in getting all the way out to St Ouen and back for no reward, so perhaps it was a lesson well learned. We gleaned in all sorts of other places after that, but only where there was no threat of upsetting the Germans. The humiliation of this little episode was not to be taken lightly.

Later I discovered the truth about the man in civilian clothes who had dismissed me so disdainfully. I now know that I had met the dreaded Wölfle, who was number two in the German plain-clothes police, the Geheime Feldpolizei. While we were fortunate never to have the Gestapo taking any part in the Occupation, the field police were still a force to be feared. Wölfle was a very clever operative. He steered clear of committing any act of violence, using far more subtle tactics on anyone who was brought in front of him. His cronies would beat someone up and then dump them at his office. 'Oh, I'm so sorry that my comrades have been a little over-enthusiastic,' he would tell them. 'Sit down, have a cigarette.... Now what is this all about?' His solicitousness often threw people off guard and they would unwittingly reveal things they had succeeded thus far in keeping to themselves. I was indeed lucky that he had believed my story, true as it was. He was known in the island as 'Wolf of the Gestapo' and was actually popular among a certain crowd, as he had his regular drink at the Caesarea pub in Cattle Street.

Simple hunger began to dominate one's thoughts, and some were ready to take desperate measures to ensure they had enough to eat—with sometimes entertaining results.

In the summer of 1942 my girlfriend of the time, named Ruth, persuaded me to join her in treading the boards. She was a member of the 50/50 Dramatic Club, so called because it used to rehearse on the first floor above the fifty-shilling tailor's on the corner of King Street and New Street. I was expected to take the role of a lover in a play called *She Passed Through Lorraine*, a romanticised and vaguely comic rendition of the story of Joan of Arc. I remember the woman I was cast opposite as being far more worldly than myself, and I was awkward in the extreme in any scenes of a passionate nature. My acting was as wooden as the stage on which I stood, and I distinctly remember the director saying to me, 'Come on Bob, haven't you ever taken a girl up onto Westmount after a dance at the Pav?' Of course I had, but I certainly wasn't going to tell them about it!

All around me the preparations were underway. In a fit of artistic generosity, the Germans allowed anyone who was in a play an extra hour of freedom during curfew, which meant we could not only rehearse but also prepare our scenery and costumes. Wardrobe mistresses stitched outfits from old curtains and worn-out remnants from previous shows while backstage workers hammered and banged to come up with a set worthy of our efforts. Anticipation was high.

One scene took place in a farmhouse, and according to directions the farmer's wife was to be seen preparing food. Since that commodity was in short supply, in rehearsals the actress concerned carefully mimed the peeling of some kind of vegetable, on the understanding that for each actual performance she would have an authentic and actual swede to practice her art upon for the sake of realism—one for the matinee and one for the evening show. Sure enough, when the day came someone with country connections brought the sought-after swedes and placed them with due reverence on the props table shortly before curtain.

Yet when the scene began, the actress appeared on stage bereft of vegetables of any description and resorted once again to her well-practised dumb show. I don't suppose a single member of the audience noticed, and even if they had I'm sure they wouldn't have cared; in fact they would have asked why such a valuable swede was being wasted as a theatrical prop! Nevertheless, after the curtain came down, instead of the usual discussion of how the performance had gone there were urgent questions about what had happened to our edible props. Finally, shamefacedly, two members of the cast admitted that in the time between the swedes being put on the props table and the show starting, they had eaten them. Raw.

The rest of the run continued with imaginary vegetables, and with hindsight I cannot see how our friendly farmer could have kept us supplied with enough for the whole run.

My cousin Jennifer Gaudin, who was a little girl during the Occupation, lived with her parents on the family farm and remembers how a German soldier used to come every week to measure carefully the amount of milk produced by the cows which they kept. One of the animals would not let the soldier anywhere near her and would in fact only allow Jennifer's father or the head dairyman to approach. Nevertheless, the Germans required a strict account to be kept of everything that was produced and the soldier insisted on seeing every can that had been filled in order for it to be requisitioned for general supply. Every farm on the island was subject to such attention, whether it produced milk, potatoes or any other kind of foodstuff which could be rationed and controlled. This became especially stringent as supplies from the outside world began to dry up and the rations became shorter, and many farmers learned to conceal some of their crops and even livestock from prying German eyes.

Chocolate was a luxury only to be dreamed of but there was one way to get yourself some, together with a nice cup of tea, if you were quite literally prepared to pay for it in blood.

Once every six months I was called to the hospital where a nurse would jab a needle into my arm and extract a pint or two of the stuff from me to be given to people whose need was greater than mine. My principle motive for going was to be of some help to people who were sick, but it didn't hurt that you were given a little document afterwards which entitled you to go to one particular shop in Beresford Street to claim a whole bar of chocolate—if it was available at the time. Before you left, your cup of REAL tea was presented to you, with milk and perhaps even SUGAR if you required it. (I had given up taking sugar before the war, when I noticed that the most 'with it' people abstained!) The system of reward meant it could be weeks before you were able to obtain the chocolate which was, as I remember, slabs of dark French Menier cooking chocolate. They were about four or five inches long and three inches wide, about the same size as a modern bar.

In summer 1944 I donated my blood as usual, and collected my slab of chocolate from what must have been the last distribution, because contact with France ceased in July that year after the Americans cut off the ports which served the island. Despite an almost overwhelming urge to wolf it down immediately, by exercising extraordinary self-control I stored it away in my room, where its presence was a constant temptation. I took it out occasionally, to look at it and make sure it wasn't melting....

On Christmas Day I made my way to Mrs Osborne's house to pass on festive greetings to her and various friends who had gathered for the occasion. As the conversation ebbed and flowed I made a careful calculation. How many people were in the room, compared to the number of squares of chocolate remaining in my bar, after giving my mother and father a little taste earlier? I had already broken it into its constituent cubes. The answer, fortunately, was 'just enough'. I waited until a natural lull in the festive cheer and said quietly, 'It's a pity none of you like chocolate, because in my pocket—!' There was no need to say any more. I was suddenly very popular, and felt like a true social lion.

Others had brought some carefully hoarded firewood, which was used to give us some warmth and cheer.

I'm not sure what we drank, as most of the wine left in the island had either been consumed by then or was being saved for the Liberation, so it is likely that we threw back some of the rough local Calvados. One of our group actually had a still and made his own, but never allowed any of his friends to drink it because he was unsure of exactly what effect it might have on their health! In fact, I remember wanting to speak to him on one occasion and managing to track him down to a rundown area of Ann Street which was ready to be demolished. When I found my way in, he seemed most displeased that I had discovered him. There he was, sitting on a stool in the middle of a derelict house, pulling pieces of wood from the banisters to feed the small fire that kept his still bubbling, while all the time reading Ovid in the original.

On that dark December night, in the blackout, with damp clothes and leaking shoes, such human contact was essential to us all. I am sure the Occupation taught many of us self-control.

Despite our discomfort I believe we were lucky to have come to our state of advanced hunger by degrees over five years, instead of all at once. By the end of 1944 we were living on about 1,000 calories a day, hardly enough to keep up a normal life under usual circumstances, yet we had become gradually accustomed to it and were able to survive. In Holland, the final bitter months of the war became known as the Hongerwinter, as cities cut off from all supplies simply ran out of food very quickly. Their daily calorific intake plummeted in a few short weeks to a level similar to, or even lower than, ours and thousands of Dutch people died as a result. Up until that point Holland had been a place of relative plenty.

A few days later when the wonderful taste of that chocolate was already a fading memory, some terrific news was announced in the newspaper. The *Vega* was coming!

The Bailiffs of both Jersey and Guernsey had told the Germans that our food situation was so serious that people would begin to die from starvation unless there was some kind of help from outside the islands. Rations had been pared to the bone and there was real concern that we had simply been cut off and left to fend for ourselves.

It was clearly to the Germans' advantage that this should not happen, and they had agreed to allow the Red Cross to get involved. Even as I had been sharing out my precious squares of Christmas cheer, the steamship SS *Vega* was sailing towards us from Lisbon bringing glad tidings in the form of thousands of specially prepared parcels crammed with every conceivable essential.

We were lucky. When the request to allow the Red Cross to help us had reached Churchill in the War Cabinet he saw that it could potentially benefit the Germans, and he scribbled in the margins of the cabinet notes, 'Let'em starve.' Perhaps he assumed that any food coming in ostensibly for us would be seized by the enemy and used to feed the occupiers instead of the occupied. The islands were of no military use to him, and I'm sure he had better things to do than to think about feeding some cut-off Germans.

Fortunately for us cooler heads prevailed, and the *Vega* sailed from Lisbon loaded with more than 100,000 food parcels similar to those sent to Allied prisoners of war, as well as two tons of medical supplies and various other essentials. It sailed under the proviso that it was a neutral ship from a neutral country, painted with large red crosses to prevent it being sunk by prowling U-boats —or indeed by Allied shipping. After sailing up through the Bay of Biscay it stopped in Guernsey first, and I remember the sense of anticipation as we awaited its arrival. I believe the organisation had realised that the need in Guernsey was even greater than ours.

It wasn't in time for Christmas, but just in time for New Year, preparing to unload on 31 December. While I know very many islanders raced down to the harbour to greet the vessel I was, as usual, at my desk in Hill Street. I couldn't just take time off to look at things like that. While there was a great buzz of excitement, I remember simply feeling a great sensation of relief, not only for my own suffering stomach but for all of us who had been enduring such hardship. It also meant far more than just some food in our bellies. It told us that we hadn't been forgotten, that the German stranglehold on our island was not absolute, and that surely the end must be in sight. While I worked on, still hungry, my mother and father joined the happy throng to collect our parcels. Each person was registered at a specific shop for rations, and the parcels were allocated around the island accordingly under the direction of volunteers from the St John Ambulance service. It had been the only uniformed organisation allowed by the Germans, and it was perhaps fitting that its members got to carry out this happy task.

When I got home my parents were waiting excitedly for me in the front room. On the table were three parcels, each the size of a shoebox wrapped in brown paper and tied with string, still unopened. They had waited for me so that we could all open and enjoy them together, although I'm sure I don't know how they fought the temptation to tear into theirs. I already had my own space on a shelf reserved for me in the kitchen where I could keep my very own, personal supplies—although there had been very little on it for a long time.

We took the string off carefully—you never knew when it might come in handy—and unfolded the brown-paper wrappings which we also put to one side. I opened the lid to see a cardboard box crammed with all kinds of packets and tins, but the one which immediately grabbed my attention was marked 'Klim'. I knew that to be dried, sweetened, powdered milk. In a flash I had grabbed a spoon from the kitchen, and began what can only be described as my Klim Orgy. Delving deeply I scooped out a huge heaped spoonful of powder and without hesitation crammed it straight into my mouth. My teeth were gummed together almost immediately, my tongue stuck to my palate and my whole mouth was one disgusting sticky, gooey mess. I could scarcely breathe. It was divine. Somewhere in the background I could hear my mother imploring me to stop, to keep the powder safe and to mix it with water according to the instructions. I decided to ignore both her and the instructions. I would continue to drink water when I was thirsty and enjoy my Klim straight from the tin in my own orgy of sweetened delight.

As I struggled to open my mouth sufficiently to cram in more powdered goodness, I rummaged through my parcel to see what else there was inside. There were all kinds of magical things that we had hardly seen for five years. Chocolate!! Canned sardines! TEA!! A tin of prunes—of which we were not in very great need, given our enforced diet of vegetables—some corned beef—and, thank goodness, some soap.

Aside from food, soap had long been one of those things we had learned to do without. There was simply none to be had, unless you had a fortune to spend on the black market, which I most certainly did not. There had been a small supply of some very bad French soap at one point, which hardly seemed to work at all. After just a few months of occupation there was simply nothing with which to clean your hands, face, body or clothes and one just had to get used to feeling permanently a little grubby. If you went to the theatre or cinema, or if you took the bus, you became very conscious of the mass shortage of soap—and of hot water. Of course there was no such thing as deodorant or anti-perspirant then, and frankly we smelt bad. Can you imagine sleeping in bedclothes that have not been washed for months on end? Even the cold-water supplies were limited to a few hours a day and you could be cut off if you used too much. After every meal there was always a rush to get the washing-up done quickly before the water went off. The luxury of a warm bath, or even a shower, was unheard of. If one wished to get clean, it was a case of standing in a basin and scrubbing down with cold water.

I clearly remember one day in spring 1945, the first warm day of the year, heading down to Havre des Pas swimming pool and jumping into the fresh cold water. Salty as it was, I felt absolute delight in rubbing and scraping my body all over with my fingernails to clean myself, and emerging fresher and cleaner than I had been for months. I still had to put my well-worn clothes back on of course…. Being truly clean was a luxury that few could afford.

The Red Cross soap, like the rest of the supplies they sent, was eked out sparingly over the next few weeks (apart from the all too tempting Klim which disappeared in very short order!). After all, we never knew if or when another shipment might arrive and didn't want to become quite as desperate as we had been at Christmas. My remaining tins and packets went onto my personal shelf in the kitchen and were consumed with great care.

Perhaps the one thing in the parcels that we could have done without was a packet of salt. Those of us who lived close to the sea could get that very easily by carrying our metal bucket across the road to the beach and scooping up as much salty water as we wished. Some people even made a living from it, and I certainly used to take some to a friend of my mother's, a Miss Picot, who lived on her own. You could use it for cooking, although we found it was far too salty to use undiluted. After some trial and error we found that it was best mixed one part sea water to two parts fresh.

The *Vega* was to be our salvation. She returned several times before Liberation, always crammed with precious parcels and I was always overjoyed to see my beloved supply of Klim restored!

Of course the Germans enjoyed very little of our new bounty. They were under strict orders that the parcels were not for them, and they were expected to cope with whatever rations they had left. They were effectively cut off from receiving any new supplies, and anything they needed had to be found on the island. Some islanders felt sorry for individual soldiers who had shown themselves to be more than usually friendly and were prepared to share a little, while less scrupulous (and less hungry) people were keen to barter their precious tins for valuable items such as binoculars.

Our joy at the *Vega*'s arrival was unfortunately soon tempered by the news that our electricity supply was to be cut off. Not just ours, but every house in the island. The gas had already been shut off and we were now to be left quite without power. Naturally Mike and René threw a party to mark the occasion, but our jollity couldn't disguise the fact that across the whole island people would be left in the depths of winter with no heat, no light, and no means of cooking unless they could gather enough fuel to burn. We were fortunate that we had an oven that could operate from burning wood and I spent most of whatever little free time I had trying to find some, despite the German ban on cutting down trees. I can remember one Sunday afternoon there was a mass cutting-down of trees at Westmount and along West Park, with several dozen people chopping and sawing away to try to gather as many branches as possible. The Germans inexplicably left them to it, but their commander Baron von Aufsess noted in his diary that he was most upset at the loss of such beautiful trees. Of course, cutting them was one thing, but transporting them home was quite another! I used to go out in the dark after I came home from work taking my bike with its trailer, into which I would cram as many logs as I could 'find'. Bellozanne Valley began just a few hundred yards inland from our house and was an ideal source, being out of earshot from most habitation. I would leave my bike away from the road, and clutching a small hacksaw head towards any tree which had branches that I could reach. I wasn't the only one and I'm sure my path regularly crossed with other people doing exactly the same thing. When I had a reasonable amount I would pack it all into my trailer and pedal home with my heavy load bouncing along behind me. It was always best to get back before curfew so I would not have to navigate the barricade by the house.

On one occasion as I made my way between West Park and First Tower I heard close to home the unmistakeable sound of sawing coming through the night air. Those responsible seemed to have no concerns about being overheard, and when I heard a great booming voice ring out I knew exactly who it was. Marjorie Baker had a voice that carried for miles, which was often used to good effect on the amateur stage. Unfortunately on that particular night her tones of almost exaggerated refinement were being used to shout instructions to some poor helpless soul explaining just how the logs should be cut. The word 'bloody' boomed out inelegantly across the night and I moved on, glad for the distraction.

My parents were always grateful for the wood that I brought back, as it meant we could keep our little stove going for as long as possible. The only alternative for cooking was to take whatever mother could come up with in a dish to the nearest communal bakehouse. Each family was allowed to take one dish a day to these places with their great ovens, which would cook them overnight for collection the next day.

While it was relatively easy for me to keep us supplied in this way, for others matters became far more difficult. I was aware of several people who burned their furniture to keep warm as the temperatures plummeted, particularly in rented properties. It was an unusually cold winter, and the thermometers fell steadily until they actually stayed below freezing for several days. Those without the facility or resources to build a fire were at great risk of hypothermia.

Lighting the house became very difficult. You could no longer flick a switch and expect light. It was falling dark shortly after four in the afternoon, and we were down to our last candle and last box of matches. Keeping the fire alight in the stove was a real challenge. To help us find our way about in the house my father had filled an old medicine bottle with diesel oil and a wick made out of an old bootlace. That threw a smelly, dirty, dim light across the room and was used sparingly. Woe betide you if you moved with it too quickly, or brushed close to it. If the flame went out we would have to use one of our precious matches to light it again and every time my father shook the box it rattled less and less. In case of emergency my father had an old torch whose battery had long since died, but he found that if he left it close to the stove the warmth would coax just a little more life out of it. Reading, writing or playing games were out of the question.

There seemed little point in simply sitting up in the dark so we would generally go to bed as soon as we had eaten what little there was, often as early as seven o'clock. I would regularly find my way upstairs using my sense of touch alone and go to sleep shivering in the gloom. Only the news from the front brought light into our lives.

In the darkest months we found working effectively in the office a challenge as the sun started to set. Often, on an overcast day, it would be more or less dark before the hour we were due to close and Miss Hunt would hunch over her typewriter squinting as she attempted to make out exactly what she was typing. The only light came from the windows in the front of the building; it could not hope to penetrate to the further recesses of the office and we became used to finding the documents we were looking for almost by touch alone.

Eventually the days grew longer and warmer and life began to resume some kind of normality. One of my strongest memories from the spring and summer of 1945 is of feeling sick any time I passed along one of Jersey's many wooded valleys, now denuded of so many of their finest trees. Lanes that were once arched over with branches and leaves were now open to the skies, and once shady spots were now in the full glare of the sun. It wasn't only caused by local people in search of wood, as during the Occupation the Germans cut down many trees themselves for fuel or to improve the field of fire around their guns. Would I ever see Jersey again as I had known it?

Chapter Fourteen

CONSPIRACY

It was in early March 1945 when Paul Casimir approached me again to ask if I might help with some more illicit translation work—although this time the words were not in Spanish.

Serving in the German Army at that time were a significant number of Russians, who were effectively traitors to their country. They served under the renegade Red Army General Vlasov, who had been captured by the Germans during the invasion of the Soviet Union. They had turned him against his former communist masters, and allowed him to raise his own force of Russians armed with German equipment to fight against their own countrymen. In October 1943 a battalion of them arrived in Jersey to bolster the defences. They wore distinctive shoulder flashes, with what seemed to be the letters 'POA' on them. We discovered later that these initials were in Cyrillic script and stood for 'Russian Army of Liberation'. These soldiers took responsibility for defending much of the island's coastline and manned many of the checkpoints from Ann Port in the east to Sorel Point in the north. They were the people the insurgents wanted to target next with their propaganda, but in order to do that they needed someone who could translate it into Russian.

Paul told me he understood I that had 'contacts' in that respect. Could I help? I was appalled. How the hell did he know? I stalled, telling him that I would have to ask around, and that I would get back to him.

I immediately went to speak to the two young men who I knew were hosting a particular friend from Russia. Dare we ask him to do this translation for us? They, quite understandably, were cautious. They approved of the cause, but wanted to know more of the risk. Who was behind it all? Could they be trusted? How well did I know the people involved, was I sure it wasn't just a trap? It was too dangerous to rush into, they argued (although the Russian in question would I'm sure have jumped at the chance). We should find out more before asking anyone to take further action. I returned to Paul with that response.

While disappointed, he understood, and told me to await further news.

A day or two later I was contacted again. Casually, Paul told me to go to the New Era Cinema in Georgetown to the east of St Helier, at seven o'clock on a certain evening. Someone would turn up whom I would probably recognise. By way of making a sign, they would be humming or whistling the theme of *Eine kleine Nachtmusik*. While this sounded very melodramatic, it was far from being so.

On the night in question I turned up at the appointed hour and loitered with my bike outside the cinema as casually as I could, sheltering from the dripping rain. I grew colder and colder as I waited and began to think I was wasting my time, when another cyclist appeared, also dripping wet, whistling softly. He needn't have bothered. I recognised my old acquaintance Norman Le Brocq. Perhaps I should have guessed.

Dismounting, he said, 'Well, you have found a good place to shelter,' and just in case I had missed his earlier efforts he began to whistle again. 'Oh,' I said. 'You are fond of Mozart....'

'Get on your bike and follow me.'

This was rather more cloak-and-dagger than I had been used to, cycling off in the dark and rain to destination unknown, but at the same time bicycles were such a regular feature of life that I'm sure we wouldn't have aroused any suspicion. We pedalled off down Plat Douet Road and then on to Rue des Pres, which at that time was like a country lane, and I made sure to keep about thirty yards behind him. He finally stopped at the back of some cottages which faced Longueville Manor. There was a high garden wall on the left, with a door, to which Norman had a key. I stopped next to him and followed him through into a garden, pushing my bicycle inside. He locked the door behind us. The blacked-out house loomed up in the darkness of the night, scarcely visible through the rain. Once again, Norman had a key which he turned carefully in the lock. As he closed the door softly, I heard a whistling sound from upstairs. Mozart again! We followed the sound upstairs in the dark, and Norman pushed open a door. A man sat at a typewriter on a desk, dimly lit by an oil light. He wore a splendid blue suit and badly dyed blonde hair. The suit had once belonged to Victor Hamon, and the hair dye had come from Mrs Osborne's salon.

He was the man whom I had been unwittingly helping.

He stood up, extended his hand, and greeted me with 'Good evening'— in a strong and unmistakably German accent. He was certainly not a Russian.

I was frozen solid. My God, I thought, I've walked into a trap! Norman, what have you done? I turned to look at him, aghast. He saw my dismay and hurried to explain. Paul Mühlbach was an intellectual, an agitator—and a German deserter. He had been sheltered in this house at no little risk to its owners, and while there he had produced countless pieces of anti-German propaganda which Norman's little communist cell had reproduced and distributed. Did I remember the fire in the German garage at St John's Road, the storage shed that burned down at Georgetown? Those, said Norman proudly, had all been brought about by the man in front of me. Somewhat shaken, I took his hand and prepared to listen to more of his story.

Paul Mühlbach (if that was his real name) had a father who was a Social Democrat leader in Koblenz. His party had been peacefully left-wing, and popular enough, until the Nazis came to power following the 1933 elections. All opposition officials were sacked immediately, and Mr Mühlbach Sr was taken to the very first concentration camp at Dachau near Munich.

The Nazis arrested Paul too, but released him when they realised there was no indication that he had done anything wrong. His father was not so lucky and died in the camp with so many others who opposed the burgeoning regime. Paul joined the fledgling resistance as an active member, and even fought briefly in the Spanish Civil War with the International Brigade. He was captured, sent back to Germany, and given the choice between following his father to a terrible death or joining the army. He was conscripted as war erupted across the Continent, but fortunately for him he escaped being sent to the Russian Front, and was instead posted to Jersey, where he determined to continue his fight against the system which had killed his father. After deserting he had committed various minor acts of sabotage, including setting fire to German-occupied buildings.

His proudest achievement was yet to come. On the morning of 7 March, dressed in his German uniform, he set fire to the ammunition store of the once-exclusive Palace Hotel in St Saviour, which was being used by the Germans as a headquarters. The fire spread and the hotel was destroyed in the subsequent blast, possibly as a result of the Germans trying to clear a firebreak among the buildings. I was in Minden Place at the time, and I not only heard the explosion but saw the smoke and flames billowing out from the site. My first thought was, 'Oh my God, it's the school,' Victoria College being very close to the hotel and in line of sight from where I was. It caused a sensation in the island, and uproar among the authorities who had no idea what had happened. Even decades after the war there was still speculation about exactly how the Palace had been destroyed.

While Herr Mühlbach and Norman were proud of the inflammatory work they were undertaking, it was not what I wanted to hear. I was determined that any efforts of mine at subverting the Germans would be made discreetly and without drawing attention to myself, or more importantly anyone who relied upon me. I concluded that it was far too dangerous to have any Russian of my acquaintance involved with these people, as under interrogation they might well give the whole game away. Some fine young men would face arrest and possible torture, and all their plans and dreams would collapse. They were less than delighted when I told them as much, although I did make arrangements to meet Herr Mühlbach again. I was escorted downstairs and out through the dimly lit garden, before making my way home with my head spinning. No-one followed me.

By early spring we were approaching the end of the Occupation, although of course we did not know quite how it would end. Some were worried that the ardent Nazi Kommandant, Vice-Admiral Hüffmeier, who was appointed at the end of February, would attempt to fight on and prevent the island being liberated without a struggle. The result could have been devastating for the civilian population.

With no indication that the Germans were prepared to end the war peacefully, Paul Mühlbach, Norman Le Brocq and the rest of their group had come up with a plan that was bold, very risky—and potentially deadly. I had met Paul Mühlbach a couple more times after our initial rendezvous, and the word on his lips was 'mutiny'. After his coercive campaign aimed at inspiring soldiers to revolt, he believed that he could actually make it happen, and overturn the Nazi rule over the island with a brief but powerful coup d'état. As we conversed in his room he assured me that he had the backing of several officers of the rank of colonel and above who were ready to turn their backs on Hitler and help to liberate the island. He even told me the same was happening in Guernsey. The more I listened to him, the more I found him convincing, in a way that my original contact Paul Casimir had never been. Mühlbach seemed very stable, not a dreamer, and had succeeded in living a clandestine life in Germany and here in Jersey.

He described how many German soldiers still harboured Marxist sympathies after their cause was crushed by Hitler in the thirties. That decade had been one where insurrections and revolt had held sway in Europe and elsewhere, and had shown how a strong minority with robust leadership could take over whole countries. More recently, we heard through the BBC that a host of German officers, including twenty-one generals, had demonstrated how deeply the army distrusted Hitler by attempting to assassinate him with a bomb at his own headquarters. Nearly 12,000 people had been executed as a result.

But while we assumed that Nazi Germany was in its death throes, there were an awful lot of Germans still under arms. Would they, as many imagined, regroup in a Bavarian mountain retreat and hold out for weeks or even months? If they did, surely the Allies would not deviate from their real work of liberating the European mainland to come to the rescue of our little island. Vice-Admiral Hüffmeier evidently had no intention of surrendering easily. We would remain occupied until the war ended, that was clear, so perhaps a successful revolt and seizure of power might just be the best thing.

It was credible that Mühlbach would be able to garner support from his erstwhile comrades as we all knew that the average German soldier was demoralised, cold and hungry, worried about the relentless push of the Red Army towards their homes and the overwhelming bombing campaign against their cities. They had followed the progress of the war, and few were still convinced of final victory or even of the chances of surviving unhurt. Everything they had been taught since they were in school was hollow and their beliefs had just been swept from under their feet.

Paul's leaflet campaign reminded them of it regularly, and his calm reasoning began to convince me of the plan.

The intention was to send the word out for a coordinated mutiny of soldiers with the assistance of the few members of the Jersey Communist Party across the island on the symbolic date of 1 May—International Workers' Day.

On that date, at ten o'clock, a sympathetic officer would fire a cannon from the ramparts of Elizabeth Castle to signal that the revolt was to begin. Common soldiers would turn on their officers, disarm them and then surrender the island—although to whom they would surrender it was a moot point. Despite only being a fringe member of their group, shortly before the big day I was allocated a job in a tense meeting at a downstairs flat in Pierson Road. I was to take myself to First Tower School on the morning of the action, despite it being a Tuesday and consequently a day of work when I should be required at the office. When the signal cannon fired I was to go into the school, approach the headmaster and tell them to keep the children inside for fear of being hurt in any action as the mutiny ran its course.

While I cannot say I was wholeheartedly behind this rather desperate venture with its associated risks, I resolved to support it in my limited task as it seemed to offer a way to bring the Occupation to a relatively quick and bloodless end without the chance of diehard Nazis prolonging it after any peace in mainland Europe. However what enthusiasm I did have for it was lost shortly before it was due to be launched, when I overheard a conversation between some of the more hotheaded leaders of the Communist Party in the room next door. It made me question my whole part in the escapade and the moral judgement of some of my comrades.

Leslie Huelin and the others were earnestly debating what should happen immediately after the Germans had finished their mutiny, and how they themselves might be able to seize control. In voices at once cocky and confident, they spoke of transforming the island into a Marxist utopia, with the old ruling order swept away. The word now was no longer simply 'mutiny', but 'revolution'. Caught up in revolutionary fervour, they discussed how to get rid of the island's leaders, to clear the way for their Red Flag to fly over the States of Jersey building in the Royal Square. Their plan, quite coldly and simply, was that the Bailiff and his deputy together with their Crown Officers and leading States members should be killed in the course of the revolt, sacrificed for a socialist ideal and clearing the way for Jersey to become a miniature communist state. They had made the preparations and approached the necessary people, and were confident that there were some Germans willing to take action with their guns.

I was horrified.

While their plot seemed outrageous, I had heard enough to convince me that they meant every word, and that Jerseymen were truly prepared to turn on other Jerseymen to take power. They fully intended to use German soldiers, products of the Nazi regime, as the armed strength with which to overturn the centuries-old system of government in the island.

I had visions of armed renegade German soldiers storming though the States buildings with machine pistols blazing, of terrified typists caught in crossfire hiding under their desks. As the day for action approached, I was placed on the horns of a terrible dilemma. Did I allow them to go ahead with their plan or could I, with a clear conscience, tell the authorities about it and risk bringing retribution upon all of our heads? What could I possibly do? For the idealistic young man that I was, there appeared no easy answer that could possibly result in a satisfactory outcome. Some might argue that I should have approached the Bailiff himself to warn him of the plot, but in that event to whom could he turn? The only possible course of action for him would have been to inform the Germans and prevent the rebellion, but in doing so he would be personally betraying some of his own people to prison and possibly to death. He would have been damned forever.

In the end I did nothing, resigned to let fate take its course; but at least I could be there to try to ensure it didn't get too out of hand. I would certainly try to keep the children at First Tower safe.

Naturally my work colleagues would need to know that I was to be absent, so I arranged to have some business with a customer close to my home early on the morning of 1 May. I went to the farm up Mont Cochon in order to discover the name of a certain cow upon which the farmer wished to extend his insurance cover, allowing plenty of time to cycle back down the hill to my station at the school which was only a few hundred yards from my home. With my mundane task complete and the farmer in complete ignorance of the day's significance I prepared myself for what the revolution might bring.

Despite being spring it was bitterly cold; I remember some flurries of snow cutting through my thin clothes and melting on the pavement as I stood there on the corner of the street opposite the entrance to the school trying to look inconspicuous. I kept glancing at my watch as the hands counted down towards ten o'clock, shuffling my feet and wondering what on earth might happen to us all. Would I be able to persuade the headmaster of the need for action, that this wasn't just a load of pie in the sky? Would maverick bands of soldiers appear with all guns blazing, would we all have to dive for cover amid fusillades of shots and broken glass, and if so would I be able to protect the children?

At last the moment approached. I prepared myself for the boom of cannon fire from the castle and the call to immediate action, yet ... as ten o'clock came and went there was nothing. Apart from a brief rattle of automatic fire from up the hill (where the present Haute Vallée School now stands) there was no sign that the Red Revolution was happening. With my nerves shredded, I waited a while longer in case there had been some simple delay. Five minutes, then ten, passed peacefully as mundane life continued all around me. The strain was immense. Had my erstwhile comrades been betrayed, or captured? Had the revolt begun without my knowledge? Were German patrols heading to capture me even as I waited? More time ticked away, and I felt increasingly cold and vulnerable loitering there aimlessly.

Finally I could stand it no longer, and picked up my bike to ride away. Nervously I headed to Leslie Huelin's flat on Peirson Road where the communists were wont to meet, but as I approached there was no sign of any activity. Pushing open the door I was greeted by a glum-looking bunch of downcast revolutionaries who had been frustrated in their grandiose plan, apparently by the refusal of the officer in charge of Elizabeth Castle to play his part. Oberst Linder had simply not fired the gun and the People's Revolt had been halted before it even began. There was an air of tragicomedy about the whole thing as their revolutionary fervour drained slowly away into the cold spring air. I had a feeling of utter relief that the crackpot scheme had failed, combined with an overwhelming sense of nervous exhaustion. I had been on pins for weeks, but now it seemed sense would at least have a chance to prevail and the Occupation might end peacefully. How different it might have been if the German officer had chosen to fire the gun, we would never know.

The revolution had melted away like the snow on the pavement.

As I mounted my bike and pedalled away down Cheapside and onto The Parade, I could not help but notice just how ordinary life was going on for everyone else, who had not the faintest idea of the drama that could have unfolded. Women walked down the pavement with shopping bags and prams, men rode past on their bicycles, shop doors swung open, and the sense of normality was overwhelming. They were completely unaware, while my mind was in turmoil at the narrow escape they might all have had. I returned to work as if nothing had happened—which of course it hadn't. My flustered face could be explained by the fact that I had just cycled back to the office into the keen cold wind, and I was able to don the appearance of slightly elevated office boy once more while inside my head was spinning. None of the people in my office had any inkling that they could have been caught up in a revolution, with our office backing onto the States' buildings and the heart of government.

In my pocket I found the document signed by the farmer just a few short hours before with the name of his precious cow; I filled in the requisite forms accordingly and resigned myself to the plodding routine of daily life once more.

Later that day we discovered that Adolf Hitler was dead, supposedly killed at the head of the troops gallantly defending Berlin. He had in fact shot himself in his bunker two days earlier. Belatedly, we celebrated.

Had the gun been fired, I do believe there would have been a mutiny—I do believe it would have happened. German soldiers were ready for it after the increasingly dire news from the front, the incessant hunger and the lack of contact with home. Even the German leader Baron von Aufsess said in his diary that he and his counterpart in Guernsey were prepared to assassinate the fervent Nazi Vice-Admiral Hüffmeier if he was not prepared to surrender; so if someone of his rank was willing to take such drastic action, it surely isn't beyond the bounds of credibility to think the average soldier may have been prepared to act in a similar way.

Would the revolutionaries have gone through with the killing of Jersey's ruling elite? I believe people such as Leslie Huelin were relying too much on the Germans to do that dirty work for them. I don't think the Germans would have had the slightest interest in killing the Bailiff nor the slightest interest in saving him either for that matter. In fact most of them probably didn't actually know who he was or what he did. But mercifully we shall never know—and the consequences had any civilian-backed mutiny failed are too awful to contemplate.

Chapter Fifteen

THE CHIMES OF BIG BEN

A s I waited nervously for the gun to fire from Elizabeth Castle to signal the beginning of revolt in our island on 1 May, hundreds of miles to the east events were taking a more significant turn as the Russians hoisted the Hammer and Sickle over the Brandenburg Gate and the Allies prepared to administer the final coup de grâce to the collapsing Nazi regime.

While the outcome of the war seemed in little doubt, we were far from certain how it might end for us in our occupied island, which now seemed far removed from the front line. Of greatest concern was the man who was now in charge of the Channel Islands. Vice-Admiral Friedrich Hüffmeier was an ardent Nazi who had told us in no uncertain terms that he would never surrender. While the Germans may not have had much in the way of food and fuel they had an awful lot of guns and plenty of ammunition, and there is little doubt they could have held out in their bunkers for a long time if the Allies had attacked. Hüffmeier had held special celebrations in Guernsey for Hitler's birthday on 23 April, and his deputy here in Jersey held an event at the Forum Cinema at which he reiterated his promise to serve his Führer until the very end. My mother never forgave Hitler for many things, but perhaps his worst offence in her eyes was sharing the same birthday as her!

The electricity had been shut off since January and we led our lives in darkness after nightfall.

At home we were now unable to cook anything to relieve our hunger unless we made the trip to the bakehouse to which we had been allocated; yet we seldom had anything worth cooking at all, so it was rarely worth our while.

Incredibly, the German whose responsibility it was to check the milk production at my cousin Jennifer's farm persisted in doing his duty and came marching down their lane just two days before Liberation. 'Why are you still doing this?' her father asked him. 'Because this is my duty,' he said. 'I have my orders and I must do my job as required.' Perhaps, rather like me when the Occupation began, he felt the need to continue with his responsibilities as though nothing untoward was happening and found some psychological comfort from the regularity of his work.

Even more keenly felt than hunger was the lack of news from our radio, which relied on mains power to make it work. Fortunately some of my friends had crystal sets on which they could listen to the BBC and get whatever information was available. We knew of the imminent fall of Berlin, we celebrated the death of Hitler, but there was great debate about whether a hardcore group of Nazis might set themselves up in some Alpine redoubt to continue the struggle. There was no mention of Jersey. Tension rose in the island as we wondered whether we could also become a final bastion of resistance for the last diehard Nazis led by the arrogant Hüffmeier. Every moment of every day we wondered what would happen to us.

On 4 May the first surrender documents were signed on Lüneberg Heath, and the BBC told us that the end of the war was surely at hand. On 7 May I worked as usual, but people came in to pay their premiums or reported their claims with one question on their lips—when would we be freed? I found out from my friends later that night that preparations were underway for the final surrender. While I was prepared to celebrate, my elation was still tinged with concern about the future of our little island when there was no guarantee that its German commander would allow it to be given up without a fight. Notices were appearing in the newspaper asking us to remain calm in uncertain times.

When I got home I found that my mother had also heard the news and was badgering my father to climb up into the loft to find the red, white and blue bunting we had displayed for the 1937 coronation. She intended to festoon the front of the house with the colours of the country.

In the office people came and went, some excited, some nervous, some sharing my apprehension of what might happen. Miss Hunt clacked away on her typewriter using some newly and expensively acquired carbon paper. We maintained our discipline and order, processing our work, until someone rushed in to tell us the wonderful news. It was over! The Germans had surrendered unconditionally and the war in Europe was finally won. Our normally orderly office broke into cheers and I thanked God that our forces had prevailed. But even as we settled down, the nagging doubt persisted: what about that bloody fool Hüffmeier?

The following morning, with things still unresolved, I walked out of the office heading for the bank to carry out some business. My way took me through the Royal Square, and I was surprised to see States' telephone workmen fitting loudspeakers to the trees all around it. I was worried. I thought this was a bad sign. Were the Germans fitting these speakers so that they could announce that while the war in Germany might be at an end, the resolution did not apply to the Channel Islands?

I hurried into the bank, where the staff were equally inquisitive. We know they are putting up speakers, they said, but why, what's going on? I shared my suspicions about Hüffmeier with them, and felt the whole atmosphere to be one of tension. Were we to face bombardment, armed struggle through our streets and the deaths of our fellow islanders before we could finally be freed?

My business complete, I headed back across the square where there was suddenly a mood of elation, people were laughing and cheering and smiling with joy. The news was that the man who had instructed the States' people to put up the speakers was the Bailiff himself; he had been given permission to do so by the Germans to enable the people to hear the Prime Minister, who would address the nation at three o'clock that afternoon! People were already streaming out of homes, shops and offices all around the town and gathering in the square in anticipation. Conscious of my duty to the office I took myself back to Hill Street quickly and told everyone inside the news, to great cheers. We decided to close the office at one o'clock so that we could play a part in this moment of such importance for our island.

The extraordinary Miss Le Seelleur was a woman who worked for another insurance company to whom I had sublet a small office in our block. She knew a boy who had a girlfriend whose father was the caretaker of the National Provincial Bank, which was situated just at the corner of the Royal Square alongside Piquet House. She arranged for us to get inside and up onto the top of the building where there was a parapet behind which we could have a pigeon's eye view of everything that was going on. Our habitual hunger was banished by the excitement, as even I started to dare to believe we might be freed without bloodshed.

By the time we locked up our office and got outside the square was absolutely packed. The Jersey grapevine had worked its usual magic, and the mood of elation was palpable. People had put on the best clothes they could find and if they didn't have actual Union flags they were waving Jersey flags instead. The noise of so many people crammed into the square echoed off the walls of the States Chamber and the buildings around it, there was laughter and singing and so much excitement, which we shared from our wonderful vantage point. What a difference to the day five years before when we had gathered here to hear the Bailiff tell us that occupation was nigh! Finally, after much anticipation, the speakers fizzed into life and we heard the voice of Winston Churchill ringing out through St Helier. After announcing the end of hostilities and congratulating the Allies on their success, he uttered the unforgettable news that 'our dear Channel Islands are also to be freed today.' The cheer that greeted him was so long and so loud that we missed whatever it was that he said next. We joined in, of course, sharing the collective outpouring of relief and happiness.

Whatever else Mr Churchill may have been saying, the reaction to the news from some people was rather comic. I could see from my elevated position people packed into Church Street by the entrance to the church, and many more crammed into Mulcaster Street. As the news spread that we were to be liberated TODAY, they began to move in one great mass as quickly as they could in the direction of the harbour and like sheep many followed them from elsewhere, not even bothering to cheer or to listen to the Bailiff who spoke next. Their enthusiasm was of course a little premature, as our liberators did not in fact arrive for another twenty-four hours!

My only sadness was that Bill was not there to witness these events with me and I wondered where he was. I believe he was in the company of another Russian, celebrating with his own countryman.

The Bailiff spoke well and took an approach of sensible celebration. The electricity would be switched back on again that evening, and he said that 'if by chance you might happen to have an electric radio you will be allowed to listen to it.' That was greeted with lots of laughter from others as well as myself who had evidently concealed their wirelesses for the past five years. Mr Coutanche also explained that the Germans had been required to lay down their arms by one minute after midnight that day and had agreed that there would be no curfew. As people cheered that news, I clearly remember him sounding a note of caution. Remember, he told us, the Germans are the only ones who are armed in this island at the moment and they still have physical control. He urged us not to spoil things with foolish behaviour. Can you imagine how I felt, having been an unwilling part of a plot just a few days before which could have resulted in his assassination so close to our moment of deliverance? If my erstwhile comrades had been able to follow through with their plan for revolt, how different might this day have been? It would not have been Alexander Coutanche addressing the crowds in peace and joy but something different altogether, and I thank God their little coup had stalled before it even began.

As the Bailiff finished, and the joyful crowds began to disperse, I remember the feelings of tension and even of joy leaking out of me as we made our way back to the office. While all around me was happiness and laughter, I simply felt exhausted and utterly drained because I had been holding so much inside me for so long. Miss Le Seelleur and Miss Hunt just wanted to get home as quickly as possible, so I put a notice on the door to say we would be closed the following day and would re-open for business on 10 May. It was the first, and only, time in the whole Occupation that we had an unforeseen closure.

I set off towards Grosvenor Street, intent on sharing the moment with my friends. The whole of St Helier seemed alive with people rushing here and there, sharing the news and celebrating. Many were pedalling furiously into the centre on their hosepipe-tyred bikes, streaming in from the edges of town to join in. Union flags and homemade flags flew, and there was not a German in sight. Even the possession of those flags could have got people into trouble a short time before but now everything was brought out of hiding.

Mike, René and Bill were of course as happy as anyone, and we talked excitedly of what might happen the following day when we were sure the liberating forces would arrive. We arranged to meet at my office in the morning before I finally made my way home to my equally jubilant parents.

Our occupiers maintained a discreet and responsible silence. As I passed I saw one German standing guard outside a gun emplacement at West Park, opposite the Grand Hotel, and having my camera with me went to take a photograph of him on this momentous day. As I prepared to take the shot he turned his back on me, and I remember thinking how very tactless I was. While for us it was a moment of triumph, for him and his comrades it was a time of defeat and humiliation and I felt his shame very keenly. My need for reconciliation had already begun even at our hour of victory.

It was only a short distance home, and the bunting from the loft flapped proudly from the windows, the colours faded but still adding a wonderful brightness to our house. My parents had heard Mr Churchill's broadcast, and the radio was still playing the Home Service from the front room at full blast with the windows open. My exultant mother had told my father to remove it from beneath the pile of untended clothing, plug it in to the newly restored electricity supply, and turn it up as far as it would go for all the neighbours to hear.

In some ways it was rather a wasted gesture as our neighbours, the

Pooles and the Carrs, had done exactly the same! We had never known that they had retained their radio sets, and they were equally surprised by ours. We had been leading a life of unnatural reticence even from people we trusted.

I remember walking around the corner into First Tower and hearing nothing but radios, people playing them just for the sake of the noise. Music, speech, laughter, every open window confirmed just how many people had managed to defy the German confiscations. At seven o'clock that night, six in England, the chimes of Big Ben rang out from radios across the island to mark the beginning of the BBC news.

As the lights blazed out in London and people danced down the Mall to celebrate VE day, in Jersey people stayed out until whatever time they liked in celebration of the end of the curfew. After excited discussion with my parents I finally went to bed in high anticipation of what the next day would bring.

Chapter Sixteen

THE LIGHTS GO ON AGAIN

The long lack of electricity and scarcity of candles meant that I was used to going to bed and waking up in semi-darkness; in fact I never drew the curtains of my bedroom for the blackout because there was never any light to show through them. On Liberation Day, 9 May 1945, I awoke at dawn and immediately went to the window to see if the morning had brought us the deliverance we were hoping for. The sea stretched out grey and empty to the horizon, and there didn't seem to be any activity anywhere to indicate that our liberators had arrived. Rather deflated, I spent the next few hours at home listening to the wireless and simply waiting for news. At about ten I took my bicycle and made my way into St Helier, joining a gathering tide of islanders who were streaming towards the harbour in hope of being some of the first to spot a Royal Navy ship. René and Bill were ready at the office to meet me together with Miss Le Seelleur and Miss Hunt, all on their precious bicycles. Mike was nowhere to be seen, perhaps with his girlfriend celebrating…. I unlocked the office door and we all manoeuvred our bikes inside, not trusting them to be safe outside even on this important day. Locking up, we made our way down to the area of the Pomme d'Or Hotel not quite knowing where else to go. Town was by now full of people milling around, all asking the same question: where should they go? There was still no activity on the sea. Where would our liberators land? Chinese whispers and the Jersey grapevine were in full effect. Some maintained they would land in St Aubin's Bay at West Park close to my house. Many believed that story and pedalled away in that direction on their bikes in excitement. Others claimed they would sail through a channel known to be free of mines and go past St Helier to land at Havre des Pas and I met some people on bikes pedalling up Hill Street in that direction to see them. The atmosphere was electric, the air buzzing with anticipation as people debated where they should go. But still there was no news!

Finally I suggested that for the first time in five years we would be able to get onto the Victoria Pier, right at the entrance to the harbour, and if we went to the end of it we would be able to see any sign of vessels entering or leaving. The others agreed to that idea, so we made our way through the throng back to the office and regained our bicycles for the short trip. Making our way cautiously down the hill in between excited people waving flags and milling about all over the place, we headed towards Commercial Buildings which ran alongside the inner harbour wall. On we rode, around the S-bend towards the harbour wall, now just a few hundred yards away. On our left, at the bottom of Mount Bingham, were the entrances to two tunnels used by the Germans. The first, opposite La Folie Inn, was guarded on this Liberation morning by two young soldiers armed with rifles who were watching the gathering islanders nervously. Bill, René and the two young women passed them safely.

But I was at the back of the group and just as I drew level with the tunnel there was an ear-splitting BANG! like a gunshot. Two passers-by flung themselves to the ground in alarm, and the two Germans swung their rifles to aim directly at me as my bike slewed to an ungainly stop. My thoughts at that precise moment have remained with me ever since. *This is absurd. Am I to be killed within an hour of our liberation, even as a British destroyer had been spotted off Noirmont Point?*

I looked down, to see the broken and useless piece of hosepipe that had exploded from my front wheel at such an inopportune moment. Glancing down the road, I saw my erstwhile companions turn and wave at me, then laugh and carry on pedalling away towards the pier. Lifting the useless piece of pipe I looked around at the soldiers. One of them seemed to be far younger than I was, perhaps nineteen, and his face broke into a smile before he started to laugh. I replied with one of the few words of German I knew. '*Kaput!*' He smiled and laughed again and as I looked at him more thoughts raced through my mind.

My God, you are thin.

You too are a victim of this war.

Ever since you were a small boy you have been taught one misguided political faith.

You have been told to report your parents if they dared voice criticism of Hitler.

Now your faith has been swept from under your feet and you know the leader in whom you placed so much faith was a fraud.

You know that your country is in ruins.

You do not know if your parents are alive.

You do not know if your home still exists.

You only know one thing for certain, that everything you trusted in has been defeated and you are about to face an uncertain future as a prisoner of war.

But … you still have it in you to be amused by my misfortune.

At that moment I wanted more than anything to drop my piece of hosepipe and walk towards him to shake his hand. To my lasting shame I did not. I lacked the courage. Why? Because this was a public place with lots of Jersey people looking on and I worried what they might think of me. To shake the hand of a Hun on Liberation Day would for many of them be simply unthinkable.

Had there been nobody around I am sure I would have done it. I failed my true instincts. What effect might it have had on him, if he was able to tell his comrades and his family that we had laughed together and that I had shaken his hand at such a time? For the rest of my long life it has been a matter of regret to me that I was not able to overcome my fear of other people's opinions for that one short moment and simply do what I thought was right.

Some weeks later I was in conversation with a rather opinionated and well-to-do lady and expressed my satisfaction and astonishment that on Liberation Day 230 British troops had been met by 11,000 Germans without a shot being fired. 'Oh yes there was,' she cried. 'My uncle was on the Commercial Buildings and he heard it!'

Picking up my damaged bike I wheeled it on down the road for another few hundred yards before turning right and onto the pier. For five years this had been a place carefully guarded with checkpoints, barbed wire and guns, but on this wonderful day there was no-one to stop me or the many other people who had crowded there to try to spot the liberating forces. Luckily my friends had saved a good place for me and we kept our eyes peeled for any sign of activity. Suddenly there was the sound of a boat's engines and we saw, very significantly, a German naval launch going out between the pierheads. Standing to attention on board was the commander of German forces in Jersey, as erect and with as much dignity as he could muster in what must have been for him a very humiliating moment. He was accompanied by two aides. Also on the boat was the Bailiff, accompanied by the two Jersey Crown Officers whom we recognised. Everyone cheered the Bailiff who was waving his hat to the crowds. If only he had known the embarrassment he was shortly to suffer.... He was of course on his way to witness the signing of the first German surrender document on board HMS *Beagle*, in his official capacity. After the war I became rather friendly with his son, who confirmed for me what I had been told had happened when the dignitaries had arrived at the British ship. While the German commander and his aides had been greeted with a guard of honour at the companionway, Alexander Coutanche and his officers had been made to wait on one side after boarding because nobody knew who he was! The Germans were taken to the wardroom where they finally managed to persuade the naval officers that the three irate men who had accompanied them on the launch were in fact the island's civil leaders, appointed by the King of England no less! In awkward haste the mistake was rectified, and Mr Coutanche was able to have his moment of glory when he took the responsibility of personally sending the signal confirming the German surrender to Buckingham Palace. His son John told me that even years after the war his father would recount the story, which still rankled with him.

After watching the launch disappear out into St Aubin's Bay, we waited for some time for any news. None was forthcoming. I became increasingly exasperated by the poor state of my bicycle and was concerned that not being able to use it might cause me to miss out on some of the day's most important events, wherever they might be. I determined to take action before it became too late. I arranged to meet René and Bill later, and began to push my wretched bike back towards my home. Somehow, unbelievably, as I cursed my misfortune and endured the constant rattle of my front wheel over the ground, I managed to miss entirely the triumphant arrival of the liberating forces and the outpouring of emotions in front of the Pomme d'Or Hotel where the Union flag was hoisted.

I was not the only one to miss it. My mother and father were at home, still with the radio on, and preparing to celebrate with the bottle of wine my father had hoarded so carefully against the arrival of this longed-for day. The Germans at the neighbouring gun emplacement were nowhere to be seen, but even if they had been I don't believe there would have been any triumphalism from us. I had been brought up not to display my emotions in public, and was regularly reminded that only common people did so. In triumph or disaster my upper lip remained stiff.

Nonetheless there was huge excitement as we shared the precious bottle with Mr and Mrs Thresher who lived upstairs, while temporarily forgetting the pangs of hunger which had long been our constant companions. We were simply too excited to eat and food had, for the moment at least, become of secondary importance.

As we celebrated I watched streams of people go past our window heading east into town. I vividly recall how most of the men appeared to be wearing brand new black-leather ankle boots which had come in on the last shipment of the *Vega*. Just a short time before we had all been walking carefully on the thin, worn-out soles of shoes which had been pronounced past it by the cobblers several times over. The day after the *Vega* came there was a remarkable transformation and everyone in the banks, shops, farms and classrooms boasted a fine new pair of sturdy boots. I was delighted to have a pair myself. I had worn out my own shoes to the extent that I had started to wear what were known as Jersey Boots. They were heavy, simple affairs made in the Summerland factory in town in response to the pressing needs of men, women and children across the island and consisted of pieces of cast-off leather nailed onto stiff wooden soles which were extremely difficult to walk in with any dexterity. I soon developed sores on the backs of my heels, and I knew one young lady near us who would roller-skate to school along the rough pavements rather than endure their discomfort.

The rattle of steel heels clattered past our window as islanders went to celebrate their liberation with the newly arrived British soldiers, and as we finished the wine I was keen to join them. First, I thought, I must fix my bike so that I can meet my friends and go out to celebrate. Fortunately my father was able to take the broken pieces of hosepipe I had brought back with me and fashion a new tyre in time for the arrival of René and Bill who were coming to meet me at the house. At that moment, on that day of all days, I wanted to be among the friends I had made and relied upon during those five long years. We had agreed to convene at the house of Bernard and Phyllis Brée. They knew all about Bill, Louisa Gould and all the other challenges we had faced together, and their wonderful house overlooking Beaumont, which they were looking after for an officer serving in the navy, was a perfect place to meet. Still riding on the right-hand side of the road, we made our way along towards St Peter before turning off into the lanes which led up towards the house. The windows and garden had a view out over the whole of St Aubin's Bay and we could clearly see the activity in the harbour as the process of liberation continued. It was a little cold though, and I remember the sense of joy with which Phyllis turned on a bar of her electric fire. What luxury, such indulgence! René sat down on a circular object which he assumed to be some kind of seat, only to leap up again, trousers steaming, when he realised it was a heater. His actions allowed us all to see the large patch covering the backside of his trousers, which had subsequently been repaired with a smaller patch on top where the original had worn through.

Phyllis opened a bottle of something she had hoarded and we were all in great spirits. Bill in particular, in his emotional way, was crying and hugging everyone in joy while we endeavoured to keep ourselves in check in a very British way. The Brée's little boy Michael ran around excitedly, and as we laughed and celebrated I felt myself finally able to believe that this could indeed be the end.

To go with the bottle, Phyllis brought out a plateful of small cakes which she had made at no little sacrifice to her store of provisions. Cakes! We hadn't seen anything like that for five years—but the extraordinary thing was that none of us wanted to eat them. Our excitement was such that all appetite had been forgotten, despite Phyllis going around with them begging us to have a taste! When we went outside onto the veranda we could hear noise coming from down the hill. Before the war there had been two blocks of flats there which were taken mostly by wealthy people who were not of Jersey stock and evacuated before the Germans arrived, leaving their flats uninhabited. The Germans decided to move the remaining people from one block and put them into the other, using the empty block to billet troops. On Liberation night lights, music and laughter rang out from the British-occupied block, while the other remained in darkness and silence.

While there was no curfew that night and I was elated that our ordeal was over I was still, as always, conscious of my duty to work. So it was that while the others prepared to continue celebrating until the early hours I called it a day at a reasonable time. As I rolled down the hill on my clunking wheels I could see lights shining out all over the island.

Chapter Seventeen

OUT WITH THE OLD

As the following day dawned I remembered my promise to our customers that we would be open at our usual time that morning despite my strong temptation to be a part of the celebrations. I swallowed whatever was available on my shelf for breakfast, grabbed my bike and began to ride towards town. As I pedalled I could not help but get caught up in the atmosphere of joy and excitement, and by the time I reached the office I had resolved that this would be the second day of unusual closure for our business. After all, who would want to come to see us on such a day? Having explained to the other staff, who were equally thrilled with what was going on, I locked up and headed back down the street towards the Weighbridge. The rest of the day is simply a blur to me. The atmosphere had not waned and I roamed wherever the spirit took me, past marching troops in khaki on Conway Street, jostling with crowds of jubilant Jersey people who had come from far and wide to celebrate. Men, women and children were laughing, crying, cheering and shouting, falling over themselves to welcome the heroes from over the sea who had come to liberate us from the Germans. Some people were waving autograph books under the noses of any soldier they could find. The soldiers themselves often seemed a bit sheepish and perplexed. They were all very ordinary-looking chaps, typical Tommies in tin hats, who seem to have been prepared to save people who had been brutally and savagely treated for five years. Maybe they had seen the newsreel footage of the liberation of Belsen and other concentration camps and were expecting the worst. They were perhaps bemused that we were not in rags and covered in bruises but happy and exultant, ready to welcome them with joy.

Some of course were even more welcoming than others. Teenaged girls and young women were most keen to be seen with their own particular Tommy, and there was quite a competition to secure one for themselves. For some it was simply swapping the colour of the uniform.

Jerrybags, as they were known, had become a firm feature of island life over the long years of occupation, although I was not encouraged to use the term by my mother. They were 'loose women', or 'not as good as she ought to be', and considered well below our lower-middle class.

It had begun early on, when the soldiers who came to the island all seemed to be impossibly tall, handsome and athletic, immaculately groomed and with impeccable manners. Who can blame a young girl if they made an impression on her? Less forgivable perhaps were the older women, many of them married, who chose to take German lovers. Some of course were very discreet and people were scarcely aware of what was going on. Others flaunted it in the High Street, walking arm in arm or hand in hand with their very own German.

Mrs —, who lived close to us, had said goodbye to her husband when he left to fight the Germans before the invasion, yet one of the Germans from the bunker opposite our house was often seen slipping in and out of her house in the dark. No-one made a fuss, and when the war ended her husband came home and the marriage continued as if nothing had happened.

To me, as long as it was discreet and unnoticed I considered it to be an unfortunate but inevitable consequence of curious women being presented with the sudden arrival of hundreds of fit, well-dressed young men. Liaisons were naturally bound to happen.

Now, while the Tommies may not have been quite as handsome or well-dressed, they were at least on the right side; and countless Jersey girls were very pleased to make their acquaintance! While I saw no evidence of islanders taking their revenge on women who had transgressed, I was told quite clearly that at least two women had to be rescued by British soldiers from angry Jersey people keen to shave off their hair. I am glad I didn't see such a thing because I feel I would have been honour-bound to have intervened. While the women may have been foolish, it was unacceptable to me that any street gang should have the right to be their judge and jury, let alone carry out arbitrary punishment. My mother would have regarded any such action as thoroughly reprehensible, equally heinous as the women's transgressions had been in the first place. Fortunately for many of them, the best known Jerrybags quickly became Tommybags and thereby gained some protection.

It was noticeable how few Germans there were about. We had been told that the authorities on both sides had come to the agreement that there should not be a single German soldier in uniform within the boundary of St Helier; and not a single British one outside it. This led to all kinds of complications as the two sides tried to come to terms with what had happened and was particularly irksome for any Jersey-born soldiers who had landed with the liberating troops. They naturally wanted to get home to see their families as quickly as possible only to be told at the boundary checkpoints that they were not allowed to roam any further. I wonder how many of them managed to exchange their uniform for civilian clothes to make the crossing…. As more Tommies came ashore the celebrations dragged on well into the night. I enjoyed it enormously while all the time wondering how on earth I was to catch up on all the work I had to do! I also wondered how our poor island would recover physically from the unpleasant changes visited upon it by our occupiers.

The Germans had turned our island into what they imagined to be an impregnable fortress whose bunkers, barbed wire and minefields had defaced our beaches, streets and woodland. We were used to seeing the Greenfly constantly buzzing around the defences, carrying out drills, standing guard or marching to and fro … and suddenly they were no longer there. The wire and barricades were left untended. There was no-one to shout if you crossed the line and approached a bunker, no-one to move you along if you were standing in the way. Naturally for some, especially boys, the bunkers and guns became an instant source of fascination and were ransacked for souvenirs and artefacts. Many an islander was seen with a German helmet, binoculars, or other item which they had 'liberated' from the abandoned defences. I watched them go into the bunker just opposite our house, but for some reason felt no compunction to follow them. I could also observe from my bedroom the bands of former Wehrmacht soldiers who were detailed to start the operation to rid us of their clutter. All over the island they ripped up railway lines, coiled up barbed wire and searched out buried mines which would have to be made safe. So many of these were laid that they were still being discovered decades later hidden in Jersey's brown soil. The soldiers, perhaps relieved to be well fed and treated humanely, used to wave and smile at us as they were driven past from their garrisons in the west to their work.

I was delighted. My beautiful island had been blighted by the Nazis' warlike apparatus and quite apart from their physical ugliness, the defences represented psychological dominance and mental oppression which simply could not have been allowed to continue. Symbolically and physically the signs of our occupation were being rubbed away. The tank traps on the beach were taken away, our wonderful sands were unspoilt once more, and it was a delight to feel the squelch of the *quoc*, or green seaweed, between my toes again.

Four days after Liberation there was more excitement on the beach. Peering out of my window in the early morning light I saw dark shapes heading towards the shore from out on the dawn-grey sea. Only about 230 British troops had arrived on Liberation Day itself and now the reinforcements were on their way. As the boats drew closer into the bay I realised they were not heading to the harbour as I expected, but sailing straight into the beach! My God, I thought, what are they doing? Don't they realise there is no depth of water here and they will run aground on the sand? Slowly but surely they ploughed on through the small waves until the inevitable happened and they ground to a halt on the beach in a line that ran right across from St Helier past my house. Then unbelievably the bows of the ships opened, ramps came down onto the sand and jeeps and trucks and men began to pour out. I watched fascinated as these landing craft, similar to those which had landed the troops to liberate

184

France, disgorged wave after wave of soldiers and equipment. Military policemen in red caps took charge and waved traffic here and there across the beach, columns of men lined up and marched off, and crowds of islanders swarmed down to cheer them ashore.

In fact, my enjoyment of the coast was nearly my undoing. With some friends just a few short weeks later I went to Beauport for a walk around the paths of the southwest, after having been told the whole area had been safely cleared of mines. I led them to the cliffs on the right of the bay where I knew there had been a path and we marched our way across the grass, when suddenly to my horror I saw a fence ahead which I did not recognise. Of greater concern was that there was a series of signs on the fence, facing away from us. We recognised those signs, despite them facing the wrong way. They had been everywhere just a month or so before. *Achtung Minen!* We had walked into a minefield that had not been cleared. I called to my friends to stop immediately and explained my error as calmly as I could. Under the circumstances they reacted very well and followed my advice to retreat down the hill following as far as possible their previous footsteps. After what seemed like an age we were sure we had come to a safe area. When I checked later, I was able to confirm that it was indeed an uncleared minefield from which we had been very lucky to escape. René was one of those with me, and how ironic would it have been if we had been killed by carelessness in such a way after the risks we had run during the Occupation!

While I had no real desire to investigate the bunker opposite my house, there was one on the cliffs at Noirmont Point which seemed rather more interesting. It was a huge, multi-storeyed observation tower with a steel cupola on top from which protruded the telescopic eyes of a sophisticated range-finding system. You could enter from the top and make your way steadily downwards into the bowels of the bunker below. It was too much to resist, and with a friend on the weekend after Liberation I rode out there to have a look. Even though it was broad daylight outside it was virtually pitch dark and very musty once you got past the huge steel doors. Groping our way down the narrow concrete stairs, holding on to the slim metal handrail, we made our way down almost to the lowest levels. Just as we were about to explore the darkened bunker rooms we heard voices echoing down from above. Young, children's voices, and light cautious footsteps. Rather naughtily we hushed each other and hatched a diabolical plan. Waiting until the voices and footsteps were almost upon us I let go with some of the very few words of German I knew, at the top of my voice. "*Raus!! 'Raus!! Verboten!! Schnell!!*' As they yelled and turned to run up the stairs, we followed them. '*Wir kommen!! Schnell, schnell!!*' Stampeding up the stairs we saw the bright rays of daylight as they flung open the door at the top and ran for all they were worth out across the common in their new Red Cross boots and I saw one of them fall and split the knee of his trousers as he lunged for his bike. As we followed still yelling they jumped on their bikes and pedalled furiously away ...

Chapter Eighteen

AN UNCERTAIN FUTURE

By the time the initial euphoria had worn off I was determined to get the office open and functioning once more. There was some degree of urgency because as the Germans left and people began to take back their homes and possessions there was a clamour to get everything insured properly. Cars were suddenly very popular again, as the vehicles that the Germans had taken from their Jersey owners had all been assembled together at Springfield Stadium, together with many other items which had no known owner, and people were buying them quickly and hurrying to see us to get them covered. It was right at this time that a rather imperious British officer came to the office and asked for me. 'Le Sueur?' Yes, I answered. 'You are required to come with me to assist in some important work. Please leave what you are doing and come this way.' What?! Just as we were starting to make some headway, what on earth could he want with me?

I was taken to the British Hotel not very far down the road from our office which had until recently been a billet for German officers—and was now a billet for British officers. But on this day it was also serving another purpose, as I gathered from the crowds of Spanish workers milling around outside. I was marched in and ushered upstairs past further lines of chattering Spaniards who were waiting at a doorway. My escort knocked and was called to 'Come!'

Inside, a harassed-looking British officer sat behind a desk laden with papers and pencils. He stood as I entered and offered his hand. Also in the room was what seemed to be a high-ranking Russian who greeted me in a rather perfunctory way. He hardly seemed aware of my presence, perhaps because he had clearly been drinking. 'Sit down, Mr Le Sueur,' the British officer said. 'We need your help with some Spanish translation.'

He explained to me that he was part of a team sent to the island to research reports of the ill-treatment and killing of forced workers and slaves, especially any Russians—in order to prove to Stalin that the British were determined to exact justice for any of his countrymen who had fallen victim to the Nazi tyranny. He wanted to ask the Spanish workers what they had seen, and whether they could identify any of the guards who might have committed such acts while they were still in the island. The only problem, of course, was that neither he nor any of his team could actually speak Spanish—and that was where I came in. He required me to help interrogate all the Spaniards who had been rounded up in the island, all of whom seemed to be either inside this hotel or gathered noisily around it. I was given to understand that a refusal would be looked upon very dimly, so I prepared to do my duty and took a seat next to the officer, facing the tipsy Russian who seemed to have no interest in the proceedings whatsoever and in fact soon lay down on the bed still wearing his boots and promptly fell asleep. It seemed incomprehensible to him that we were even bothering to concern ourselves about people who had failed in their duty to the Motherland to fight until the last bullet. I was given to understand that he was the military attaché to the Soviet Embassy in London. Uncle Joe Stalin had already washed his hands of hundreds of thousands of men who had dared to allow themselves to be captured and I'm sure this man felt the same way.

Sadly, I was not able to be of much use. The British major particularly wanted to ascertain the truth of stories that Russian people had been beaten to death and their bodies disposed of in liquid concrete being used for the construction of the island's defences. While many Spaniards said they were aware of beatings and abuse, none of them could—or would—say that they had actually witnessed any such deaths. I had myself always been sceptical of these rumours, because while I feel sure that there were some Organisation Todt foremen capable of doing this, I wondered how it would be possible to throw a body into liquid concrete that was already full of reinforcing rods. Try as we might, not one of them gave us anything which could be used to identify a single German who had disposed of any Russian in this way. To my despair this took several days, and all the while the work at my office was piling up higher and higher. I had become a cog in the military machine and it seemed in no hurry to let go of me. Finally I went to an acquaintance of mine, an elderly man who had lived in South America and spoke quite fluent Spanish. Would he be interested in doing his bit for King and Country, I wondered? Fortunately he was, and the next day I marched him into the British Hotel and announced to the British officer that he was my replacement, starting immediately. The Russian didn't seem to care. I thought myself well rid of the drunken Major Gruzdev and hoped I would never see him again—only to find very soon afterwards that he had been assigned a Russian translator of his own. Bill.

Bill, like Paul Mühlbach, had declared himself to the British authorities as soon as they arrived, hoping no doubt to be well treated and allowed some freedom. He stayed on with Mike and René at Grosvenor Street until the vodka-swilling Gruzdev arrived and finally realised he needed a translator. Could the British help him to find one? Checking their records they realised that Bill was an obvious choice and he was installed with due solemnity in the Fort d'Auvergne Hotel at Havre des Pas where the Russian also had his quarters. For some weeks he was based there and managed to stay in touch with me and his other Jersey friends, only to come to me one day with his concerns about a list he was helping to compile for the major. Recording the names of every single Russian in the island, the list had been compiled by combing all the German camp records and details which had been supplied to the British. What alarmed Bill was that he was on the list too—and there seemed to be no differentiation between any of the names upon it. Some may have been civilian prisoners, some may have been officers, some may have been escapees like him—but to the Russian bureaucrats they were all the same. Those who had joined General Vlasov's forces as part of the German Army and who as such could perhaps legitimately be seen as traitors were there. Even the women who had fled Russia at the time of the revolution and were now naturalised British living at Snow Hill were initially on the list, despite having risked their lives to shelter escapees. To the Russian mind, it appeared, that if you were born Russian you stayed Russian—and you belonged in Russia. We were not overly concerned when Bill was finally shipped away, without much warning and without a farewell party, as we believed that he would be returning to a reformed, modernised Soviet Union. In fact, he was headed first to England and it was to be a long time before he was able to tell me the full story of what happened next.

On being docked in Southampton Bill and his companions were told that they would be taken on trucks to a transit camp where they would await transport back to their homeland. Of course, they were not told that as people who had spent time as prisoners of the Germans they were all under suspicion. The Soviet attaché warned them that as they drove through the English countryside there would be people waiting for them at each village who would wave and smile and perhaps even throw them cigarettes—but this was all put on, a show to pretend that the English were now their friends when in fact they were not. Bill knew this to be a lie and hoped very much that he could stay in England. Once at the camp they were told in no uncertain terms that this was to be their home until they were shipped to Russia—and on no account were they to leave. One man who actively took great exception to that instruction was George Koslov, the Russian who had been sheltered by Louisa Gould's sister before I arrived there with Bill. George was certainly not prepared to be taken back to face goodness knows what treatment from Stalin, and he chose to make a break for it, as we will see.

Bill, on the other hand, as an official interpreter, had a certain degree of freedom and was able to get to a public telephone from where he called René Franoux who happened to be in London at the time. He asked him to visit him at the camp urgently. René went the next day, and later explained to me what transpired. Bill had told him about an extraordinary meeting he'd had with an Englishman who worked in the camp kitchens. The man, who was obviously some kind of agent, had beckoned to him and then led him away from the camp to a spinney of trees where they could talk unobserved and beyond the range of any secret microphones. The man, who looked the picture of innocence in his kitchen clothes, asked Bill if he would like to have an English bank account into which money would be put from time to time and would always be useful if and when he came back to England. His unsubtle attempt at recruitment went rather over the head of Bill, who explained to the man that he already had an English bank account, thank you, in Jersey, and had quite a few pounds in it too after all the artwork he had sold. (It was still in my name as he obviously couldn't have opened it under his own.) Bill didn't understand what the man was driving at, especially when he asked him to be a 'sleeper'—the secret service term for an agent who might be inactive for years until called into action. Bill's understanding of the term was that it referred to someone who liked to stay in bed!

As Bill recounted the story, René realised that the man was clearly an MI6 agent hoping to set Bill up as a source of information about Soviet Russia. If only he had known, as we did, that Bill was just about the last person you would choose as a satisfactory spy. Irascible, inflexible, given to mood swings and emotional in temperament, he would have drawn far too much attention and would not have been able to keep quiet about his role. Perhaps we were naive in our youth, but we really hoped that after the elation of mutual victory there could be some kind of mutual respect and a new dawn in Anglo-Soviet relations. There was certainly an assumption on our part that it would be quite easy for Bill to move from the Soviet Union to other countries should he wish to, and perhaps even return to Jersey where there was a girl whom he hoped to marry. Sadly it was not to be. After spending some time in the camp he was bundled once more into a train to the south coast and then a ferry across the sea. From there he and countless others were transported across northern Europe and across the border into the Soviet zone of occupied Germany. Shortly afterwards his lover in Jersey received a hastily written letter from him with a British Armed Forces stamp on it, posted in Berlin. He'd handed it to a British soldier he'd met in the street and asked him to post it, explaining that he was forbidden to write officially and had to resort to subterfuge to get his message through. He loved her, he wanted to marry her, but things were difficult and would she wait for him, he would return as quickly as he could? There was no address for her to reply. All over the Continent there were similar tales of separation and loss as millions of men and women were uprooted and pulled apart by the aftermath of the war and the beginning of the Cold War. Alas for Bill, the object of his desires had already moved on and had formed a serious relationship with a British soldier who had come over with the liberating forces, so perhaps it was as well that she was unable to respond to him. It was twenty years before any of us saw or heard from him again.

Paul Mühlbach was another who came to see me at the office shortly after Liberation. I was sitting at my desk working at the backlog of business when there was a tap at the window, and there in plain sight at last stood Paul, still wearing my friend's nice blue suit but with the ill-applied hair dye mostly gone. He explained that he had officially declared himself to the British and was now a prisoner of war, although he wasn't being held in any sort of camp. Rather, because of his story, they had arranged some temporary accommodation for him before his imminent transport to England. As the clamour of my customers grew more urgent he strained to get his head up to the level of the window to explain when he expected to be taken away and what might happen to him. Unfortunately because of the noise of customers behind me and the incessant ringing of the telephone I couldn't hear everything he was saying or indeed spend much time with him, something I very much regretted for some time afterwards. After everything we had been through together there was now a real warmth between us and I counted him as a friend. Leaning out of the window I implored him to contact me when possible as he knew my address and to stay in touch. After all, we had come through some extraordinary times together, working with a common aim against a common enemy and that can form a very strong bond between people. I never knew whether he was simply a dedicated individual with strongly held beliefs or if he was a small cog in the bigger Communist machine hoping to establish dominance over Europe, but I would certainly miss him. Finally I had to say goodbye, as the call of business was becoming too strong to ignore, and he went off on the next stage of his life's adventure.

Some weeks later I finally heard from him by mail. He had landed a most interesting job, working as an inspector of the units of the British Army who were trying to re-educate German prisoners of war in England. Starting with those who had been prisoners the longest, they taught the virtues of democracy, an independent judiciary, the concept of presumed innocence until the proof of guilt, freedom of ideas and of expression and speech; all of those things that had been brainwashed out of most Germans by the oppressive Nazi regime. It was referred to as 'de-Nazification'. Paul was told to visit the unit in Colchester where this work was being done particularly well by a combination of British and former German officers. Sure enough, when he got there he found that one German in particular was most effusive about the wrongs of the Nazis, and how western democracy held the key to happiness and prosperity in the world. He explained at length to his quite literally captive audience that they must abandon their faith in the now dead Führer and embrace democracy for the good of the world. Paul immediately recognised this paragon of liberal thought as none other than former Hauptwachtmeister Heinz Carl Wölfle—the second-in-charge of the Geheime Feldpolizei in Jersey, scourge of any attempts at civil insurrection, and he of my failed attempt to glean a few fragments of sustenance from a field in St Ouen. This amused me greatly and taught me that there is a certain kind of individual with the right abilities and charm who can talk his way into, or indeed out of, any situation. Paul ensured that Herr Wölfle didn't hold his new post for very long, which is a shame because apparently he was doing it very well!

Eventually Paul was released from captivity and returned to Koblenz where his mother and sister were still living. I had several letters from him and managed to eke out some more of his Occupation story of which I had been unaware at the time. Extraordinarily, he seemed to have been in regular contact with the senior American officer in the US prison camp at Mount Bingham. (Some of the Americans had either been brought from St Malo as German captives after the fighting in France in August 1944, or been rescued from the sea after crashing in their aircraft. A significant number, however, had been taken prisoner in a daring raid by the Germans who had sailed across to attack Granville in early March 1945.) While the Germans were still in charge he had found a way to make contact with the prisoners; I am told that Colonel Reybold was sure that if the communist-led mutiny had gone ahead, the Germans guarding the camp would have joined it and released their captives.

Paul stayed in touch with the Colonel after the war and wrote to him asking if he could visit America at some point. Was he, as a dedicated communist, hoping to see for himself the land of western capitalism in order to understand how to bring it down—or had he been recruited himself by western intelligence? I never found out. Shortly afterwards he crossed into East Germany, contact between us ceased immediately and I never heard from him again. If he was working for Allied intelligence then perhaps a double agent ostensibly working for the British had already denounced him to the Stasi, the East German secret police. The spy Kim Philby had been responsible for similar actions and I have always wondered if he could have been the one to betray Paul.

George Koslov was another Russian I knew who had been transported to Guildford with his fellow countrymen from Jersey. I'd met George at Ivy Forster's house soon after Louisa Gould had been compromised and had moved him away from there very quickly to another hiding place before entrusting him to others for the rest of the Occupation. He'd done well and been sheltered by a better class of people including the island's chief surgeon, Mr Halliwell. In fact, some Germans were due to be billeted in Mr Halliwell's house and came to inspect it, whereupon they were introduced to George as the surgeon's gardener. George was moved on as soon as they left, and once the Germans returned they asked where he had gone. Mr Halliwell informed them that George had been rubbish as a gardener and had been sacked, which they were quite happy to believe! George's itinerate life led him to a former army officer's house, then to a house shared by two doctors in Bonne Nuit, and eventually to a butcher's in St Martin where he had to work hard for his keep. Full of delight, he once regaled me with the tale of a funeral cortège which he joined on its way from St Martin to St Helier. The local carpenter made the coffin, there was a glass-sided horse-drawn hearse and carriages full of mourners all in black behind—one of whom was George. People doffed their hats, including some German soldiers, as they passed by at Five Oaks. The hearse finally reached its destination in town with due pomp and ceremony before being taken into the funeral parlour ... where the coffin was carefully opened to reveal a freshly slaughtered pig ready for distribution to certain hungry and wealthy people who were in great need of meat.

He was a very different character to Bill, far more intelligent, lively and with an overwhelming personality. He was also very good-looking and a serial philanderer who never seemed to be without a girl who simply couldn't resist the charms of a man on the run. After Liberation he was one of the many Russians rounded up under the tender care of Major Gruzdev and shipped off to Guildford.

When they got to the camp, George was under no illusions about what was in store for them when they finally returned to Mother Russia and resolved to attempt to escape, come what may. His first try got him nowhere and meant that he was held in handcuffs for the onward journey across the Channel and onto a train, where he was watched by armed guards as the carriage trundled inexorably eastwards. He described everything that happened next to me later, and his story is one of daring and excitement equal to any novel or film. Seizing a moment during the night when the guards were distracted, he managed to kick one of them between the legs, put his foot through a window and hurl himself out into the darkness. He knew that if he let his body go limp there was at least a chance that he would land with bruises but hopefully without anything broken, and be able to make some kind of getaway. It worked. Picking himself up he fully expected the train to be screeching to a halt on the assumption that the injured guard would pull the communication cord; but it puffed inexorably onwards into the gloom and was soon lost to sight. He was lucky. It didn't have far to go until it crossed from the western area of Germany that was occupied by the Americans and British into the Soviet zone, and I have little doubt that as a troublemaker he would have quietly been made to disappear once behind the barbed wire.

His adventure was not yet over, however. Waiting in a forest until dawn, he set off with the sun at his back until he came to a road which he followed to a farm which still bore the scars of war. Germany in the summer of 1945 remained in chaos as the country picked itself up after the conflict and he found the farm in rubble and populated only by dead animals. Finding a rough metal post he rubbed his handcuffs up and down on it until he broke himself free and started to walk further along the road. Eventually a British army jeep spotted him—he was wearing old British battle dress—and asked him who he was and where he was bound. 'I am Polish,' he told them, 'I am separated from my unit, can you help me?' The Tommies agreed, loaded him into the jeep and took him to their camp where they introduced him to the officer in charge as a misplaced Pole. But George was nonplussed when the officer immediately greeted him in fluent Polish! He was unlucky to have stumbled upon one of the very few British officers who actually spoke that language, and realised he would have to come clean. George told him the full story, including his escape and hiding in Jersey. All he wanted to do, he said, was to avoid being retaken by the Russians and eventually to seek protection in Britain. If he was returned to Russia, he would be in severe trouble. Luckily for him, the officer was sympathetic, despite a firm undertaking between the British government and Stalin that all liberated prisoners of war would be repatriated. He was given a job in the kitchens while things settled down on the understanding that he would eventually be able to return to Britain and ask for asylum. Had it been Bill, he would have cried with relief and knuckled down to a few months of peeling potatoes, happy to do what he was told, but George had far too much charm, imagination and drive simply to wait around. Besides, there were no girls in the camp.

He managed to abscond without much difficulty and headed north in the hope of stowing away on a boat headed across the Channel, but his luck ran out when he was picked up by military police at a Belgian port, where the authorities decided that they should follow the rules and hand him over to his countrymen. After spending the night in a cell he was loaded onto a jeep and driven to Brussels where the commissars were waiting. As usual though he managed to work his charm, and when the jeep slowed down for some lights he simply leapt out and ran for it. He expected the soldiers to make a screeching turn and come after him but they simply drove on to a place where it was safe to manoeuvre and came around very slowly. I'm sure that thanks to George's charm their supervision was perhaps not quite as strict as it could have been and they seemed in no real hurry to pursue him. Dodging between the few cars that were on the street hooting at him, he turned repeatedly left, right, right, left, until he came upon a side street that led onto a huge building that looked like a church. In he went with sore legs and heaving lungs, and hid inside a large cupboard at one end. Immediately a voice behind a velvet curtain said, '*Oui, mon fils?*' … it was of course a confession box and George certainly had a lot to confess. By now exhausted and very frightened he told his story to the priest, who gave him the sympathy he needed. He was taken to a small room up a spiral staircase in the clock tower and told to stay there until it was dark; some food would be brought to him. The priest was as good as his word and returned with two bicycles, one for each of them. George was used to riding from his time in Jersey and followed at a discreet distance until they arrived at the priest's own house, where he was made welcome. Finally, after so many lucky escapes, he resolved not to look a gift horse in the mouth and to do as he was told. His knowledge of French, picked up before the war at his upper-middle class home in St Petersburg, where everyone had French maids and governesses, stood him in good stead and he was able to converse with those who came to see him. After he was finally freed his favourite place became Sark. He loved the solitude.

George's end was suitably poetic. He died in Bavaria just a few years ago in a castle which was a home for elderly men, in a room which had its own TV and telephone, all paid for by the German state. He told me they looked after him very well.

Chapter Nineteen

.... THE COST

As the business began to establish a routine we also had to say goodbye to Jean Le Seelleur, who had rented the spare office space in the building on behalf of her company for the duration of the war. I would be sorry to see her go, as she was a smiling, cheerful soul who seemed dedicated to both her work and her husband. I was therefore astonished to be told by someone else, shortly before she left, that she had in fact been the courier who had taken clandestine messages from Paul and his communist comrades to Colonel Reybold at the American POW camp! She had smuggled them rolled up inside the handlebars of her bike and had flirted with her innocent-looking, pleasant face at the Germans manning the barriers nearby. Some people might have sniffed at her behaviour, thinking she was a Jerrybag, but in fact she had been risking an awful lot taking messages from a secret communist group to a camp full of American soldiers. The consequences had she been caught were unthinkable—yet none of us had the faintest clue that she was engaged in such activities. Full of admiration for her pluck and her secrecy I asked her about it in the office before she left. She simply giggled and turned back to her papers.

I believe that she was typical of the people who really did any kind of work that could loosely be described as resistance in the island. The only ones that I heard actually claim to have been resisters were those such as Leslie and Norman, or people who had never, as far as I knew, lifted a finger to do anything of any consequence. One should remember that any kind of real resistance was simply impossible in an island where one in every five people was a German and there was no chance of any arms drops or support from the mainland. Even if there had been, any kind of collective action, armed or otherwise, would have been utterly futile in such a small island where there was nowhere to hide, prepare or train. In fact there was very little attempt to claim that Jersey had any kind of resistance movement, perhaps because people were just relieved that it was finally all over and their daily lives could resume once more.

I did not want to describe myself as a *resistant*, whatever the cachet attributed to that title after the war. I was not described thus by anyone else, I was not part of any organised band, and only helped on the fringes of one small group engaged in the occasional activity. To be a resistant implies a full-time dedication to the task, at the expense of everyday life; I always tried to put my family and my duties at work first.

My parents had known about Bill shortly before the end. Certain that the Germans were at their last gasp, I asked my mother if it might be all right to bring a friend home to meet them. He came on his bike and I made the introductions, only for my mother to pick up on Bill's accent immediately. 'You're foreign, aren't you?', she asked. The penny dropped. 'I knew there was something, Bobby!' she exclaimed. 'I thought you knew a Russian!' Mothers, as any child knows, can be very perceptive. I think in hindsight she was a lot brighter than I was, a gentle person who never talked unnecessarily and was extremely good at keeping a secret. She assured us both that she would never tell a soul. My father on the other hand was shocked. 'Oh my goodness, you were taking a risk! Thank heavens you weren't caught!' Thank heavens indeed. I cannot abide physical pain and I am sure that if the Germans had questioned me with any kind of brutality I would have been prepared to tell them anything they wanted to know, some of it true and some of it false, in order to make it stop. I had ensured that no-one who was involved in looking after Bill or any of the other poor souls knew any more than they had to. What they didn't know they couldn't tell. I had seen at once very early on the need for secrecy and it had stood me in good stead.

Of my Jersey friends who had been arrested, it was not long after liberation that we had distressing news. Harold Le Druillenec, sentenced to five months in prison at the beginning of July 1944, had ended up in the appalling concentration camp of Belsen after being processed through several other Nazi camps. He endured hunger, extreme thirst and barbaric treatment but somehow managed to survive. When the camp was liberated he was eating grass to keep himself alive, and was thought to be the only British person to come home from that dreadful place. He gave a long and detailed description of his ordeal to a war crimes tribunal. I rarely saw him once he returned to Jersey, but those who did told me that he talked often and with bitterness about his experience.

Of Louisa Gould, the news was even worse. Sentenced to two years in prison, she was shipped to France on 30 June 1944 and dragged through the Nazi penal system. From a prison in St Malo she was taken, together with her brother Harold and Berthe Pitolet, to Jacques-Cartier prison in Rennes. In a terrible irony, the prison was bombed in an RAF raid on the nearby railway station and some of the old walls were so badly damaged that some prisoners were able to escape—among them Berthe Pitolet, who pleaded with Mrs Gould to come with her. Mrs Gould could not be persuaded and insisted on staying and awaiting her fate. The younger woman crawled through a hole in the wall, losing a shoe in the process, and ran off through the burning streets of Rennes to eventual safety. The city was liberated a short time afterwards, but it was too late for Mrs Gould. Pushed into a train with hundreds of other prisoners, she was carried for miles across France towards the Swiss border, where incredibly the train drew to a halt immediately next to another going in a different direction—and in the truck opposite her was Harold. They managed to exchange a few words and Mrs Gould gave him some cigarettes, before the trains went clanking on their way. Harold's train was taking him towards Belsen—while hers was headed for the infamous women's camp at Ravensbrück. In poor health, unable to work, she was killed there in February 1945. A French-Jewish woman who knew her in the camp and heard her story had the theory that the name Gould appeared similar to the Jewish name Gold, and the Germans may have suspected her of altering it to avoid detection. I am certain that if they had confronted her and asked, 'Are you a Jew?', she would have spat in their faces and cried 'That's no business of yours!' I'm sure that she would have been able to demonstrate the authenticity of her Breton maiden name ending in '-ec' had she chosen to, but she was never one to bow to that kind of oppression.

I was enormously sad that such a heroic, warm-hearted and loving woman could have met such a wretched end. I was told of it by her sister's family, the Forsters, and we mourned her loss together. In doing something for another mother's son, she had paid with her life.

Was it worth it? I'm sure she would have said yes. At certain times in life when there is a strong point of principle involved there must not be any compromise, and she never compromised on her feelings at all. While what happened to her was desperately unfortunate, her actions exposed her to such risk and she was well aware of what could befall her.

While her capture may have been inevitable, it was distressing to be told that the blame for her betrayal may have lain at the door of her neighbours. It appears that a letter was sent to the Germans informing them that Mrs Gould was sheltering a Russian. After the war our old friend Heinz Carl Wölfle, of the German Field Police, helped British officers who were investigating the case. They found the original letter, and another confirming receipt of reward money, and Herr Wölfle identified the handwriting as that of two sisters who lived close to Mrs Gould in St Ouen—Maud and Lily Vibert. Many have since wondered why they were not questioned or prosecuted over these unproven claims, but I don't see how the Jersey authorities could possibly have done so. Galling though it may be to some, there were very good reasons for their forbearance.

To begin with, if they had arrested them, what could they have charged them with? There was no Jersey legislation to cover this kind of situation, as the island had never imagined that it would be occupied. In order to be charged with a crime, you have to break a law—but there was no law to break. Moreover, they would have had to send a local centenier to arrest them, as only the parish police have the right of arrest in Jersey. What would he have told them they were charged with? Even if the matter did get to court, which is highly unlikely, the chief prosecution witness would have been none other than Hauptwachtmeister Heinz Carl Wölfle, and a good defence lawyer would have argued that his evidence was surely inadmissible in a Jersey court. While there was certainly an appetite in the island to visit justice on anyone who had betrayed their fellow islanders, in this case there was very little that could be done.

Let us not forget that all through the Occupation some Jersey people had been defying the Germans in all kinds of ways, by hiding slaves, listening to the radio, or selling things on the black market. Very many of them were victim to the same attempts at betrayal, and the archive is full of badly written notes suggesting the Germans look beneath the floorboards of a certain house or ask Mrs So-and-So where she got that piece of bacon. While Jersey may have had its brave people willing to take risks to defy the occupiers, there were inevitably those who went the other way. Most of the denunciations were acts of petty revenge, spite and unpleasantness; the wife whose husband had an affair, the farmer in a dispute over land with his neighbour, the jealous work colleague or bitter lover, all could find a way to take revenge by writing an anonymous letter to the German commander's headquarters at Government House and they did just that, *just as they would in any society under such circumstances.*

After the war there was, if not solidarity and forgiveness, then a sense that one could not live in such a small island with mutual hatred forever, and there seemed to be a tacit understanding that we would have to move on with our lives.

Chapter Twenty

REDEMPTION

Twenty years after the end of the war Bill was living in Siberia, impoverished and under constant KGB surveillance due to his past association with decadent westerners such as myself. He was not allowed to take on a job of any significance or to live in any homes which were remotely desirable. He had finally given up on ever being reunited with his love in Jersey and had married, only for the union to fall apart under the pressure of constant observation and state oppression which wore out his poor wife's nerves. Then early one morning there was a hammering at the door and two men with revolvers pushed their way into his little apartment. 'Pack a small bag,' they told him. 'You are coming with us.' He knew what that could mean and begged permission to go to the lavatory. One of the men followed him and made it very obvious that there was little point trying to get away. They escorted him outside where a car was waiting and put him between them on the back seat in the time-honoured manner for policemen who were concerned their quarry might try to get away. But rather than taking him to a prison or punishment camp, they headed to the airport, where they took seats on a civilian flight once all the other passengers had boarded. Their seats were right at the back and once again he was in the middle with their revolvers poking him through their overcoats. Naturally they had not seen fit to tell him where they were going but as the plane took off the sun was rising and he worked out that they were heading west, away from the dawn. The question was: to what destination?

It turned out to be Moscow. Disembarking last, he was marched through the airport and into another car, which finally stopped outside a large building, once very grand, perhaps the town house of a Muscovite aristocrat in the days of the Tsar. Still the bruisers on either side would not tell him what was going on. They took him up the stairs, through some double doors which were opened for them and into a large sparsely furnished room with wide picture windows on one side. Opposite them was another set of double doors which were opened—and in came Norman Le Brocq and Harold Le Druillenec! 'Bill!', they both exclaimed, and greeted him with open arms. Their instant recognition of him confirmed his story to the KGB observers who had previously held him under suspicion of spying. That was no real surprise, given that he was an intelligent man with good English and was therefore an ideal candidate for recruitment by MI6—which, of course, had almost happened when he was in the Guildford transit camp. He had told his interrogators of his resistance to, and escape from, his German captors and given details of the few of us who had helped him to stay hidden in an attempt to clear his name; and to test him they had gone to the trouble of flying Norman and Harold all the way from Jersey to meet him. For Bill it was a wonderful opportunity. Not only did he meet his two old friends again but once the shadow of suspicion lifted from him he was effectively rehabilitated in the eyes of the Russian authorities, and whatever modest civic rights Soviet citizens were allowed he was now given. He could seek better employment, and a better home to live in—and at last write letters to people outside the Motherland. It was lovely to hear from him again even though he very obviously had to be careful what he said.

Norman, I'm sure, relished the chance to see the beating heart of the communist ideal in action during his visit to Moscow, and I expect Harold was held in high regard by the Russians because of his survival in a Nazi concentration camp. He'd also got to know Bill.

Shortly afterwards I was asked to accept a token of gratitude from the Soviet Union, in recognition of what I had done, along with nineteen other islanders who had contributed to the well-being of Soviet citizens during the Occupation. Rather than fly to the Soviet Embassy in London, an official was to come to Jersey—and to present us each with a gold watch in a ceremony at the unlikely location of the Ommaroo Hotel. I spoke to René about it as he was one of the lucky twenty. Mike Frowd, however, was not, which I thought was very wrong as he had exposed himself to equal danger. Many of the others had been members of the (very small) Communist Party in Jersey during the war, while others I simply did not know at all, although that could of course be because like me they had managed to keep their underground activities to themselves. After some well-meaning speeches, I took my turn to be presented with a heavy gold watch by the Soviet official and I remember trying to joke with him a little when he asked me whereabouts in Jersey I lived. 'I live at Le Bourg,' I told him, 'which I suppose makes me Bourgeois!' My attempt at humour was greeted by the stony silence of disapproval. The Cyrillic inscription on the back proclaimed that the watch was a gift to Robert Le Sueur from the Supreme Presidium of the Soviet Socialist Republic, and its elegant design sat comfortably on my wrist right up to the time when it stopped working. I took it with me on my visits to Russia in case I got into any trouble....

It would still be another quarter of a century before I would finally meet Bill again. It was in 1992 when the Soviet Union was becoming so desperate for foreign exchange that it not only allowed but positively welcomed tourists—provided they came with a carefully supervised package tour and a wallet full of money. They even allowed individual travellers and I dreamed up a rather complicated plan not only to see Bill, but also to fulfil my ambition of visiting southeast Asia. The intelligent thing to have done would have been to fly to Bangkok and start from there, but I decided to take the ferry to St Malo and then travel by train all the way to Hong Kong, passing through Russia and seeing Bill on the way. I started to make my arrangements in September 1991 for travel in the New Year, because the Soviets would not let you cross their borders as a tourist unless you could supply them with a full itinerary of every journey you would make and every place where you would stay, booked and paid for in advance. In other words they would know exactly where you were at any given moment. It was an auspicious time to be planning such a trip because behind the Iron Curtain great cracks were appearing in the Soviet structure and the whole edifice was about to implode. I was fortunate that I postponed my initial plans until the New Year because on 25 December Gorbachev resigned, the all-powerful Hammer and Sickle flag was pulled down from the Kremlin, and just nine days later I was on the ferry from Jersey with a small travelling bag and one other very heavy sack. The following morning I was on the first of many trains that would take me towards Hong Kong on a journey that would need a whole month to complete. I could have made it much more quickly, but I had resolved to see some sights on my way and planned several interesting stopovers. In Berlin I explored a city which was still getting used to unity, the Wall having fallen such a short time before, while in Warsaw I saw how the patriotic Poles had rebuilt their wonderful old streets which had been flattened in the uprising at the end of the war. In Moscow I spent hours revisiting the Pushkin Museum, one of the greatest in the world.

I had in fact been to Moscow on a previous occasion. In 1985 I had a call from Norman asking if I knew of anyone who had sheltered Russians during the war that was still alive. After all these years, he still didn't know the true extent of what I had done for Bill and the others. He'd been contacted by Moscow to find islanders who might want to come to a conference of people from different countries who had been in the war, in an attempt to forge some new relationships. I did of course know a few people and I went to visit them to ask if they would like to attend. By that stage the Cold War was well into its thaw, but even so people would not easily be persuaded to travel to Moscow and none of my Jersey contacts were interested. Many of them of course were simply too old to undertake such a trip. Finally Norman put me in touch with the Russian organiser of the conference who was under obvious pressure to find someone, anyone, who met the criteria and could join them in Russia. Some days later he called to tell me that he had enlisted the national secretary of the Royal British Legion and an RAF pilot who had been given the Order of Lenin—and would I perhaps like to come? I am always a sucker for a new experience and a free trip and sensed the poor fellow was in a bit of a jam, so I accepted. The trip over was notable for the time I managed to spend with the MP Dennis Healey, who happened to be on the same flight as me to Moscow. We had chatted after I approached him in the lounge after recognising his eyebrows, and we ended up sitting together on the flight. It was then that I recognised that in the Soviet Union some people were indeed more equal than others as the Aeroflot plane had both Economy and Club class—and we were ushered into Club. The conference itself was an absolute farce but it did give me the chance to visit some cultural icons including the Pushkin, where I saw wonderful post-Impressionist paintings which had been locked away in a cellar during Stalin's time as they had been deemed unsuitable by the Soviet authorities. The wealth of the collection overwhelmed me. Such was my first impression of Moscow and it was interesting to go back and compare it seven years later after the state had crumbled.

After weeks of travel I arrived at a station bearing the name 'Novisibirsk' in the depths of Siberia and took a deliberate deviation from my declared itinerary by asking the woman at the desk for a ticket to Tomsk. I might have asked her for a ticket to the moon as she found me completely incomprehensible and I was compelled to ask around the station for some help. 'Does anyone here speak English?' I asked the various passengers waiting on the platform. To my relief one young man told me that he did, and he actually went to the desk and bought the ticket for me after embarrassing me by calling me 'Sir'. Once on the train I was treated like a Martian by the other passengers who had probably never even met anyone from outside their own country. The Russian trains had a kind of corridor going down one side with compartments opposite, but unlike those on British trains there was no door to close for privacy. I shared with a man whose friendly peasant face gave him the appearance of someone who had just stepped out of a painting by Breughel. At one point he pulled out a large flask and disappeared off down to the samovar at the end of the corridor before returning and offering me a drink in simple sign language. We shook hands and watched the desolate countryside flash by on the single-line track. Bill of course knew that I was coming and I found myself wondering how the last forty years of suspicion and oppression might have altered him; would he still be the buoyant individual who had flung out his legs in a Cossack dance at the flat in Grosvenor Street, or would his spirit have been ground down by the KGB's constant vigilance?

When the train drew to a halt I stepped off—and there he was, unmistakably Bill. Still constrained by my mother's insistence that one should never, ever show emotion in public, I politely offered him my hand only to find myself enveloped in a tight bearhug and my face being smothered in wet kisses. It had been nearly five decades and thousands of miles since he had last spoken to me in our little island and now here we were on the frozen platform of a railway station in Siberia. He was overcome; I kept my upper lip stiff, in accordance with my upbringing, despite the waves of memories which flooded though my mind.

After a brief journey through the bleak frozen streets we arrived at his little flat where I was to sleep on the settee, since they had only one bedroom. Bill's new wife Nadia had now taken over the hugging duties and alternated between flinging her arms around me and urging me to eat something. I already knew though how meagre their supplies were as a result of both poverty and a lack of availability and so I finally opened the heavy grip bag that I had lugged with me all the way from Jersey. Shortly before boarding the boat I had been to my local supermarket and loaded up with foodstuffs which carried a good food value for their relative size and weight—cereals, dried fruit, tea, coffee, nuts—and also practical things such as ladies' tights, at which Bill's wife burst into tears. When I mimed 'shopping' to them I demonstrated walking down a supermarket aisle, picking something up, looking at it, and then putting it back on the shelf, only for her to flinch noticeably. The idea that you could put something BACK on a shelf! In Russia, if it was there you took it even if you didn't need it, because you never knew when it might become available again. The nuts had been on offer because I'd bought them just after Christmas and I opened a bag of them to share. Nadia looked at them with some mistrust as she had never seen peanuts before, and I had to pop one or two into my mouth before she would start to eat them. 'Be careful,' Bill urged her, 'don't eat them all at once!' I also astonished them when I brought out some writing paper with envelopes whose gummed seal had perished and would not stick. Wishing to seal the letters I had written, I pulled out a partly used roll of Sellotape, only to find Bill pushing a well-used pot of glue and a brush upon me. He had never seen such a wonder as Sellotape before. 'Where did you get that?' he asked with eyes wide. He was even more taken aback when I told him that it was made in Nairobi—in Africa! He could not comprehend that his country had managed to send men into space, yet it did not have anything so simple as Sellotape. 'Be careful!' he urged me, 'THEY might not allow it!' Ah, the miracle of Communism.

Their simplicity humbled me, as they tried to press upon me every small delicacy they possessed, including a packet of Earl Grey tea which had been given to them the previous year by someone who had been to the Soviet Embassy in the UK. No matter how often I said 'Niet, niet' in my faltering Russian, they insisted on offering me all of the little they had.

Of course we talked over old times for hours in between hugs and the three days I had allowed to stop there went by very quickly. I was concerned that I should at least attempt to stick to the plan I had outlined to the Russian authorities, so I left with Bill on a train to Irkutsk from where I could continue my journey. I remember walking with him around a lake on a beautiful sunny day when the air was so still and dry that you could hear gentle crackling sounds coming from all around as the ice froze upon the trees, every twig was outlined in white and the smoke from the chimneys went straight up into the air. I didn't feel the least bit cold and took the hood off my parka to enjoy the freshness of it all, only for Bill immediately to make a fuss and tell me to put it back on again. I didn't want to cause a scene and so did as I was told. By way of explanation he showed me a thermometer. It read minus twenty-seven degrees. Bill exclaimed dolefully that they were suffering from global warming and that it was an unusually warm winter because the water at the bottom of the dam hadn't frozen yet! Apparently children at the local school are not allowed to go out to play if the temperature falls below minus thirty.... I certainly felt warmer than I had on the day I left Jersey when a damp chill wind made it feel far colder than the nine degrees registering on the thermometer.

Naturally when the time came for me to board the train there were more emotional scenes; tears, hugs and kisses from him and a very stiff upper lip once more from me. I boarded the train which was full of Americans, Swedes, Japanese, Mexicans and French all making their organised trans-Siberian excursion. Bill was taken aback by the number of foreigners who were now coming to his country.

The train became a travelling village as it trundled through the deserted white Siberian landscape and the different compartments intermingled with parties where a lot of alcohol was consumed in the spirit of international cooperation. The exception were the reserved Swedes who kept themselves to themselves, pining perhaps for their silent lakes. Every mile onwards was another mile away from my friend Bill and I wondered if I would ever see him again. As it happened, I would—back in the island of Jersey.

In May 1995 it would be fifty years since the Liberation and the States of Jersey were determined that it should be marked with suitable solemnity and celebration. Deputy Jean Le Maistre was head of the committee responsible, and wondered if it would be possible to bring Bill back to the island where he had been a slave and a runaway five decades before. Russian people were no longer under the heel of Communism and passports were far more easily available to those wishing to visit other countries, so we were optimistic that a trip could be arranged. Sure enough after managing to negotiate a long and complicated journey, Bill returned to Jersey in considerably more comfort than he had left, together with a university professor named Felix Tarasenko and a TV cameraman.

But what a shock it was to him. Where fifty years before there had been grey austerity and constant suspicion, there was now prosperity and freedom. Brightly lit shops sold luxury goods of a quality and quantity unheard of during the Occupation—or, for that matter, in the country he had just left. Where bicycles had been virtually the only mode of transport, thousands of cars, lorries and motorbikes now made every street a noisy and dangerous hazard. The population had almost doubled in size, new buildings had sprung up everywhere, old buildings had simply disappeared. Bill, always an emotional man, was overcome.

His feelings were heightened still further when we went to the flat he had shared with Mike and René. Some weeks before the visit I telephoned the current owners to ask if we might go inside together to relive some of our wartime stories. The Spanish woman I spoke to was delighted to hear our tale, and excited to welcome us into her home. The only serving member of his wartime hosts Mike Frowd, with whom I was still in touch, came also. René by this time was dead. All of our memories came flooding back, as we walked around saying, 'That's where René's bed was ... that's where Bill slept on the floor ... up in the attic was where he hid from the Germans ...'. Mike laughed ruefully as he looked at the windowsill where he had managed to grow six lettuces to supplement their meagre rations. As Bill looked around with tears in his eyes, the owner was goggle-eyed at our tales of a world so different to her own. She kept saying, 'But my flat is so ordinary, I can't believe these things happened here!'

She knew a little of my story, and asked me about other people that I had helped. What about Yevgeny, Mikael, George? Mike was aghast. 'Who were those people?' he wanted to know, 'were you helping them too?' Yes, I said, I knew them and had moved them around the various safe houses that I knew with people whom I could trust. 'But René and I never knew that! We never knew you were helping anyone other than Bill!' Fifty years on, Mike was only just discovering the extent of my nefarious activities and it came as a great and perhaps rather unwelcome surprise. During the Occupation I had of course kept all of them on a 'need to know' footing. 'I don't suppose I told you,' I said to him. 'You were doing something very dangerous and there was always the chance you could have been picked up. They could have used brutal methods against you to find out who else was involved, and I know that under those circumstances I would have told them anything they wanted to know to save myself any further physical pain. Under that sort of interrogation you might say absolutely anything, but you could not divulge what you did not know. In all our best interests I never told you more than you needed to know. Whenever I moved one of these other men I told whoever he was to stay with that he was to be moved within six weeks; and I did not want to know where.'

The owner of the flat was almost as astonished as Mike at this exposure of secrets that had lain between us undiscovered for so long. What a moment it was.

Another moment of a different nature occurred on 8 May, the day before the anniversary. The authorities had agreed to put a memorial plaque on the wall of what had been Louisa Gould's house in St Ouen. The ceremonial unveiling was due to take place at eleven o'clock, so I made it clear to my three Russian guests (who were staying in my house) that we would have to leave by ten at the latest. Unfortunately they appeared to have no appreciation of the need for punctuality. 'Are you all ready??!!' I demanded with increasing frequency as the hour for departure drew closer. The professor was prepared at a reasonable hour and finally Bill presented himself at the front door in the nick of time. But where was the TV man? By that time I was living in a house which backed immediately onto the beach on the east coast of the island, and it was the professor who thought that might be the answer. Sure enough, he shouted excitedly from the beach and pointed out to sea. There, about fifty yards out and happy as a sandboy was our missing Russian enjoying an early morning dip despite the chilly sea. The situation quickly became farcical as we waved at him to come back to shore quickly, only for him to wave back at us happily and carry on swimming.

When we finally got him ashore and crammed him, still wet, into some respectable clothes, we piled into the car and set off at breakneck speed. I drove like a maniac, determined not to be late to a party at which we were effectively the guests of honour. After defying the speed limit across the northern parishes we arrived only to find there was nowhere to park. Screeching to a halt as close as I could to the house, I pointed them in the right direction and yelled, 'Now just get out and go!!!!' By the time I got there the ceremony had started. Despite it all, the TV man appeared to be blissfully ignorant that his refreshing dip had been the cause of such chaos.

Once the short service was over we were able to go inside thanks to the kindness of the owners, and revisit the events of fifty years before. The shop had long since closed and the building was now a private home, but Bill's room was still there. Of course it was another very emotional time for us all, especially when we remembered what fate had befallen Louisa Gould, who had been taken on the journey to her death from that very place. Close by, we visited René Le Mottée's house, where Bill met those he had known as children who were now in their sixties but still remembered him being there. They made a lot of fuss over him.

More difficult was a visit to Ivy Forster's home. Her time in prison during the war had not dampened her spirit and she had become Jersey's first female member of the States and a well-recognised island figure. By this time though she was in her late eighties and needed to be treated with great diplomacy. Her son was understandably concerned about how she might react to us all trooping in to see her, and suggested that Bill alone might go in. He knew that it was because of him that her sister had been killed, and found the meeting very difficult. As they spoke, I sat on the verandah of the house together with the TV man and the professor. The TV man in particular was astonished as he looked down on the busy roundabout at West Park. He had never seen so many cars. He was equally staggered by the opulence of the Grand Hotel where we had been the guests at a special dinner, and had almost certainly never set foot in such a place in his life. During that meal, Bill had sat next to a young man with a foreign accent. He was German.

I arranged a meeting for Bill with the woman he had professed undying love for all those years ago—and her husband. It turned out very amicably, and I don't know if the flame was still there after all that time. She had been so sweet to him, mending his trousers and looking after him in a hundred little ways that must have endeared her to him very much during his darkest moments; but I fear his passion had always been unrequited.

He also met Harold Le Druillenec's widow. Her husband had been through the hell of Belsen because of Bill, and the last time she had seen the Russian he had been with Louisa Gould. Bill found all of this very hard indeed to cope with and the meeting was far from easy for him.

George had also made the journey to Jersey and joined us on several of our visits, although he was understandably less shell-shocked by it all than Bill. George had, after all, escaped a life under Communism, settled in Germany after the war and had changed very little. In fact, I was to regret sending an attractive widow friend of mine to pick him up. 'Never ask me to give that man a lift again!' she said. Why on earth not, I wondered. 'Because we were only part way down Mont Felard when I felt his hand on my leg! I had to slap him off and I thought we would crash!' Ever the ladies' man, George was up to his old tricks again.

We spent our spare time going back to our old haunts, such as the house at Archirondel to which we used to walk for tea and the occasional overnight stop. To show them something of the new Jersey I also took the three of them to visit the Orchid Foundation, where experts grew blooms of such beauty that they won prizes in international competitions. Looking at the myriad colourful blossoms, Bill was confused. 'But what are they for?' he asked. I told him they weren't for anything, simply to look beautiful. 'Yes, but what are they for?' he asked again. Coming from a country where everything had to have its practical purpose, he couldn't understand that one would spend time and money on something purely for its aesthetic value. It was all so different for him. I remember him looking at the apples and pears in the fruit bowl on my table. 'Did you grow those yourself?' he asked in wonderment. I told him that no, I had of course bought them in a shop. 'But how can that be? They are not in season?' When I explained that they had simply been imported from abroad he was astonished that such things were possible. In his country such luxuries had been unheard of, especially in Siberia.

The TV man insisted that we see a little of the poorer side of Jersey, as he harboured a suspicion that I had somehow only shown him the wealthiest, most privileged side of our island. Willingly I took him to one of our States' estates where people paid rent according to their income. To my delight, as we drove slowly around the flats, two boys came out of a doorway carrying wetsuits and surfboards ready to get into the sea. I was even happier when they informed us that they had saved up for their equipment by working in part-time jobs. To the TV man this represented jet-set glamour and he made sure to film them for his programme. He had a further question. To whom did all of the cars belong? When I told him that they belonged to the people who lived on the estate, he looked grave. 'I would rather be a poor man in Jersey,' he said, 'than a rich man in Russia.' All through his visit he was suspicious about why people were so friendly to him, from the veterans of the Arctic Convoys to Mr and Mrs Malet de Carteret, the owners of St Ouen's Manor who hosted a reception to mark the anniversary of the Liberation and to commemorate Louisa Gould and what she had done. The reception was held in a huge marquee in the grounds and the Russians simply did not know where to look. One special guest was Louisa Gould's former maid, to whom Bill had a certain attachment while he was living at the house in St Ouen. She was now respectably married to a man from St John, but she and Bill managed to have a long conversation about old times. Poor Bill was still terribly confused—largely because he simply could not comprehend how HE could possibly be socialising with people of such quality in such a fine house. 'I should not be here!', he kept repeating as he was greeted by the great and good of the island. He thought himself far beneath them. Mrs Pat Malet de Carteret had her suspicions. 'No wonder they caught Mrs Gould,' she said. 'Everybody in this place knows who you are!' Surely, he thought, the grand house and high-class people were all a deceit to have him believe all the people in Jersey were fabulously wealthy? 'It may look wonderful,' I told him, 'but look down in the moat over there and you will see the Seigneur's washing drying on a line. They have no servants, they have to fend for themselves just like the rest of us.'

Liberation Day itself, the fiftieth anniversary, was a huge occasion for the island and Bill and George were given a VIP seat up with the dignitaries. This was almost too much for Bill, as I took a seat with the rest of the hoi-polloi in Liberation Square. While George looked content that his worth had been recognised, Bill looked completely lost. As the lengthy ceremony unfolded I watched him in the roped-off area, staring with wide eyes and wondering how on earth he had come to be there. But more was to come. When the ceremony was over, a sharply dressed man with an earpiece came over to me. 'Are you the man who was involved with the Russian prisoners?' he asked. I replied in the affirmative. 'Please bring them this way,' he said. 'There is someone who would like to meet them.' I guessed who it was. Prince Charles, the son of the Queen of England, was the guest of honour, and he wanted to meet Bill—and of course George too. For Bill, it was almost too much. George naturally took it as his due. The Prince was wonderful with them and spoke with an easy candour. Despite being pressed to many other appointments that day he stayed and chatted with them, asking questions and displaying a knowledge and understanding of the Occupation that showed his interest in our island's history. Finally he was urged onwards to meet the great and the good. 'It's a shame I have to go,' he told them, 'I would have liked to hear much more of your stories.' He shook hands with them very warmly. Bill was left in a daze from which I'm not sure he ever truly recovered....

My last sight of Bill was at the airport as he prepared to say goodbye. A hopeless traveller, I had to give him step-by-step instructions simply to get him through to his aircraft. Follow the arrows, I told him, they will lead you to Heathrow. After turning to wave goodbye, he shambled off in completely the opposite direction and I had to call him back, 'Bill, Bill....' Eventually he got aboard and was off. During the flight the pilot announced that he was proud to have on his aircraft a man who had fought with the Soviets during the war, been wounded, captured and lived as a brave escapee in Jersey. There was great cheering and Bill realised that the English were capable after all of showing emotions. He was not used to such acclaim.

The professor met him at Heathrow, thank goodness, to shepherd him on his way back to Siberia. He never returned to Jersey again.

After the splendours of my gold watch and the public recognition I been given on the anniversary of Liberation Day I thought I had received quite enough for my exploits—after all, I had never done anything except out of a sense of duty to help my fellow human beings. But one day in spring 2013, sixty-eight years after the Occupation ended, I received a telephone call. I picked it up as normal. 'Hello, Bob Le Sueur.' 'This is John McColl,' was the reply. *Sir* John McColl was at that time the Lieutenant-Governor of Jersey, effectively the Queen's official representative on the island. I thought it was probably a prank by a friend of mine who is very good at imitating voices, and I was very tempted to say that I was in fact Prince Charles, but fortunately discretion got the better of me. 'Yes, Sir,' I answered. 'How may I be of service?'

His reply took me greatly by surprise. He wondered if I would kindly accept being made an MBE! He explained that I was due the honour not only for my work helping people during the war but also for my work with the National Trust, Trees for Life and the Société Jersiaise. I did not feel I could accept straight away, because it troubled me that there were other people in Jersey during the Occupation who had taken far greater risks than I had, and they deserved such elevation before me. After reflecting for twenty-four hours, however, I called back to accept but on the understanding that it would be on behalf of Mike, René and all the other brave souls who had put their lives on the line all those years ago but were no longer around to be appreciated. I was entertained to see that affixed to the official envelope from Buckingham Palace, inviting me to the investiture, was a *second-class* stamp. Perhaps it was one of Charles' cost-cutting exercises?

Come the day, and I attended the palace duly excited. The function room was vast and it seemed an immensely long walk to the platform when my name was finally called. The Prince himself was to pin the honour upon me, and he immediately spoke to me in a very relaxed manner. His first words came as though he was in the middle of a train of thought. 'And so you are the chap who is ninety-three and helped some of those poor wretched slave workers in Jersey during the Occupation?'

I had been told that if you were addressed, you should first respond with the title 'Your Royal Highness', but he had so surprised me with his use of the word 'chap' and the fact that he knew my age and who I was that all convention was forgotten. 'Sir,' I said, 'You may remember …': I got so far before realising my mistake, but like Corporal Jones in *Dad's Army* I told myself not to panic. 'You may remember you came to Jersey to help us celebrate in 1995, and on that occasion you may recall there were two of those slave workers in the crowd at Liberation Square.' He then astonished me by recalling the occasion perfectly, and repeating what he had said to them. 'And was that you standing alongside them?', he asked. I told him it was, and looking intently at me he said, 'Ah, if only I'd known!' A flunkey then moved towards us with the cushion upon which rested my medal, and the Prince clipped it on my jacket himself. I had been warned not to shake hands with him too firmly as he would be shaking so many hands that day, but he extended both his hands to mine and took my right hand with a very firm grip. 'Thank you so much for making the effort to come,' he said. 'It has been a delight to meet you.'

I remember moving backwards thinking that I must not fall over, reflecting that he probably said something similarly generous to every recipient. I did not walk out of there. I believe I must have floated through the archway and back into reality when I was asked to sit at the back of a roomful of other people who had been honoured.

I believe that in less formal circumstances I could have formed a good relationship with this well-educated and informed man.

EPILOGUE

It was two or three days after Liberation. The snow flurries and spiteful wind of just a few days ago had gone, to be replaced by clear skies and the promise of a beautiful spring as flowers blossomed all over the island. In less than two weeks I had gone from desperate plans of doomed revolution to peace, freedom, and optimism for what lay ahead, in a great spiral of emotions.

I walked through town, made curiously empty by its lack of German soldiers, and found myself drawn towards the building near the harbour where so many of my friends had assembled to be taken away to an uncertain fate in Germany all those months ago. As I stood there with memories rushing through my mind, two aircraft in formation suddenly zoomed over Fort Regent to my left, flying low in the blue sky, and I flinched, pulling my head down and my shoulders up in a reflex action born of long habit. But as they roared out to sea with the sun glinting off their wings before turning back towards me, I saw something very clearly.

They were Spitfires. They were ours.

As they roared back over the harbour and pulled into a climb right over my head, something snapped inside me. Almost without realising it I found myself sobbing uncontrollably, great heaving sobs that racked my whole body, tears pouring down my cheeks unchecked as I cried with distress, unable to stop. What was wrong with me? I had disciplined myself never to betray any emotion in public, yet here I was practically on my knees in the centre of St Helier. All of the secrecy, tension, falsehoods and oppression which I had stored up for the last five years were finally bursting out and I was helpless.

Through my own sobs I became dimly aware of someone close by. It was another man, of perhaps forty years old. Like me he had his eyes up to the sky. And like me he was crying fit to burst.

ACKNOWLEDGEMENTS

The publishers would like to thank Bob for finally agreeing to have his invaluable recollections put into print.

Thanks to Chris Stone for his dedication in helping Bob to tell his story, John Nettles for his foreword, Ian Ronayne for editing, Dinah Bott for proofreading, Roger Jones of Seaflower Books for origination of the print edition and Steve Foot for eBook conversion.

Thanks also for kind permission to reproduce the photographs in this publication: Bob Le Sueur, Tracy Mourant, BCA Film.co.uk, *Jersey Evening Post*, the Channel Island Occupation Society (Jersey) and the Channel Island Military Museum.

About Bob's co-author:

Chris Stone is a BBC journalist who has lived in Jersey for more than twenty-five years. He has made many radio documentaries about the experiences of Jersey people during the Second World War, and written three other books about Jersey men who fought in it. He continues to regard them as heroes, even if they protest otherwise.

Also written with Chris Stone and published by Seeker Publishing:

Stinker's Nine Lives, Dangerous Driving, Bomb Doors Open

FURTHER READING AND INFORMATION

There is a wealth of material about the Occupation, some written at the time and some written far more recently. Some is meticulously accurate and of great historical value, while other work is perhaps clouded by the mists of memory and time.

As a starting point, Michael Ginns' monumental *Jersey Occupied* is an exhaustive but very readable account of many aspects of the island's experience between 1940 and 1945. He was accounted by many as Jersey's foremost Occupation historian for good reason.

Cruikshank's *The German Occupation of the Channel Islands* is the official account of the story but for more personal memories of people who lived through it we have many contemporaneous diaries and accounts, from Leslie Sinel to Nan le Ruez.

Mark Lamerton's *Liberated by Force 135* is a detailed exploration of how the islands were freed, and has been republished with many new images and documentation.

Other recent scholarly works include Madeleine Bunting's *The Model Occupation*, which attracted the ire of both Bob Le Sueur and Michael Ginns for its allegations of complicity on the part of the island's government and apathy on the part of the populace. It is still a necessary read for those wanting to consider both sides of the argument.

John Nettles, much loved for his portrayal of the eponymous detective in *Bergerac* but also a history graduate, produced *Jewels and Jackboots*, which considers events in Jersey and the other Channel Islands through the eyes of both occupier and occupied.

All of these publications and many others have informed and inspired my work with Bob on this, his personal story.

There are also many articles and photographs online which are a godsend to a researcher in a hurry.

For example, the Frank Falla Archive *https://www.frankfallaarchive. org* provides information on the people from the Channel Islands who were deported and imprisoned, such as Bob's friends Louisa Gould and John Max Finkelstein. Dr Gilly Carr has done a wonderful job of making the site very detailed yet highly accessible.

Jersey Heritage has a wealth of documents and pictures in its archive, a number of which can be found online: *https://catalogue.jerseyheritage.org.*

The Jersey War Tunnels have told the story of the Occupation for years in an immersive and informative way and have myriad stories of the people who lived through it—on both sides: *https://www.jerseywartunnels.com.*

The Société Jersiaise is always a good source of knowledge not only about the Occupation but the whole of Jersey's long and colourful history: *https://societe-jersiaise.org.*

A trip to Jersey Library gives you access to the entire wartime archive of the *Evening Post* (renamed the *Jersey Evening Post* after the war), which at once shows the Germans' attempts to mislead and subdue the Jersey people and the people's attempts to survive and endure. My thanks to the staff there for their patience in reminding me to use the film reader!

And the Channel Islands Occupation Society has a wealth of resources for those wanting to find out more, or to experience life from the Occupier's point of view inside their carefully restored bunkers: *https://www.cios.org.je.*

The phrase used by Louisa Gould to explain to Bob why she risked her life to help Russian Bill gave the title to a film in which she was played by Jenny Seagrove. *Another Mother's Son* shows the hardship of life under the Nazis, and the impossible choices some people had to make.

But perhaps the best way to find out more about what the average islander went through under German rule is to ask them. There are still those, such as Bob, who remember what it was like to go to bed in the dark, hungry. Those who remember the crash of hobnailed boots, the demand for papers, the worn-out shoes and the misery of the slaves.

There are also those who remember the Germans who helped them fix their bikes, turned a blind eye when they were late for curfew, sang, played music and opened doors for ladies. Their memories are just as important.

If you want to find out more about the Occupation, ask them before those memories are gone.

ABOUT THE AUTHOR

Bob Le Sueur was born in Jersey two years after the end of the First World War.

He was educated in the island at Victoria College before starting work as an office boy at the local branch of the General Accident insurance company.

At the outbreak of the Second World War in 1940 he was left to run the business as self-appointed manager after other staff members joined up or left for the mainland.

During the five years of the Occupation he offered safety and shelter to many escaped Russian slaves and helped in the publication of numerous subversive documents undermining the morale of the Germans and their supporters. He played a role in the failed mutiny shortly before the Liberation.

After the war he left for Scotland to work at General Accident's head office in Perth, before returning to the island to become an English teacher at Hautlieu School.

Since retirement he has worked extensively for many local and international organisations, including the Channel Islands Occupation Society, Men of the Trees, Amnesty International and various overseas charities. He has travelled at length across Eastern and Western Europe, North and South America, Asia and Africa.

Among many awards he was presented with a gold watch by the Soviet Union in recognition of his clandestine activities and in 2007 was chosen to be the subject of the Jersey Heritage Trust Portrait Commission. In 2013 Prince Charles made him an MBE.

Bob Le Sueur lives on the south coast of Jersey.